Praise for *Capital Evolution*

"*Capital Evolution* offers a vision for achieving economic growth while revitalizing the middle class, promoting equity, protecting the planet, and overcoming political polarization."
—**Suzanne DiBianca, Chief Impact Officer, Salesforce**

"At PayPal I learned firsthand that the invisible hand of the market doesn't work for everyone. For too long, we've overlooked the plight of the working class and the result has been a society that is completely out of balance. In *Capital Evolution*, Seth and Elizabeth tell the compelling story of how and why capitalism needs to change. This is an important book for anyone who cares about the future of our economy and our democracy."
—**Dan Schulman, former CEO, PayPal**

"In *Capital Evolution* Seth Levine and Elizabeth MacBride explore the long strange trip by which America has arrived at such a bewildering and precarious stage in its history. And having documented that journey, they go on to present a vision of an alternative economic future—Dynamic Capitalism—and the political and economic building blocks required to achieve it. Their insights, observations, and recommendations are not only fascinating and provocative but amount to an urgent must-read blueprint for restoring faith in business-centered capitalism—and even American democracy itself."
—**John R. Dearie, President, Center for American Entrepreneurship**

"Tectonic shifts are reshaping capitalism. *Capital Evolution* brilliantly navigates this new world of complex change with fresh insight and sharp storytelling that is both pragmatic and optimistic. Levine and MacBride have written a blueprint for a more inclusive, resilient capitalism. Practical and forward thinking, this is essential reading."
—**David Smick, Global Macroeconomic Strategist and *New York Times* Bestselling Author, *The World Is Curved***

"*Capital Evolution* is a clarion call for us to join the movement to reimagine capitalism—interrogating our past, confronting our present realities, and putting forward new forms and alternatives to our current form of capitalism. Levine and MacBride nuance the ways that capital has shaped our American society and call us to be intentional about our individual role in shaping, evolving, and reforming capitalism versus succumbing to its 'invisible hand.'"

—**Nate Wong, Partner, The Bridgespan Group**

"Over the past few centuries, capitalism has evolved to become the best economic system and wealth creation engine in the world. Seth and Elizabeth masterfully break down what is needed for its next evolution in this nuanced and timely book."

—**Javier Saade, Managing Partner, Impact Master Holdings**

"*Capital Evolution* builds on the sharp analysis of *The New Builders*, offering a courageous and compelling road map for how capitalism can evolve to meet today's challenges and shape a more resilient future. Levine and MacBride trace the roots and failures of neoliberalism—rising inequality, a decimated middle class, and deepening political divides—while presenting a hopeful alternative: dynamic capitalism. Defined as a renewed social consensus that prioritizes inclusivity, adaptability, and shared prosperity, this new framework centers long-ignored externalities like climate and equity as core business strategies. I finished the book feeling curious, excited, and ready to roll up my sleeves."

—**Kate Williams, CEO, 1% for the Planet**

"An important and courageous book, this relatively brief 16-chapter treatise addresses changing tides surrounding American capitalism. As a former investor myself, I couldn't be more hopeful about some of the early signs based on this reading.

MacBride and Levine have captured a burgeoning movement among elite finance professionals. The authors offer a slew of possible financial solutions to aiding and sustaining the rapidly diminishing American middle class. The challenges, according to authors MacBride and Levine, is agreeing on how concerns like shareholder value and stakeholder capitalism might realistically be extended to expand the social contract."

—**Pia Sawhney, Cofounder and Partner Emeritus, Armory Square Ventures**

CAPITAL EVOLUTION

Also by Seth Levine and Elizabeth MacBride

The New Builders:
Face to Face with the True Future of Business

CAPITAL EVOLUTION

The New American Economy

SETH LEVINE | **ELIZABETH MacBRIDE**

Matt Holt Books
An Imprint of BenBella Books, Inc.
Dallas, TX

Capital Evolution copyright © 2025 by Seth Levine and Elizabeth MacBride

All rights reserved. Except in the case of brief quotations embodied in critical articles or reviews, no part of this book may be used or reproduced, stored, transmitted, or used in any manner whatsoever, including for training artificial intelligence (AI) technologies or for automated text and data mining, without prior written permission from the publisher and the authors.

Matt Holt is an imprint of BenBella Books, Inc.
8080 N. Central Expressway
Suite 1700
Dallas, TX 75206
benbellabooks.com
Send feedback to feedback@benbellabooks.com

BenBella and *Matt Holt* are federally registered trademarks.

Printed in the United States of America
10 9 8 7 6 5 4 3 2 1

Library of Congress Control Number: 2025025528
ISBN 9781637747780 (hardcover)
ISBN 9781637747797 (electronic)

Editing by Lydia Choi
Copyediting by James Fraleigh
Proofreading by Marissa Wold Uhrina and Cheryl Beacham
Indexing by Elise Hess
Text design and composition by Aaron Edmiston
Cover design by Brigid Pearson
Printed by Lake Book Manufacturing

Special discounts for bulk sales are available.
Please contact bulkorders@benbellabooks.com.

To the tens of millions of people working in businesses big and small across America. We see you.

To Greeley, Sacha, Addy, and Amanuel for being exactly who you are.

To Lillie and Quinn, as always.

CONTENTS

Introduction   1

Section I: UNDERSTANDING CAPITALISM

Chapter 1   Standing at the Precipice   13
Chapter 2   The Beauty and Fallacy of Milton Friedman   25
Chapter 3   The Politicization of Business and the Fallacy of Woke   43
Chapter 4   Capital Fundamentals   57
Chapter 5   Is Capitalism Exploitative by Nature?   69

Section II: THE PREVIOUS CONSENSUS CANNOT HOLD

Chapter 6   Class Matters   87
Chapter 7   Mid-Century Mirrors   99
Chapter 8   A New Narrative   115
Chapter 9   The Climate Fallacy   129

Section III: THE MESSY MIDDLE

Chapter 10	Government Is Not the Problem (But It's Not the Solution Either)	147
Chapter 11	The Heart of Finance	163
Chapter 12	Values	177
Chapter 13	Global Blind Spots	191

Section IV: NEW BARGAINS, NEW POSSIBILITIES

Chapter 14	More Middle-Class Capitalists	203
Chapter 15	Policies and Leadership	217
Chapter 16	Reclaiming Dynamism	231
	Epilogue	241
	Acknowledgments	245
	Notes	249
	Index	263

INTRODUCTION

If you ask people what the future of capitalism looks like, a surprisingly large number will respond with a question of their own: Is there a future for capitalism at all?

The last century saw American-style capitalism trounce communism as countries across the globe shifted toward freer markets. The world financial system and increased trade tripled the global middle class, dramatically reduced the number of people living in extreme poverty (and lifted a billion people out of poverty entirely), raised average life expectancy, and enabled unprecedented technological advancements.[1]

Despite these achievements, an increasing number of people question whether capitalism's costs outweigh its benefits. In a world where many people feel trapped by their circumstances and where concerns about the environment are tied to the idea of consumption, "capitalism," typically poorly defined, often receives the blame. What was once a near consensus around the benefits of the American free-market system is now the subject of meaningful debate.

We pointedly saw this in the 2024 election, where Donald Trump rode a wave of economic anxiety to reelection as president of the United

States, capitalizing on a rising fear of globalism and a building populist sentiment. This was part of a broader worldwide trend in election after election away from incumbent parties, reflecting a clear sense among voters that *something* was wrong, even if they often couldn't put their finger on exactly what that something was. We are living through a time when seemingly fundamental assumptions about the nature of our economy, as well as the United States' role in the world, are being called into question.

The United States remains the world's most successful economy, viewed in terms of GDP per capita, sustained GDP growth, and the innovation and profitability of our largest companies.[2] Nevertheless, across the US political spectrum it's now popular to question the foundation of our economic system and suggest that capitalism is irredeemably flawed. Polls find nearly half of young professionals, people you'd assume are on a comfortable upward trajectory through the global economy, have a negative view of capitalism.[3] The number of people in the United States with a positive view of capitalism has declined by 8 percentage points to 57% in the past five years. Even in the worlds of academia and policy, where the idea that American-style free markets should rule the world has long held sway, capitalism is up for debate.

As two pragmatists with long careers in business journalism and international finance, we started working on this book when it became clear to us that the rules that had long governed the relatively staid world of business were changing. We were living in an era of "white rage," in a "world on fire," in which "greedflation" could lead to the "end of capitalism as we know it."[4] Business was taking on the cast of America's fractious politics. Companies were responding to various critics by changing their hiring practices, acting to lower their environmental impacts, adopting long-term orientations, or, in some extreme cases, suing the government over the limits of its control. Many firms were being called out in the public arena, not just by activists advocating boycotts or pundits taking companies to task on political talk shows but also with threats of violence, even death, against CEOs and their families. Business decisions that had previously gone unnoticed or were relatively uncontroversial were suddenly subject to the weaponized language of politics. The role of business in our society was coming under growing scrutiny.

We witnessed these changes not just through our research but also firsthand. Companies Seth works with in his job as a venture capitalist started asking for advice in navigating what felt like a choice between staying focused on their business or bowing to the ever greater pressure—from peers, from employees, from society writ large—to weigh in on the social issues of the day. Elizabeth's work as a business journalist and consulting at the World Bank brought her face to face with the fact that companies—despite growing in size and number—were not creating enough jobs, especially well-paying ones. Conversations in boardrooms and in leadership meetings had changed as more and more companies grappled with issues outside of their core scope of business.

Hidden Economic Pain

It was tempting to dismiss criticism of individual businesses, but the reality on the ground suggested to us that something more serious was happening. Americans are dying from opioids, alcohol, and suicide at rates so high, they are lowering the average US life expectancy.[5] Black Americans and others continue to face steep economic obstacles because of systemic racism. Young people, the same ones dissatisfied with capitalism and ready to give it up entirely, are part of a generation that can't afford to purchase a home or pay off their college debt—a generation that spends hours immersed among the doomsayers of social media.[6]

For more than two years, we read, researched, debated, and talked about the future of the American economic system with the smartest people we could find, including the CEOs of some of the world's largest companies, academics, researchers, policymakers, business owners of all stripes and political persuasions, and workers at every level of the corporate hierarchy. This research led to surprising conclusions and changed our perspectives about the challenges facing our country. One point that felt less surprising than inevitable after our years of research, however, was that the rise of the populist wing of the Republican Party and the return to power of Donald Trump were the outcome of decades in which both political parties ignored the economic issues facing the middle class. While this is not a book about politics, much of what we discuss in the pages that follow can provide answers for people across the political spectrum trying to better understand how we landed at this moment in our history.

As we researched this book, we came to realize just how little we understood the immense challenges many people face while navigating life in America. Elizabeth heard from her two sisters, both public high school teachers, about the strain placed on school systems that are being called upon to cope with rising tides of economic pain. In the suburban district where one of Elizabeth's sisters teaches, so many families are losing their houses that the principal developed a form letter to notify teachers. Imagine being newly homeless at the age of 16 or 17; imagine being the parent of that child; imagine being the teacher asked to grade a student who has no place to sleep at night. We could see and feel that basic systems across our economy and society were no longer working for most Americans. It's surprising to see this side of America if you're from Washington, DC, or Boulder, Colorado (where we both live), or from one of the relatively small number of cities that have thrived over the past 50 years.[7] As a population, we are becoming more insular in our relationships, largely spending time with people who look and think like we do, while consuming media that confirms our worldview. The information ecosystem has changed so much that most local newspapers, which previously filtered news up to the national stage, have all but disappeared as sources of real reporting. Many of us don't see the true picture or the wider context. In a country of some 340 million, *despite the robust economic statistics*, tens of millions of people feel insecure and find it impossible to get ahead.

These factors created the conditions for the emergence of Donald Trump's style of populism and help explain the broad coalition that came together to support his reelection in 2024. Failing to understand these factors—or worse, dismissing them entirely—serves only to fan the flames of the populist movement that is taking shape across America and other parts of the world. Indeed, doing so only bolsters the movement's main arguments.

By nearly every measure, inequality is heart-poundingly high. If you're the kind of person who worries about revolutions, you may be concerned. Between 1978 and 2018, CEO compensation increased by more than 900%, while worker compensation rose by just 11.9%. Across the United States, in land that was once derisively known as "flyover country," factories are slowly disintegrating into hillsides and the vinyl is peeling from houses in once-middle-class neighborhoods. Though there are signs of hope in these places and plenty of humanity—a new small business opening its doors, a neighborhood block party, a new state park—many people inhabiting these communities appear to be filled more with American Exhaustion than the American Dream.

It may surprise you that against this backdrop, we emerged from writing this book with a feeling of optimism. We see a path forward—one that addresses the inequalities that the last 50 years have created and capitalizes on the unique strengths of the American economy and the American people. Yet one of our first conclusions was how much America still needs capitalism. It is the most nimble form of economic governance yet discovered, and the best system devised for funneling resources to good ideas. It can be, and often is, a force for progress and for good in the world. As we heard from leaders from across the country and across the political spectrum, we cannot solve the world's daunting problems without the speed and efficiency of functioning markets. America also needs to rebuild and protect its middle class, which is one of our greatest assets and the foundation of any stable democracy. This is both a moral and a practical imperative. Capitalism can and should deliver a rising standard of living and a chance at happiness for the people living under it.

Capitalism Can Change

Our second conclusion was that capitalism can change—and needs to do so. It may surprise you to hear that capitalism itself is in the midst of a transformation and, in fact, doesn't have a fixed definition. We've all but taken for granted that unfettered free markets, limited government, and a laser focus on sending profits to company owners are what define capitalism. But that's not actually the case. Capitalism has existed in different forms across time and geographies and with different emphases on labor, capital, and productivity. We needn't be limited by old ways of thinking. Nor do we have to completely tear capitalism down and replace it with something altogether different to address our current challenges.

The problem with our current system isn't capitalism itself. Instead, it's the *kind* of capitalism we've been practicing that is.

For more than 50 years, the US form of capitalism has been dominated by a singular set of ideas, known as the "Washington Consensus," "neoliberalism," or "Friedman-style economics," that latter two of which are how we'll generally refer to it in this book. These ideas were outlined by Milton Friedman and his peers and disciples, and evangelized most famously by Ronald Reagan. Capitalism—defined by neoliberalism—feels like it's always been this way because for many (if not most) of us, it has.

But the neoliberal era is coming to an end. What replaces it is up to us, but in these pages, we describe a new consensus emerging, what we term "Dynamic Capitalism." In fact, this is our third broad conclusion: that a new system is already taking shape. Dynamic Capitalism acknowledges the more complex world in which we live and, importantly, recognizes that businesses are the most powerful actors in our new economy—in many cases, more powerful than governments. The fact that America's most successful companies have more power to shape people's lives than our elected officials is a problem. So, too, is the expanding power of a very small number of ultra-rich, generally unaccountable business leaders.

We should not be surprised that this is the current state of affairs. Indeed, Donald Trump's election can be seen as the culmination of the past 50 years of rising corporate power and a fractured and inefficient government. Trump is a leader who rose to power entirely through the business and entertainment worlds by virtue of his mastery of today's information systems. He is a curious figure to have emerged at the crossroads of a change in how we view and practice capitalism. In many ways, he's a symbol of both the old guard and the new, embracing aspects of the neoliberal worldview of limited government and unfettered markets while also taking up the populist mantle and calling out how the past 50 years have harmed many Americans, especially the middle class. His complex relationship with neoliberalism mirrors society's broader uncertainty at this pivotal moment, as long-held beliefs are being challenged and reevaluated.

When we viewed American capitalism through this lens, it became clear why so many people are questioning whether our current economic construct is sustainable and why, in turn, their dissatisfaction has launched us into a period of transition and upheaval. Our country is at a transformative moment, one that offers meaningful opportunities to rethink existing systems and structures while reconsidering the relationship among companies, consumers, and government. But this transition is also fraught with challenges and faces resistance from those with an embedded interest in the status quo or for whom change simply feels too risky. As we continued our work, tracing the patterns of this change became our quest.

Throughout *Capital Evolution*, we'll introduce some of the people grappling with the new American economy. The complexity of today's business world presents an opportunity for skilled, pragmatic business leaders, as well as land mines for those who struggle to find the appropriate balance among the multiple stakeholders they must consider when making decisions. Profits remain important, but the success of a business—the responsibility of a business—doesn't end there. Dynamic Capitalism will reward leaders who are grounded in their values, who can express those values clearly to guide the organizations they lead, who avoid toxic politics, and who can engage people who have a variety of views and ideas. It recognizes that government is neither the problem nor the solution to most of society's challenges, but unlike neoliberal capitalism—which in many ways views government as the enemy—Dynamic Capitalism looks more pragmatically at government interventions in our economy. In most cases, we believe that the role of government should be limited to the smallest imposition necessary to obtain the desired outcome. Still, government clearly has a role to play in our economy as a facilitator of Dynamic Capitalism and an enabler of the free movement of labor and capital.

At a certain point in our research, we paused to ask a basic question, one that has echoed across the country for a decade or more: How did we get *so* divided? Capitalism has evolved in the past, but rarely are transitions so disruptive that they seem to threaten the foundations of our union. As we looked deeper into the past for answers, we discovered echoes of our current reality.

Capital and Labor

Although the 2024 presidential election wasn't explicitly framed in these terms, much of the core debate centered around the dynamic between capital and labor and the resulting consequences for our economy. We'll explore this connection and discuss ways we and others are thinking about how to reshape this dynamic while addressing key challenges facing our rapidly shrinking middle class.

When we started writing this book, we didn't realize that we were already part of the movement to transform capitalism. The process of researching and writing was revealing, both because it changed many of our initial views and also because it put a more structured framework around a set of loosely knit ideas each of us had been pondering for years. This book is a call for other business leaders to consider where they stand and to be more conscious about their actions. It is a call for political leaders to acknowledge the changes that are taking place across our economy and to better understand the underlying reasons for them. It is a call to managers and employees to take up the mantle of change and embrace their agency and power.

The success of Dynamic Capitalism—and ultimately, the United States—will require us to travel outside insular bubbles, embrace core values, think longer term, form new coalitions, and recognize that America faces meaningful challenges to the economic primacy we've enjoyed for much of the last century. We hope this book becomes a call to action to push Dynamic Capitalism ahead while avoiding the temptation to roll back many of the changes already starting to take hold across our economy. Our concern is primarily with the business sector because that's where our expertise lies, but more importantly, because after 50 years of shrinking government, business has in many ways become the most functional power in the world. We're not here to dictate what business leaders' ethics should be—there is plenty of room for differences. However, businesses and their leaders clearly must be driven by a clear set of values to successfully navigate an ever more fraught world.

A New Era for a More Complex World

We stand at a crucial moment of reckoning for America, as the world's economic leader. We must take decisive steps toward revitalizing our dynamic economy. A strong middle class is essential for driving the consumption of goods and services, while an educated population is vital for building a skilled workforce. As businesses and their leaders move beyond the shareholder-first model that has dominated the past 50 years, more organizations, managers, and employees are openly bringing their values into the workplace. These values are diverse and increasingly reflect broader societal issues, including the environment, the boundaries of free speech, and reproductive rights—many of which take on a distinctly political cast.

Change is taking hold among businesses, both big and small. Among established companies and startups. In the US and worldwide. In fact, we found the beginnings of a consensus emerging—one that often spans political divides and is spreading across businesses of all shapes and sizes. Dynamic Capitalism is a journey of fits and starts, one that is clearly not a straight line nor unfolding in perfect unison or harmony. However, the next era is unfolding both in America and globally, and it will shape our lives for decades to come.

Section I

UNDERSTANDING CAPITALISM

Chapter 1

STANDING AT THE PRECIPICE

Jamie Dimon is one of the most famously diligent executives in American business. He has to be. Dimon leads one of the world's largest banks, a behemoth with 320,000 employees in 100 countries that moves $10 trillion daily. JPMorgan Chase is so large that when there's a run on a regional bank, Dimon gets a call for help from the US treasury secretary. The last time it happened was in 2023, resulting in JPMorgan leading a private-sector bailout of First Republic Bank.

Every week, Dimon runs risk scenarios to test JPMorgan's resilience amid global events: interest rate increases, bank defaults, global pandemics, and any number of other negative externalities that could have meaningful consequences for the company's business. That's because Dimon recognizes that JPMorgan, which has roots in the Industrial Revolution that helped America become the world's superpower, is more vulnerable than it may seem. Though it is among the world's largest banks, it is the only US bank among the world's five largest (the other four are Chinese banks—a testament to the size of the Chinese economy). Because JPMorgan banks small business owners, homeowners, and depositors across America, it is vulnerable both to the myriad factors that affect its customers' well-being as well as the US economy more generally. Dimon described to us how this position allows him to see firsthand the challenges of those who are struggling to keep a toehold on the American Dream, pinched on one side by reduced job prospects and on the other by rising costs of living, all while stretched thin with debt.[1] More than almost any other kind of business, banks are tied to the health of their communities. And Dimon's identity ties him even more to the success not just of JPMorgan but of America.

The World's 10 Largest Banks

Rank	Company	Headquarters	Assets (US$B)
1	Industrial and Commercial Bank of China Ltd. (1398-SEHK)	China	6,303
2	Agricultural Bank of China Ltd. (1288-SEHK)	China	5,623
3	China Construction Bank Corp. (939-SEHK)	China	5,400
4	Bank of China Ltd. (3988-SEHK)	China	4,578
5	JPMorgan Chase & Co. (JPM-NYSE)	US	3,875
6	Bank of America Corp. (BAC-NYSE)	US	3,180
7	HSBC Holdings PLC (HSBA-LSE)	UK	2,920
8	BNP Paribas SA (BNP-ENXTPA)	France	2,867
9	Mitsubishi UFJ Financial Group Inc. (8306-TSE)	Japan	2,817
10	Crédit Agricole Group	France	2,737

Figure 1. Source: S&P Global.

Back in 2019, he was the chairman of the Business Roundtable (BRT), a group of America's top corporate executives and one of the world's most quietly powerful lobbying groups. From this position, Dimon led a change that would become a flashpoint in an increasingly politicized debate about the role of corporations in our society. In hindsight, this period during the first Trump administration was a turning point between the previous world order, governed at least on the surface by democratic norms and mid-20th-century institutions, and an era in which large businesses have a much bigger and more overt role in our society. Of course, large companies have exerted influence on American life for decades. But over the past five years, it has become clear just how much business has become the dominant force in our society, holding sway over many of the critical issues of our time.

Companies have long been the beating heart of capitalism. Their purpose and structure have had a singular focus for the last 50 years: short-term profits delivered to shareholders. Dynamic Capitalism asks us to reconsider this focus. How should we create market-based systems that fairly distribute the profits of corporations to a wider base and that take into account longer-term measures of success? Put succinctly, if the biggest economic question of the last 50 years was about the role of *government* in the economy, the biggest question of the next 50 will be about the role of *business* in our economy.

Optimists by nature, we have called the new systems that are emerging "Dynamic Capitalism." But the contours of these systems—and its winners and losers—are still in question. It is the nature of these new systems that we will explore throughout this book.

The Purpose of a Corporation

When Dimon was chair of the BRT, he was approached by a columnist from *The Washington Post*, Steve Pearlstein, who challenged him about the Roundtable's then-definition of the purpose of a corporation. It seemed, according to Pearlstein, to have become out of date. Ultimately, Dimon and the CEOs of the BRT responded in a way that both changed 50 years of near-universal dogma and effectively asserted their position as the dominant force in American society.

Pondering Pearlstein's question, Dimon went back to read the BRT's *Statement of the Purpose of a Corporation*. At the time, America's rising political fractiousness was becoming tougher for JPMorgan and other companies to navigate. Every remark that Dimon made was parsed for its political implications. Activists on both sides of the political spectrum combed JPMorgan's public filings and press releases and scrutinized every business decision, looking for things they disagreed with. Environmentalists criticized JPMorgan for not being eco-friendly; at the same time, when the bank added renewable-energy projects to a portfolio that included plenty of fossil-fuel-related businesses, a raft of conservative state attorneys general went after it for not sufficiently supporting oil and gas.[2] The bank was being called upon not only to shore up the Treasury but to be a leader on economic and social issues as well.

The BRT's *Statement of the Purpose of a Corporation* had changed a few times over the years but generally made clear that the primary role of a corporation and its managers and directors was to maxamize profits to shareholders. Since the early 1970s, this idea has been central to American capitalism. "The paramount duty of management and of boards of directors is to the corporation's stockholders," the most recent BRT statement read.[3] Shareholder primacy, as this idea is known, leaves corporations free of responsibility for anything but profits.

In reality, of course, the idea of shareholder primacy has always been somewhat of a myth—at best, imperfectly practiced but, more realistically, completely unattainable. Corporate executives are human; their decisions are subject to many factors, only one of which is the bottom line. They hire their friends or are reluctant to lay people off. CEOs keep factories in their hometowns, make ego-driven bets, and engage in corporate buyouts to help companies run by CEOs they know. Corporate boards approve compensation packages that don't pass the test of reasonableness. Most corporate decisions are driven to some extent by emotion and bias (both good and bad). This is the reality of how business works, even if some would prefer more black-and-white thinking.

But for the past 50 years, shareholder primacy has been the central idea underpinning America's approach to business. To Dimon, this seemed to be hopelessly simplistic. When he or CEOs like Mary Barra of

General Motors, Mark Zuckerberg of Meta, or Harold Hamm of Continental Resources come to work, they worry about competition, globalization, and whether their companies will be around 10 years from now. "CEOs walk into the office every day," Dimon told us. "You think about 'How am I doing for customers? How's my product and service versus the competition? How do I get my employees better trained, with better products, better services, better equipment? How do I compete in the other parts of the world?' Shareholder value is an *outcome* of all of that . . . And matter of fact, if you do any one of those things poorly, you fail."[4]

CEOs get paid to look around corners and ensure their companies are successful in the long run. This involves understanding a complicated landscape that encompasses not just shareholders but other stakeholders. Recognizing this, and the overly simplistic reasoning of the BRT's then current *Statement*, Dimon began lobbying his fellow CEOs for an update—one that would reflect the reality of an increasingly complex business landscape. What he saw around the corner were new risks that required a new approach.

As a result of this work, the Roundtable released a new and updated *Statement* in 2019, signed initially by 181 member CEOs and eventually by nearly all the 200 or so BRT members (the BRT doesn't publish its precise number of members). "Americans deserve an economy that allows each person to succeed through hard work and creativity and to lead a life of meaning and dignity," said the new statement. "We commit to deliver value to all of them, for the future success of our companies, our communities and our country."[5]

The Measure of Success

The problem the CEOs were trying to tackle wasn't just a superficial concern over politics. The politics of blaming either "white men" or "immigrants and DEI" was obscuring a much more complicated story. They were aware—as many leaders across society have been—of the broad decline of dynamism in the American economy and the risk this decline poses to our shared future. Dynamic economies develop and embrace new technologies at higher rates, weather economic disruptions better, and bounce back faster from recessions. Dynamic economies benefit from the greater movement of people and their ties to broader communities. They create more and better jobs while offering greater career advancement opportunities, chances to start companies, and ways to capitalize on new ideas and inventions. Dynamic economies are especially good at creating job opportunities for marginalized workers, setting them on a course to advancement. Ultimately, dynamic economies use free market systems to deliver a better quality of life for the vast majority of people, not just those who are already advantaged.

We often celebrate America as a land of opportunity, where hard work and industry come together in the notion that anyone, anywhere, can become successful here. It's why so many people from across the globe fight for the opportunity to immigrate to the United States. But today, America is losing the broad-based economic dynamism that has been such a defining feature of our economy. In 1940, 90% of children would go on to outearn their parents; today, only 50% of millennials (those born between 1981 and 1996) are expected to do the same. It's now easier to climb the economic ladder in Sweden, Germany, France, and Japan than in the United States. The richest 1% of households had 15 times the combined wealth of the bottom 50% in 2021. That same 1% holds about one-third of the country's assets. And the gaps may widen as the top quintile of earners take an ever larger share from everybody below.[6] This declining dynamism has had negative repercussions for large segments of American society, harmed our democracy, contributed to rising polarization, and undermined American business interests.

Shareholder primacy and the idea that businesses could focus on short-term profits alone, leaving the responsibility for the rest of society up to institutions and government, won the latter part of the 20th century for America and helped create some of the largest companies in the world. But what the CEOs of the Roundtable realized was that what worked in the 20th century wasn't working in the 21st. Their new *Statement* challenged 50 years of corporate dogma and suggested that rather than shareholders being the sole beneficiaries of a business, companies should consider a broader set of stakeholders, including employees, vendors, and communities.[7] If society was struggling to function, business would have to step in.

Although the statement seemed innocuous on the surface, it ignited a firestorm. In retrospect, that's because it signaled a critical change of philosophy for many in the business community, and the start of a new era. In essence, the Roundtable CEOs were calling for a new form of capitalism—an evolution from the overly simplistic black-and-white thinking of neoliberalism to something more nuanced, less rules based, and more long-term oriented, in which business leaders had more responsibility and more power as unelected decision makers. Capitalism has always been more fluid than many give it credit for. Norms and laws shift within the business community and in relation to governments and society. Society evolves and ebbs and flows, as do the constructs that underpin it.

Academics and activists on America's political left dismissed the BRT's shift as merely performative—words on a page that were unlikely to bring about meaningful action. Meanwhile, America's right-wing political community took the move differently: They hated it. Conservative activists criticized the Roundtable CEOs for bowing to political correctness and labeled them "woke," a moniker soon championed by the political right to encompass any move by corporate America they disagreed with. Some extremists targeted signatory companies for boycotts and singled their leaders out as anti-American. In at least one case, which we'll talk about in chapter 2, a CEO's family received death threats.*

In retrospect, shareholder primacy and the old system of capitalism rest on three assumptions that have been growing ever shakier: (1) that companies will create enough decent-paying jobs to support communities (and that people holding those jobs will, in turn, rear law-abiding citizens and consumers), (2) that stockholders are reasonably rational and reward companies that are well managed, and (3) that government is strong enough to police a sufficiently fair market (and that markets also self-govern and prevent bad actors from running rampant). When assumptions as basic as these come into question, economies lose their dynamism.

By 2019, as Dimon and his fellow CEOs debated the role of corporations in our society, all of these assumptions were being called into question. The introduction of new technologies in recent decades has divided labor markets, in which the skills of a few people, including CEOs, engineers, and other "thought workers," have become more valuable, while the skills of many others have become less so—a trend that appears to be accelerating. The breakdown in information systems and the proliferation of unreliable information made it harder for people to make informed decisions about companies and their governance (or anything, for that matter). And the US government, weakened after decades of creeping corporate power, was failing to police monopoly and other forms of entrenched influence, resulting in fewer innovative companies reaching the market. Power—both corporate and governmental—was becoming ever more concentrated. Many Roundtable CEOs felt deep conviction over their role as longer-term stewards of their businesses and the key stakeholders surrounding them. Many also likely recognized that

---

* See the next chapter when we introduce Dan Schulman from PayPal, a signatory of the new BRT statement, who told us about the death threats he faced after some of his controversial decisions.

this moment granted them an opportunity to become even more central actors in not just our economy but also our society as a whole.

Examining the roots of this next phase of capitalism, as we do throughout the book, showed us that the hue and cry over "woke" capitalism is more political than substantive. The actual conflict is better described as between those who make decisions for their short-term interests—safely ensconced in the cozy rationale that the "markets know best"—and those whose orientation is more long term. Between those who delude themselves with simple thinking and those who see the complex fabric that comprises our business and social landscape. With America teetering on political dysfunction and authoritarianism rising worldwide, companies and business leaders have been shifting for some time to assume more responsibility for their communities—in ways both recognized and more subtle, and in ways you may or may not agree with. This change in business culture has often been dismissed entirely or turned to political ends. The BRT's action should have sparked a conversation about these changes, but instead, it became one more sign that we're on a knife's edge. Rather than an honest dialogue about the future of capitalism, it created a stalemate between a left wing that sanctimoniously wants to jettison capitalism—in favor of what is never clear—and those on the right who refuse any discussion about changing it. Political division is common in American life and history. But what was uncommon about this moment was that the politicization of our national conversation infected the business world and the ability of change makers in our culture to find consensus or compromise. With democracy and broad prosperity so inextricably linked, doing so is critical.

Why We Need Dynamic Capitalism

All of this change and uncertainty adds up to an environment fraught with challenges, which have only grown as the second Trump administration has unfolded. Leaders swimming in a sea of change need to understand it better to navigate this moment successfully. As a society, we are struggling to find a consensus, if such a thing is even possible in our current state of political instability and unrest. But, having talked to dozens of business leaders, academics, politicians, workers, and researchers, we believe such a consensus about the future of our economic system *is* starting to emerge, based on the ideas of opportunity for more people, expanding ownership, limited government, and a more cautious stance to global engagement (although not an overly protectionist one, as some have argued for). Seen through this lens, the turmoil unleashed by President Trump in his second term is a sign of neoliberalism in its end state. A populist, militaristic leader has created a Frankenstein version of neoliberalism, with a smaller government used as a tool to punish opponents and reward allies. But the forces at work today, and the potential for a new consensus, are larger than any one leader.

In the first part of this book, we describe the birth of neoliberal capitalism and how we arrived at our current contentious moment. Importantly, we'll directly address whether capitalism is inherently exploitative and argue for why we think the best path forward lies not in replacing free markets but embracing them. In the middle of the book, we explore the roots of our division and the history that brought us to this moment. We'll then turn to the stories and strategies of those leading the movement toward Dynamic Capitalism and the various ways they are working to shape a new narrative. We pay special attention to the challenges of being a corporate leader in an environment where there is rising pressure to speak out on issues that don't necessarily relate directly to a company's operations. Relatedly, we'll discuss a few notable controversies that occurred when CEOs have waded into public discourse and debate.

Certainly, the government has a role to play in our path forward, but the changes brought about by Dynamic Capitalism need to be bottom up, not top down. We'll talk about the role of government in shaping (as well as staying out of the way of) this new system. Given the fossil fuel underpinnings of our economy, we'll also address questions about climate and how Dynamic Capitalism must help us move away from a dependence on extractive technologies while recognizing that this transition needs to be undertaken carefully and thoughtfully. The free flow of capital is critical in any capitalist system, but our current system is becoming ever more concentrated, with a small number of firms wielding unprecedented power, supposedly on behalf of their underlying investors. We'll question that assumption and propose ways to rethink the relationship between investors and the intermediaries who control the vast majority of investment funds.

One of the most interesting ideas we encountered in our research is the need to develop more of an ownership economy. We will discuss various ideas to promote this concept, including devoting a full chapter to ideas centered around creating more owners and capitalists. This is important as new technologies, including artificial intelligence and quantum computing, continue to replace jobs. In the book's last section, we'll offer suggestions on how to encourage and shape Dynamic Capitalism, including policy prescriptions and opportunities for individual action.

The Path Forward

This is a heady book, but we've done our best to make it approachable. Neither of us is an economist, and because of that, our treatment of the underlying economic issues is more common sense than academic.* Like you, we are concerned citizens who want to better understand how we came to this moment and how we move forward—together.

New eras arise from the remains of old ones and weave together

---

* That said, we talked to a number of economists in our research for this book.

threads of the past to create a new fabric. In the coming pages, you'll meet some of the leaders and ideas coming together today, from Silicon Valley to Rochester, New York, to Washington, DC. And we hope that you'll recognize, as we did, that you have the power to be a part of this change. In fact, you may already be.

Chapter 2

THE BEAUTY AND FALLACY OF MILTON FRIEDMAN

In 2019, Dan Schulman, then CEO of PayPal, asked for a report on how the company's employees were doing to help him prepare for a town hall–style company meeting. As he looked through the pages of the report, he was shocked. Many of the company's 23,000 employees, particularly those in entry-level jobs or who worked in PayPal's call centers, were clearly struggling.[1] Some were choosing between health benefits and putting food on the table. One customer service representative in Omaha was selling his blood plasma twice a month in an attempt to make ends meet.[2]

Schulman was stunned. He'd thought of PayPal as a company that treated its employees well. And he thought he'd been doing his job by benchmarking the company's compensation against its competitors'. Schulman's thinking at the time, which mirrors that of many executives and board members, is telling. He assumed that markets work. That if PayPal was meeting or topping its competitors' pay, *everyone was fine*.

"We all have a dependence on market data," he told us. "We benchmark on market data. That's how all compensation elements are done. If you're paying at or better than what your competitors are paying, and you're able to attract the best and most highly skilled workers, then obviously your odds of being a successful company improve. But after we surveyed our employees, I really realized that certain elements of capitalism needed an upgrade, that the hand of the market does not work for everyone."[3]

Across the country, hundreds of thousands, if not millions, of business leaders share the thinking that if the free market dictates it, it works.[4] You can trace this widespread belief back to Milton Friedman, whose ideas have dominated boardrooms and corporate executives' mindshare for the latter half of the 20th century and into the 21st. This ideology doesn't question the primacy of "markets" and certainly does not encourage corporate leadership to question prevailing wages (Friedman was famously against a minimum wage, for example). What is good for shareholders, the Friedman view espouses, is good for everyone.

Schulman ultimately rejected the black-and-white idea that he and the company should leave it up to the markets to set wages; in his view, the markets had failed. With the approval of his board, he came up with ways to set pay and benefits that fall into a much grayer territory. His actions were dictated partly by what he believed to be his greater responsibility, but also by his vision for the kind of company he wanted to create. These changes—which included paying many workers weekly instead of bimonthly, boosting the company's contribution to healthcare costs, and raising compensation—not only impacted tens of thousands of PayPal workers but also served as a model for other businesses. He described it as one of the most important things PayPal and its board did during his tenure.

In America, Schulman and other CEOs are on the front lines—and as the death threats he and others have experienced show, "front lines" is more than just a metaphor—in one of the most important and contentious battles of our times. In that fight, there's no more symbolic or polarizing figure than Milton Friedman.

Some people see Friedman as a hero whose 1970 manifesto clearly articulated a worldview that accelerated capitalist ideals and economic freedom around the globe. Others see him as a villain whose cynical and single-minded view of how companies should act led to the collapse of responsibility in the business world, accelerated climate change, and sparked massive social and political inequality. Because of the immense impact of Friedman's philosophy on generations of business leaders, it is important that we take a moment to better understand this thinking, and especially the context in which his ideas were born and the conditions in which they spread.

The Friedman Doctrine

Friedman is most closely associated with the idea that the sole focus of every business should be to maximize shareholder value—"shareholder primacy." His seminal 1970 essay, published in *The New York Times*, described his rationale for why businesses and their leaders should only focus on maximizing returns to owners.[5] The title, "The Social Responsibility of Business Is to Increase Its Profits," aptly describes his views on the subject. Friedman argues this point emphatically:

> *In a free-enterprise, private-property system, a corporate executive is an employee of the owners of the business. He has direct responsibility to his employers. That responsibility is to conduct the business in accordance with their desires . . . the key point is that, in his capacity as a corporate executive, the manager is the agent of the individuals who own the corporation . . . and his primary responsibility is to them.*

Friedman believed that an executive spending company money on social causes is, in essence, spending somebody else's money for their own purposes:

> *Insofar as [a business executive's] actions in accord with his "social responsibility" reduce returns to stockholders, he is spending their money. Insofar as his actions raise the price to customers, he is spending the customers' money. Insofar as his actions lower the wages of some employees, he is spending their money . . . What does it mean to say that "business" can have responsibilities? Only people can have responsibilities.*

His work, and that of other economists at the University of Chicago, became the foundation of neoliberal capitalism, representing a shift in thinking about how the economic system should express society's values. Neoliberal capitalism is centered on the idea that human well-being can best be advanced by a combination of social and economic freedoms, characterized by strong private property rights, free markets, and free trade.

After Friedman's essay, neoliberal capitalism emerged as the dominant definition of capitalism around the world. It was initially spread by Ronald Reagan and Margaret Thatcher, but since then, it has been advanced by many academics and politicians from across the political spectrum. Based on America's strong track record of economic growth, and buoyed by the international financial system that America has a dominant hand in maintaining, countries worldwide adopted the ideas Friedman and his neoliberal peers advocated.

Friedman in Historical Context

Born in 1912, Friedman was the child of Jewish immigrants to New York City. The first part of Friedman's life was shaped by two world wars, which upended the social and world order that existed at the time of his birth. After receiving a BA from Rutgers University in 1932 (at the age of 20), he earned a master's degree in 1933 from the University of Chicago, where he would later return to teach, and with which he is so associated that many of his ideas came to be known more broadly as the "Chicago School" of economics. Later, in 1946, he received a PhD from Columbia. He won the Nobel Prize in Economics in 1976 for his work on consumption analysis, monetary history and theory, and the complexity of stabilization policy.[6]

In 1947, he was among the 36 men who met at the Mont Pelerin Hotel outside of Montreux, Switzerland, to frame a new economic system that they believed would shape the postwar world and deliver broad prosperity, not to mention create the economy necessary to pay for the rebuilding of a decimated Europe. It was the first meeting of what became the Mont Pelerin Society, a group that still meets regularly and strongly espouses economic freedom, generally standing against measures that would constrain the actions of businesses, especially government regulations and trade restrictions.[7]

That first meeting included a collection of some of the most famous economists not just of the time but, in retrospect, in history. Their view from the ashes of Europe would shape the world economic order for decades. Ludwig von Mises was appalled at what National Socialism had done to Europe. Friedrich Hayek was terrified of the rise in the east of Soviet collectivism. Milton Friedman argued that individual freedom was the essential precondition for economic decision-making. Citing the murders in Germany and Russia of millions of people who dared oppose collectivism, they believed that the path to happiness lay in encouraging private ownership and individual freedom, both in the political and economic sense. For Friedman and the other men assembled at Mont Pelerin, economic and political freedom were linked. In fact, they might have been one and the same. The founding statement of the society explained,

> *The central values of civilization are in danger. Over large stretches of the earth's surface the essential conditions of human dignity and freedom have already disappeared ... The position of the individual and the voluntary group are progressively undermined by extensions of arbitrary power [as well as] ... a decline of belief in private property and the competitive market.*[8]

While it was some 20 years between the meeting in Montreux and his authoring of the Friedman Doctrine, which he outlined first in his book, *Capitalism and Freedom,* and then more succinctly in his 1970 *New York Times* essay, these early experiences shaped Friedman's view on the role of individual actors (including corporations) and his work on what we now refer to as supply-side economics and monetary theory. His academic work focused on the relationship between inflation and employment, and many of his arguments ran counter to the mainstream economic ideology of John Maynard Keynes, which Keynes had developed in the aftermath of the Great Depression and posits that governments have the ability to stabilize economies by stimulating demand, which in turn creates full employment and keeps prices stable.

Friedman, in contrast, believed that there was a natural rate of unemployment, below which inflation would increase significantly. He was a vocal proponent of free-market principles and favored limited government intervention and minimal regulation of private markets. With this worldview, he served as a key economic advisor to US President Ronald Reagan and British Prime Minister Margaret Thatcher. His libertarian leanings came through on issues such as conscription (he once called his role in helping to eliminate mandatory military service in the United States his "most important accomplishment"), taxation, exchange rates, and the minimum wage.[9]

Friedman's thinking proved irresistible to the policymakers and business leaders of the time. It was appealingly simple, and it connected the ideology of American political thought—ideals like free speech and freedom of assembly—to the economic sphere.

As we researched this book, we looked at his ideas in the context of his experiences and the time in which he proposed them to better understand why now is the time for new thinking. When Friedman published his essay, men were the primary breadwinners, women cared for children and the elderly for free, and people could expect to work for only two or three employers in their lifetimes. In a smaller and tighter-knit country, executives had a much better window into the rest of society. Corporations were at the center of community life, and the benefit of those corporations was intertwined with the stability of the economy as a whole. Public-company shareholders were primarily individual investors, as money market accounts and stock funds were either yet to be invented or had not achieved widespread adoption. Friedman and the other economists meeting in Montreux were very much the products of their era's turbulent political environment. The world was grappling with critical questions of how societies should organize themselves after the war. Capitalism versus communism, as well as individual rights and action versus collectivism, were the key debates.

Several decades later, Friedman, still struggling with these same fundamental questions, wrote his *Times* essay in the midst of the Cold War and at the height of European socialism. It was this framing and context that produced Friedman's thinking about the political economy and the role of corporations. When businesses were allowed to compete unencumbered by regulation, those with the best ideas or products would win, he thought. Government intervention, in Friedman's view, was akin to state planning and communism. He didn't have examples of different forms of capitalism, as we do today, which offer us the idea that there is potential for variation and nuance. Nor did he seriously consider government as a funder of innovation, which turned out to be a critical oversight. That said, even in his original 1970 essay, Friedman acknowledged that some corporations might have a purpose beyond profits, a tacit acceptance that his theory was neither truly an overarching framework for business nor as simplistic as many have since made it out to be. Typically lost in critiques of the Friedman Doctrine is his nuanced view about those things that appeared to be "social responsibility" but were, in fact, in the long-term best interests of the corporation. As he wrote in the *Times*,

> *it may well be in the long-run interest of a corporation that is a major employer in a small community to devote resources to providing amenities to that community or to improving its government. That may make it easier to attract desirable employees, it may reduce the wage bill or lessen losses from pilferage and sabotage or have other worthwhile effects. Or it may be that, given the laws about the deductibility of corporate charitable contributions, the stockholders can contribute more to charities they favor by having the corporation make the gift than by doing it themselves, since they can in that way contribute an amount that would otherwise have been paid as corporate taxes.*[10]

Even Friedman acknowledges that we live in a complex world.

The Overly Simplified "Beauty" of Neoliberal Capitalism

Though Friedman became the standard bearer for his ideas about how to bolster freedom by segregating business from society, he was one of many people thinking along the same lines in the early 1970s. Business leaders from across the political spectrum tend to despise chaos and unrest, which make their jobs that much harder. The 1960s had been a decade of upheaval in American life, including the Civil Rights Movement, the rise of feminism and women's empowerment, the assassinations of Martin Luther King Jr. and John and Robert Kennedy, and protests against the Vietnam War. The government enacted or expanded a number of programs, including Medicare, whose implementation fell heavily on private businesses, adding to the strains of earlier social programs.

In August 1971, Lewis F. Powell Jr., who was about to be elevated to the Supreme Court by Richard Nixon, sent a confidential memo to the US Chamber of Commerce, arguing that criticism of and opposition to the US free enterprise system had gone too far and that "the time had come—indeed it is long overdue—for the wisdom, ingenuity, and resources of American business to be marshaled against those who would destroy it." Powell argued that individual action was insufficient. "Strength," he wrote, "lies in organization, in careful long-range planning and implementation, in the consistency of action over an indefinite period of years, in the scale of financing available only through joint effort, and in the political power available only through united action and national organizations." The national Chamber of Commerce, he argued, should try to change how individuals think "about the corporation, the law, culture, and the individual."[11]

The Chamber of Commerce subsequently expanded its base from around 60,000 firms in 1972 to over a quarter of a million 10 years later. Along with the National Association of Manufacturers (which moved to Washington in 1972), it began to lobby Congress and engage in research that would be disseminated to the public.[12] As the Chamber of Commerce expanded to represent the broad community of businesses, the Business Roundtable, representing executives only, was established in 1972.

All this worked. The mainstream business community adopted the thinking of the newly minted "neoliberals." In 1976, in a paper that did more than any outside of Friedman's itself to advance the Friedman Doctrine, Michael Jensen and William Meckling argued that companies could easily get distracted from their mission of maximizing profits by "frivolities" such as charitable contributions and "personal relations" ("friendship," "respect," and so on) with employees. Their *Theory of the Firm* suggested that companies that didn't focus exclusively on profits ran the risk of being too community or employee minded. In their writing, Jensen and Meckling also argued in favor of compensating executives with rich stock option packages to "align" their incentives to that of the company's financial performance and creation of shareholder value (as measured by stock market gains), laying the groundwork for the rapid rise of executive and CEO compensation that would occur throughout the last part of the 20th century and into the 21st.[13]

American public opinion moved toward neoliberal capitalism too. In just one example of the extent to which Friedman's views became popularized, in 1977 a television version of Milton Friedman's book *Free to Choose* was produced, funded with a grant from Richard Mellon Scaife, an American billionaire and the principal heir to the Mellon banking, oil, and aluminum fortune that dated back to before the Industrial Revolution.[14]

None of our recounting of this history and context is meant to excuse the harm that has come from Friedman's thinking (and his own efforts to popularize it), as countless adherents to this dogma used the veil of the Friedman Doctrine to justify actions that compromised any number of other stakeholders, such as the environment, employees, or community, in the name of profits. But it was the rigid adherence to short-term profits, adopted conveniently by many of Friedman's adherents, that has led us the farthest astray. Even Friedman acknowledged that short-term decision-making at the expense of longer-term benefit is not in a company's best interest.

Companies exist to perpetuate themselves and create long-term sustainability. In fact, that's necessary if they are to stay in business. Most companies actually fail at this, and in many respects, this failure is the result of short-term thinking trumping longer-term planning and investment.

Friedman's ideas—which evolved in an ivory tower—eventually became less and less practical for companies working in the real world. This is the most pernicious effect of Friedman's views. Too many have taken his ideas to an extreme that even Friedman likely didn't envision, at times to their grave detriment.

American companies today exist in a world of constant change, which partly explains why short-termism became so appealing. Even companies that appear to be stalwarts of our economy are not immune. As just one example of this process in action, consider the rate of turnover among companies on the Fortune 500 list of America's largest corporations. With a half-life of just 20 years, the list is in constant flux.[15] This isn't due to a lack of effort to generate profits but to a lack of foresight and investment into their longer-term future. In today's economy, too many believe these ideas are in opposition—often citing Friedman as the (incorrect) reason to focus on short-term gains.

Keeping shareholders happy in the short term often seems like the right thing to do, especially when considering how you keep your job as CEO, executive, manager, or employee, but it rarely actually is. Clearly, many companies and corporate executives don't understand or even consider the longer-term consequences of their actions, and as a result, they fail to make the investments necessary to keep their businesses thriving. It's perhaps a testament to the US form of capitalism that our economy has so readily created new businesses and given them paths to become large companies.

Jack Welch and the Fallacy of Short-Term Thinking

No company better personifies the Friedman Doctrine taken to its extreme than General Electric under Jack Welch. Founded in 1889 by

Thomas Edison, the Edison General Electric Company brought together a handful of business ventures that Edison had been working on, then acquired several more in related industries. (Welch, who would later go on a historic acquisition spree, surely must have appreciated that GE was founded as an immediately acquisitive company.) In 1896, GE became one of the original 12 companies comprising the Dow Jones Industrial Average, and it remained on that list for 122 years (although not continuously). Over the many years of its existence, GE operated in an array of markets, from lighting and power generation to heavy industries to medical devices and aviation.[16]

Having joined in 1960 as a junior engineer in GE's Pittsfield, Massachusetts, operation, Welch rose quickly. He headed GE's plastics division (1968) and its metallurgical and chemical divisions (1971), and became group executive in charge of GE's chemical, metallurgical, medical systems, appliance components, and electronic components businesses. In 1977, he was named head of the consumer products and services division, and in 1979, he became vice chairman and heir apparent to CEO Reginald Jones, whom he replaced as CEO and chairman in 1981.[17]

The business world and an admiring media knew Welch for his hard-charging leadership style and his view that GE should only compete in industries where it could be the number one or number two market participant. He had a reputation for extreme candor and instituted a policy of firing the bottom 10% of the GE workforce annually, regardless of the performance of the business. His cost cutting earned him the nickname "Neutron Jack." GE was relentlessly acquisitive under Welch, buying more than 600 businesses during his time as CEO, including RCA, NBC, and Honeywell International. During Welch's 20-year reign, GE's stock price rose an average of 25% per year, a performance unparalleled in corporate history.

This growth in earnings and profit came at a cost, including significant employee turnover and job losses (under Welch, the company let go of some 250,000 employees). Most importantly, the GE that Jack Welch built turned out to be a house of cards. The pursuit of quarterly earnings led the company to adopt accounting practices that were nefarious and, in many cases, both misleading and illegal. The company eventually paid a $200 million fine after a Securities and Exchange Commission investigation found that it had deceived investors through fraudulent reporting. Much of what Welch created evaporated, along with the stock price he fought so single-mindedly for. Once the most valuable company in the country, GE is a shadow of its former self. In 2018, it was removed from the Dow Jones Industrial Average.

Earlier leaders of GE had been different. In 1927, GE's then chairman, Owen D. Young, encouraged businessmen to "think in terms of human beings—one group of human beings who put their capital in, and another group who put their lives and labor in a common enterprise for mutual advantage." He derided those who "devise ways and means to squeeze out of labor its last ounce of effort and last penny of compensation." GE's 1953 annual report described how the firm worked "in the balanced best interest of all." This included paying taxes, paying suppliers fairly, and taking care of its employees.[18]

But under Welch, GE—indeed the entire country—turned a new page, embracing the neoliberal approach and Friedman's doctrine to an alarming degree. Approaching business with a singular focus on corporate earnings and stock price, Welch failed to understand the consequences of his short-term thinking. GE is an extreme example, partly because the market rewarded it for its execution of Friedman's principles so richly and for such a long period of time before the bottom fell out, and partly because when its reckoning finally came, it fell so far and so hard. However, Welch also played a particular role in the history of American CEOs as the poster child for the Friedman era. At his height, Welch was considered to be among the greatest CEOs of the modern age.[19] His influence on business, politics, and the world economy is hard to overstate. This was especially true in the realm of corporate idealism. In fact, it was Welch who led the effort at the Business Roundtable in 1997 to change their statement on the purpose of a corporation from the more nuanced view its members previously espoused to the more strict, Friedman-compliant view that "the paramount duty of management and of boards of directors is to the corporation's stockholders ... The interests of other stakeholders are relevant as a derivative of the duty to stockholders."[20] Companies (and societies) worldwide are still grappling with the repercussions of Welch's hold on the American business psyche.

The Meaning of Milton Friedman

Friedman clearly believed deeply in the concepts he outlined in his 1970 essay. He lived another 36 years and never publicly revised his views on the singular purpose of corporations. In many respects, he doubled down on them, despite some of the ways in which their implementation was clearly running astray from his thinking. His influence was far reaching and extended beyond political boundaries. When Friedman died in 2006, Larry Summers, Bill Clinton's treasury secretary and a senior advisor to President Obama (and, subsequently, president of Harvard University), said, "Any honest Democrat will admit that we are now all Friedmanites."[21]

From the beginning, Milton Friedman's views were oversimplified. Friedman himself made space for long-term thinking, although that part of his essay didn't tend to get as much attention. It's important to remember that he, too, was shaped not only by WWII but by the big government programs of the 1960s, whose flaws were already apparent at the time of his seminal essay. This is part of the essence of capitalism: It evolves in reaction to problems that earlier iterations create. Understanding what Friedman actually believed and putting it properly into the context of the time is important if we are to both critique those who put his ideas into practice as well as reject those ideas for our present era.

It's easy to look at the Friedman Doctrine and declare it ill-conceived, even heartless, but our view is a more nuanced one. We certainly don't think that Friedman was correct in how he described the role of businesses. But his view was more complex than he is often given credit for—the difference between the soundbite version of his nearly 3,000-word essay and the fuller, more discerning read (not to mention his much lengthier treatment of these questions in *Capitalism and Freedom*). Understanding Friedman's views in context provides a framework from which to consider how they might naturally change or evolve over time, as even he acknowledged capitalism itself does. One of the fundamental theses of this book is that viewing capitalism as a static concept is more of an academic or parochial way of thinking. The reality is that capitalism is quite dynamic.

Better Pay, Better Benefits

After PayPal's Dan Schulman had his rude awakening that relying on market forces alone to determine his employees' pay wasn't working, he decided to approach the question of compensation from a different perspective. This, he came to believe, was not just for the betterment of the affected employees but for the benefit of the entire business. He didn't undertake this process lightly, nor did he assume that simply raising pay was the right answer, at least not in the absence of other measures. Not surprisingly for a technology company, the process PayPal embarked upon was data heavy and started with a more detailed analysis of the true financial health of the PayPal employee base. The company engaged with academics and nonprofit organizations to develop a new metric of financial health—net disposable income (NDI). NDI measured how much money each employee had left over after paying basic expenses—food, housing, gas, taxes, and the like. By PayPal's formulation, an NDI of below 20% was problematic.

With this more precise measure, PayPal surveyed its employees again, and the results were alarming. Fully half of the company's employees had NDIs of around 4%, which explains why so many reported financial stress and were struggling to pay for even basic necessities (or selling their plasma). Schulman set the company along a path to increase NDI for all employees to above 20% and authorized a multifaceted program to do so. First, despite already paying above minimum wage in all its markets, PayPal increased pay across the board. They also instituted a stock-option program that included all employees, not just company management. However, survey data revealed that simply raising pay would not be enough, so PayPal also initiated a comprehensive financial literacy and financial management program for its employees. This would help them better manage their expenses and develop savings plans that would help build wealth to insulate them from unexpected expenditures. Last, PayPal became determined to help solve what they learned from their survey data was the number one issue confronting their employee base: healthcare costs. These expenses were eating into employees' wages and significantly lowering their NDI scores. This is not an uncommon experience, but those in higher income brackets easily overlook the considerable effect of healthcare costs. To address this, PayPal reduced these costs for its lowest-paid employees by some 60%. Schulman told us that from his perspective, this was probably the most dramatic and impactful part of the PayPal program.

The changes instituted by Schulman cost tens of millions of dollars, a relatively small amount considering PayPal's net income, which has ranged from $2 billion to $4 billion over the past five years. Schulman says the investment has been well worth it. "I believe very strongly that the only sustainable competitive advantage that a company has is the skill set and the passion of their employees," he said.[22] Employee engagement "skyrocketed," he told us—and employee churn went down dramatically.[23]

Schulman sees no trade-off between building a company that creates value for shareholders while considering other stakeholders. "This whole idea that profit and purpose are at odds with each other is ridiculous," he said.[24] One quickly learns when talking to Schulman that he strongly believes in a values-driven approach to business and also that he's as comfortable defending his actions through the lens of long-term value creation as he is talking about them from a principles perspective. When the chance came to vote on the Business Roundtable's new statement, Schulman was quick to sign on.

The practical effect of the 2019 statement on actual business practices, including for the companies whose CEOs signed on, is debatable. But the statement certainly raised the question of whether the age of the Friedman Doctrine was finally over, while helping to shine a light on that doctrine and the man behind it for a new generation of business leaders, many of whom were unfamiliar with his work even if they practiced his teachings.

This is the strength of capitalism writ large. It can transform itself from within, and when individuals with the power to do so decide to make changes, they can move quickly and decisively.

Chapter 3

THE POLITICIZATION OF BUSINESS AND THE FALLACY OF WOKE

In 2018 and 2019, another influential member of the Business Roundtable, Larry Fink, founder and CEO of the investment firm BlackRock, weighed in with his views on businesses' role in society. In his 2018 annual shareholder letter, he called for companies to adopt a greater purpose and to serve stakeholders as well as shareholders. In his 2019 letter, he called for CEOs to be leaders in a divided world.

BlackRock is the world's largest investor, owning shares in thousands of companies globally. Fink wrote that it was crucial that businesses make "a positive contribution to society" and told CEOs he would ask for their specific plans to do so. He said he would hold them to account for adopting a purpose (or more than one) and taking meaningful steps to further it.[1]

Four years later, in the summer of 2023, Larry Fink told an audience of wealthy and influential people gathered for the Aspen Institute's Ideas Festival in Aspen, Colorado, that he was embarrassed to have been part of the movement toward stakeholder capitalism, at least in the way it had turned out.* "I'm ashamed of being part of this conversation . . . when I wrote these investment letters, it was never meant to be a political statement," he said.[2]

The story of what happened in the years between Fink's bold pronouncements and his public retreat is a cautionary tale for business leaders, though also a reassurance for people who worry about businesses' growing power. It gives us hope that when companies do take a stand, they can coalesce change. Though, as Fink acknowledged, the process isn't pretty. Ultimately, the stories that follow of what happened to three powerful CEOs who took stands for what they believed was social progress are also a sign of what's to come. Companies need to consider the long-term effects of their decisions and actions while including stakeholders other than shareholders in their thinking. But those decisions will be open to criticism and challenge, and there are limits to how vocal companies can and should be in today's cultural debates. In our current politicized environment, business has become political too. As we write this, in the spring of 2025, the politicization of business has become even more extreme, to the point where companies are being targeted and persecuted by the government for any number of practices that the current administration deems wrong. This is an unprecedented governmental intrusion into private businesses. Although alarming for any number of reasons, the politicization of business is both threatening *and* a sign that we're in the midst of creating a new social compact. The debates about the limits of corporate power and when stakeholder advocacy turns into corporate activism are important but as yet unsettled ones.

---

* It's rare to hear a businessman as powerful as Fink admit to being ashamed. Perhaps he felt a degree of comfort or intimacy because of the setting. Or maybe he had simply reached a point of exhaustion, having become a lightning rod for criticism around stakeholder versus shareholder capitalism. After the session, Elizabeth asked Fink about his previous comment, and he backtracked: "I'm not ashamed. I do believe in conscious capitalism."

Masters Reshaping the Universe

With a stake in thousands of companies, BlackRock is the world's largest financial manager, with over $11 trillion in assets under management as of the end of 2024.[3] Because of this position, Larry Fink and BlackRock carry immense sway over nearly every sector of the global economy. Fink's annual letter, much like those of Warren Buffett and Jamie Dimon, has become required reading for business leaders and aspiring capitalists the world over.

In his 2019 letter, Fink argued that

> [P]urpose is not a mere tagline or marketing campaign; it is a company's fundamental reason for being—what it does every day to create value for its stakeholders. Purpose is not the sole pursuit of profits but the animating force for achieving them. Profits are in no way inconsistent with purpose—in fact, profits and purpose are inextricably linked. Profits are essential if a company is to effectively serve all of its stakeholders over time—not only shareholders, but also employees, customers, and communities.[4]

While Fink had talked about a company's purpose in prior CEO letters, in 2019 he staked out new ground in a way that had been previously unheard of for a mainstream investment management company—let alone the world's largest asset manager. His 2019 letter mentioned "purpose" 18 times and referenced "stakeholder" 6 times.

The letter reverberated across the business landscape and ignited almost immediate controversy. Attorneys general in nearly 20 states (all Republicans) pushed back. Some called for boycotts or divestment of state assets from BlackRock funds. Others passed laws trying to codify Milton Friedman's notion of shareholder primacy more firmly into state laws. There were calls for Fink's resignation.

While the backlash against Fink and BlackRock was meaningful—in Aspen, he noted, "Our business was hurt; we lost $4 billion because of 90% misinformation"—the pain was fleeting.[5] Fink and BlackRock retreated from some of their public championing of the ideas of stakeholder capitalism but not their substance. BlackRock and Fink continue to maintain pro-stakeholder views. The company was coming off its best year ever, Fink said, with $400 billion of net capital inflows, $200 billion of that in the United States. And Fink has doubled down on some of his thinking, calling in 2020, for example, for meaningful corporate action around climate change ("Climate risk is investment risk," he wrote).[6]

It is a bold step for leaders of financial institutions to talk about the importance of managing businesses with a broader view toward purpose. Just as bold is their advocating that stakeholders such as employees, customers, and communities, in addition to shareholders, should be considered in any investment analysis. Many argue that this purpose and broader outlook is a better path toward more widespread societal prosperity and, ultimately, better investment returns. Finance often lags behind other sectors of the economy in advocating for change of the type that Fink describes. Moreover, it often finds ways to relegate new thinking to the corners of the investment world where it can be effectively marginalized. Not so in this case.

Fink isn't the only CEO to run headlong into a backlash and the new social conservative movement against "woke capitalism." The core of this anti-woke, socially conservative movement looks familiar, including opposition to abortion rights, LGBTQ+ rights, and affirmative action. There are also signs that the movement is aligned with fossil fuel companies seeking to slow or resist the transition to alternative fuels.* Others pushing back are taking closer aim at corporate interests they feel are

---

* For example, the Heartland Institute, a conservative think tank funded largely by the fossil fuel industry, published a number of opinion pieces and reports decrying the dangers of "woke capitalism."

straying too far from their traditional lanes when they, or their leaders, speak out on social issues, although these same groups don't seem to object when companies address conservative-aligned topics.

While much of the backlash comes from the right side of the political spectrum, the left also engages in the politization of business. Liberal-leaning states have long exercised the power of their purses to influence companies on issues such as gun reform and climate. California, for instance, does not do business with underwriters who also underwrite gun companies' debt. Just as on the right, powerful groups on the left seek to impose their version of political correctness on businesses—calling out those that don't meet their standards for worker compensation, transparency, diversity, or politics. Look no further than efforts to support the Green New Deal—a sweeping and generally unrealistic set of corporate and environmental goals that would dramatically change the business landscape.

There is nothing wrong with political groups from either side trying to influence the government—or businesses, for that matter. That's the way the American system has always functioned. But to the extent that the toxic political and information environment keeps Dynamic Capitalism from happening, America will be worse off. It's not the government that's getting in the way in the stories we relate next—it's politics.

Cat-and-Mouse Games

The Walt Disney Company's presence in Florida dates to the mid-1960s, when the company purchased more than 27,000 acres of undeveloped swampland near Orlando. In 1971, the doors to Walt Disney World opened, and it quickly became a major tourist destination. Today, the economic impact of Disney World on the Florida economy is staggering. With four theme parks, more than two dozen hotels, and a local workforce of some 70,000, Disney is responsible for more than $75 billion in annual economic impact and nearly $6 billion in local and state tax revenue, according to a 2019 study by Oxford Economics.[7]

With this backdrop, consider the fight that embroiled Disney and the state of Florida. The dispute originated with a Florida law, the Parental Rights in Education Act, referred to by many critics as the "Don't Say Gay" bill.[8] The legislation prohibits the teaching and discussion of sexual orientation and gender identity to early elementary school students.

The 2022 bill was immediately polarizing. Leaders from many sectors spoke out about the bill and its ramifications. Some teachers were fired, and many reported feeling intimidated. Disney CEO Bob Chapek initially said that the company would not take a public stance on the legislation, but he later reversed his position after facing pressure from employees and LGBTQ+ advocates (more than 1,000 employees walked off the job in protest that March). The Disney announcement also included a pledge to donate $5 million to activist organizations supporting LGBTQ+ rights and a pronouncement that Disney would suspend all political donations in Florida. Chapek said that Disney would work to defeat discriminatory legislation in the future.

This wasn't the first time Disney or its executives spoke out on political issues. In 2016, Bob Iger (then and now the CEO of Disney—Iger took over when Chapek was fired over the fracas in Florida) spoke out against President Donald Trump's executive order banning travel from several Muslim-majority countries. And in 2020, Disney donated millions to support organizations working to fight racial injustice in the wake of the George Floyd murder.

But by 2022, the environment had become even more politicized. Disney found itself facing an opponent with political aspirations, Florida Governor Ron DeSantis, who had a more attuned sense of how to use social issues as a political wedge.

The outcome for Disney was quite different than those of its prior political forays. In response to Disney's actions, DeSantis ordered an investigation into the special tax district, the Reedy Creek Improvement District, that gives Disney certain privileges and significant autonomy over its properties in Florida. Ultimately, the Florida legislature passed a law to dissolve the district and replace it with one controlled by local officials. DeSantis framed the issue as one of political correctness gone awry and painted Disney as bowing to political pressure from its employees and others. Culturally, Disney itself became a wedge issue, with conservatives vowing to boycott the theme park. Meanwhile, Disney countersued, claiming the Florida law disbanding Reedy Creek was unconstitutional.

In March 2024, the state reached a settlement with parents and social advocates who argued that the law went too far in restricting kids' freedom to learn at school. The law prohibiting the teaching of sexual orientation through eighth grade remains on the books but now explicitly says students and teachers are allowed to talk about gender identity and sexual orientation as long as it is not part of formal classroom instruction. It's hard to say whether Chapek's high-profile stance against the law helped or hurt, but it is clear that Disney, as a corporate citizen employing thousands of Floridians, suffered because of it.

In May 2024, Disney and Florida also reached a settlement to end their litigation, with the company agreeing to spend $17 billion on Disney expansions with the state's approval. The theme parks are now overseen by a government board.

This was a fight about the role of business in our broader society and what happens when those in power feel that a company has stepped over the line. DeSantis, who was married at Disney World and who represents a state where Disney is a major economic driver, capitalized on an opportunity created by Disney itself when it decided to step into the political arena over a controversial issue. Disney was "suckered," to quote one Fortune 100 CEO we spoke with about the matter, who believes Chapek confused values for politics and bowed to pressure in a way that painted himself in a corner.

These days, CEOs are being asked to navigate fraught waters, often with little guidance as to the new cultural norms or boundaries. Employees, consumers, and society as a whole now expect companies and their CEOs to take public stands on private matters, leaving many at a loss for what to do.

The most lasting damage of the Disney fight was to the public school system, and not only in Florida. Public attention focused on a governor angling for a political platform who backed a powerful corporation into a corner. Meanwhile, laws that keep teachers from exercising their professional judgment about how to teach complex issues like race or sexuality have proliferated, and the authority of locally elected school boards to manage their own systems has been undermined. Seventeen states passed measures restricting the way teachers speak about "divisive issues," affecting a third of all public school teachers in the United States. The restrictions also came from the left-leaning side of the political spectrum, who claimed they wanted to protect students from discussions that could upset them. Teachers reported that limitations placed on how they can address race- or gender-related topics harmed their working conditions, and they worried about the consequences of such limitations for student learning.[9] Teachers were particularly concerned about the effect on their students' ability to develop critical thinking skills to analyze America's complex history.

In other words, across the country, our public school system, which was already at the center of our sputtering engine of meritocracy, came out even worse for wear. This is often the upshot of the culture wars: Those with power fight, while those in the middle bear the cost.

Both Sides of the Table

Walking into one of Chick-fil-A's 2,600 restaurants can feel, for some, like a bit of a culture shock. While the interior looks similar to other fast-food restaurants, if perhaps cleaner, the feeling is different. Employees say "my pleasure" instead of "you're welcome," and you will likely find flowers on your table. If you order takeout, employees will often walk your food out to your car. These seemingly small gestures are a nod to Chick-fil-A's founder, S. Truett Cathy, and his guiding principle to put "purpose front and center [at Chick-fil-A] because it helps us to steward our business and our work to positively influence everyone we meet."[10]

Plenty of businesses and CEOs use terms like "purpose," "culture," and "values," but Cathy and Chick-fil-A take this concept to a different level. In Cathy's view, Chick-fil-A exists "*to glorify God* by being a faithful steward of all that is entrusted to us" (emphasis added).[11] This is why Chick-fil-A remains a private company—it's easier to implement a vision in which God is a critical stakeholder as a privately held business than as a public entity beholden to a larger group of shareholders. Chick-fil-A makes decisions that support its mission and vision, but that at times can run counter to maximizing profits. For instance, the restaurants are closed on Sundays—something that, without question, prioritizes values over the bottom line.

These religious undertones have led to controversy for the fast food chain from both the left and the right. Cathy was a devout Baptist and openly expressed opposition to gay rights and same-sex marriage. In 2012, the company was criticized by LGBTQ+ advocates for Cathy's support of organizations that opposed marriage equality and for his foundation's roughly $2 million in donations that year to further that view. While the business itself never expressed a position on LGBTQ+ issues, as a closely held company it was tied to the public statements of its founder and to those of his son, Dan Cathy, COO of Chick-fil-A at the time (now the company's CEO). Chick-fil-A was the subject of boycotts by some and held up as a bastion of corporate responsibility by others.

In the years since the initial controversy, the company has sought to distance itself from political issues and stopped funding the organizations that originally caused the business to come under fire. More recently, they made statements that further clarified their intent not to fund organizations that stand against LGBTQ+ rights. They also reportedly declined several requests by political candidates to use the restaurant as a backdrop for campaign events. "Chick-fil-A is about food, and that's it," a company vice president reportedly said.[12]

Despite Chick-fil-A's efforts to stay out of the press for its political views and the religious views of its founders, the association between the business and its religious underpinning remains an enduring part of the company's history and, to some extent, its present as well. And in today's more polarized world, it serves as a reminder of the challenges of navigating complex and often quickly changing social issues.

Supported by many on the right side of the political spectrum for what they saw as the company's views on LGBTQ+ rights, Chick-fil-A found itself crosswise with that same group several years later around questions of corporate social responsibility and its efforts to promote diversity. The later controversy stemmed from the company's appointment of a vice president of diversity. The company had created this position nearly three years before it was picked up by right-wing social media, and the person who filled it had been at the company for nearly 15 years prior to taking on the role. It's not entirely clear exactly what angered those who opposed the move, other than, in an era of increasingly polarized views about culture, it signaled to those who disagreed with it a capitulation to political correctness. "Chick-fil-A has gone woke," tweeted one conservative political influencer.[13]

The use of "woke" to describe the company underscores the weaponization of this term. This isn't surprising, but it is a reminder of how challenging it is for companies to navigate the political landscape. Companies are often criticized for actions they've been taking for years. Budweiser came under fire for the use of a transgender social media influencer years after they had started working with people in the transgender community to promote their products. Target had been selling Pride merchandise for many seasons when it capitulated and removed LGBTQ+ items from certain stores' shelves after a social-media-inspired backlash. Corporate decisions such as these go beyond dollars and cents, but they are massively influenced by marketplace dynamics. In the case of Budweiser, the company saw its market value drop by more than $1 billion immediately following the controversy. For Target, the economic impact of their Pride controversy was also significant. In the quarter that followed, Target's sales fell by 5.4% and its profits fell by 8.9%, the largest decline in sales and profits for the company in more than a decade.[14]

That a company like Chick-fil-A can find itself in the crosshairs of activists from both the right and the left underscores how challenging the current environment can be for businesses to navigate. On one hand, companies are under greater pressure to participate in public discourse. On the other, some people lie in wait to pounce on them for any actions or statements they feel are against their worldview. This is not to suggest that companies shouldn't be held accountable for their actions, especially when those actions are direct and overtly political. But the nature of accountability has shifted to such an extreme that companies are beginning to be labeled as either "red" or "blue," depending on how the public mob interprets their behavior.

What's a Business Leader to Do?

As companies get caught up in this debate—pulled in many directions by constituents who have differing opinions on just about every subject imaginable—what are they to do? The question has become even more difficult in 2025, which has already been marked by attacks on businesses, universities, and law firms perceived to be political or cultural opponents of the current president.

We posed this question to many of the business leaders and CEOs we spoke to. Jamie Dimon of JPMorgan told us, "Don't allow yourself to be weaponized by somebody else. Don't let them force you to take a position that you didn't really think about, that you don't really completely agree with."[15] He further clarified, "We don't just spout out opinions because we feel like it. And we frame our statements in terms of our values, not our politics."

Values and politics are becoming conflated more and more, making Dimon's advice harder for business leaders to follow. However, having posed this question to dozens of corporate leaders with varying perspectives on how politically active they or their companies should be, we believe that Dimon's view—if somewhat aspirational—is the right framework from which companies should consider these questions. Overstepping boundaries should be a conscious decision. Too many are being baited into politics in ways that don't serve either their or society's best interests. Companies comprise constituencies (employees, customers, suppliers, etc.) with varying perspectives and views on the complex issues facing society today. Morphing them into bully pulpits only feeds the culture wars and rarely changes minds. Asserting a clearly articulated set of values from the outset can and should serve as a north star as businesses react to current events and might buffer their temptation to get drawn into political debates. Companies make their greatest impact through their business operations, not the public statements they make on any given issue of the day. We disagree both with those who believe that corporations should take strong stances on political issues, as well as those who believe they should "shut up and put up."*[16]

If there is a path to be found through the messy middle, CEOs are most likely to find it by sticking to a few core values.

---

* Presumably Mitch McConnell, who declared this, meant that he wanted companies to stop talking about issues that were in opposition to his policy aims, while continuing to support him and other Republicans financially.

Beyond Labels

When Larry Fink took a step back from his public leadership on stakeholder capitalism, he singled out a particular concept: ESG. Blackrock is still making investments based on long-term viability of ideas and companies, which partly depends on building thriving societies and communities. But the Environmental, Social, and Governance movement, he said, had been misused by the right wing as a tool in its cycle of labeling people as enemies and then inflaming the public against them—and misused by the left, which expects companies and wealthy people to bear the costs of fixing big problems. "In my last CEO letter, the phrase ESG was not uttered once because it's been unfortunately politicized, weaponized," he concluded.[17]

The ESG movement can trace its roots back to the social and environmental movements of the 1960s and 1970s as issues around environmental stewardship and social causes became mainstream topics across society. The ideas underpinning ESG gained momentum in the 1980s within the framework of Socially Responsible Investing (SRI), spawned in that decade as pressure mounted for companies to divest their operations in apartheid South Africa. The anti-apartheid movement was successful in changing some corporate behavior, and many of its tactics were adopted by groups who wanted to encourage companies and investors to consider the environmental effects of firms' actions. In the mid-1990s, the US Social Investment Forum Foundation took its first inventory of all "sustainable" investments in North America, meaning that some companies were considered "good" investments not based on returns but because they treated the environment well. The year 1997 saw the founding of the Global Reporting Initiative, with an initial focus on environmental concerns. Then, a 2004 United Nations Global Compact report titled *Who Cares Wins* used the term "ESG," vaulting it into the popular lexicon.[18]

The goals of the ESG movement are generally laudable—a sharper focus on the impacts of companies that are typically not captured in their financial disclosures, combined with a recognition that the governance structures that guide corporate decision-making are critical to how businesses are able to address these concerns. The goals of increased transparency, accountability, and reporting around the environmental and social impacts of a business's operations make sense. Companies regularly rely on "externalities"—inputs to production for which they don't directly pay, and therefore don't show up on their financial statements—and we agree with the idea of increased reporting so that investors, as participants in a free market, can make informed decisions about their investment choices.

That said, it's certainly possible (indeed, we would argue likely) that a decade from now, we will look back on the early 2020s as the high point of the ESG movement. This isn't because corporate practices related to environmental action, fair governance, and the acknowledgment of the importance of constituencies other than shareholders will fade away. However, ESG as a broad movement failed to brand its efforts and create an effective framework of measurement. This resulted in an environment in which companies could easily abuse the ESG label, making the movement a ready target for pushback. Because ESG has been weaponized, we believe it's time for us to move past it. "ESG," "woke," and other politicized terms work against the progress that many proponents are seeking and drive a wedge between them while obscuring the real work being done. The ideals of ESG will be better served in the long run by framing the underlying issues in a new light and using new language.

Business leaders would be wise to avoid politics and divisiveness, not least because Larry Fink was right: In an era when governmental effectiveness is declining, much of the action to build a new form of capitalism will need to come from the business community.

Chapter 4

CAPITAL FUNDAMENTALS

HBS—Harvard Business School—has produced many corporate titans over the 115 years of its existence, and many government policymakers, too. Yet even here, at one of the bastions of American capitalism, some central tenets of our current economic system are being questioned. In a 2022 profile of one popular seminar course, Capitalism and the State (known more informally as CATS), student Ethan Rouen described the environment on the Harvard campus: "I will say, though, that if you look at the courses being offered, the institutes being created and speakers we bring on campus, there is a huge demand both from the faculty and the students for rethinking the obligation of the corporation to society."[1]

Professor Debora Spar teaches CATS. She makes no assumptions about the perspectives her students bring. "This course tries to help my students think critically about how capitalism works," Spar told us, "what's working, what's not working, and whether there are ways to make it better. But where we start is more fundamental—really understanding how capitalism operates. As one of my students said to me the first year I taught the course: 'Everybody's telling us it's our job to remake capitalism, but nobody is telling us what capitalism actually is.'"[2]

At the beginning of each semester, Spar challenges her students to define capitalism. The ideas vary from class to class and are often debated and rehashed. After all, capitalism as a system has been around for hundreds, if not thousands, of years, and people in power in any given era often adopt a self-serving belief in a "natural" order of things. For much of Harvard's history, the definition of capitalism, while fuzzy, was taken as a given, or at least an idea that business students ought not to waste time questioning. The job of the business leaders being trained at HBS was to succeed within the system. Today that is changing, as students talk about capitalism as part economics, part social norms and ideas, and part a philosophical construct. Especially when viewed through the lens of time, capitalism turns out to be quite fluid.

Most classes come to a general consensus that "the only thing that is fundamental to capitalism is that the market sets prices," Spar said.[3] Notably, profit seeking, often a critical construct of capitalism in the world of think tanks, isn't part of that definition. The HBS students nearly universally leave room for companies to exist for purposes other than profit. This updated concept of markets widens people's mindsets beyond the single-minded notion of shareholder primacy that helped define neoliberalism. Markets, after all, inevitably involve multiple players.

The writing of Bruce R. Scott, also of HBS, is another good starting point as we explore thinking about capitalism more broadly. Scott's work on national strategy seems highly relevant today as the United States seeks to adapt to rising challenges from other countries. "Capitalism," he wrote, "is an indirect system of governance based on a complex and continually evolving *political bargain* in which private actors are empowered by a political authority to own and control the use of property for private gain subject to a set of laws and regulations. Workers are free to work for wages, capital is free to earn a return, and both labor and capital are free to enter and exit from various lines of business" (emphasis added).[4] Renowned sociologist Max Weber similarly pointed out that capitalism is more than just a way of doing business; he described it as "a mode of organizing society."[5]

The notion of a "political bargain" is not mentioned as much as it should be in discussions of how capitalism operates. It is a critical feature of any capitalist system—perhaps *the* critical feature. Too often, capitalism is defined solely in economic terms, but in practice, it is the enablement of markets that actually underpins capitalist systems. And if capitalism is as much a philosophy as it is an economic system, it is the differences in underlying philosophies that produce such wide discrepancies in how capitalism is put into practice. In the United States today, politicians have been weaponizing these differences, turning them into questions of ideology.

Pillars of Capitalism?

But politicians often distort the historical record. Far from being fixed, capitalism exists on a continuum, the extremes of which aren't even recognizable as sharing the same underlying principles. Indeed, it is the breadth of these ideas that gives capitalism its power. That two interpretations of capitalism can simultaneously differ so significantly in their implementation and yet share fundamental organizational tenets is at once maddening yet incredibly powerful. This is what makes Professor Spar's course so widely appealing among Harvard students. She encourages open-mindedness toward a concept many students may have assumed was not up for debate.

Along with the free functioning of markets, the idea of predominantly private control of assets is another critical pillar of capitalism. Without private property ownership, governments would be the only economic actors. Property includes both hard assets, such as land, and intangible assets, such as stocks and bonds. The free functioning of markets includes concepts like competitive markets, where firms and individuals are free to decide where and how to compete; market-based pricing mechanisms, where buyers and sellers determine prices and the allocation of resources instead of a centralized entity such as a state; and the open and free choice among market actors about both where and how to apply their skills on the production side of the market, as well as those actors' ability to make free and independent decisions about investment and consumption.

As we consider capitalism through the lens of our combined nearly 60 years in business, and having talked with hundreds of people from across society and the political spectrum, we keep returning to Professor Scott's idea of capitalism as a political bargain—an agreement between and among people that ultimately defines how our economy functions and the role of various players in the system, from individuals to corporations to governments. The idea that capitalism is more a philosophy than an economic model underpins our working definition of capitalism: *a consensus between different elements of society that ultimately creates the conditions for a market-based economy.* This definition purposely leaves plenty of room to debate key aspects of capitalist systems. But it is the interaction between the elements of these systems that ultimately creates the conditions for capitalism to thrive and that define their varying degrees of power. *They are part of the political bargain.*

Indeed, a few of the ideas we just listed still seem inviolate in the United States, including the concepts of the market and private ownership of property. But others are in the midst of serious societal debate and renegotiation. We've already discussed how many core ideas from neoliberalism are being reconsidered, often centered around whether companies have obligations to a broader set of constituents beyond just shareholders. However, a wider set of issues is in play, including questions about the limits of government intervention in social issues and the economy. For instance, rising concerns about the environment have resulted in local, state, and national governments, as well as organized groups of citizens, mobilizing to change long-established business practices, such as sending fossil fuel emissions into the air. Other examples include the government's role in curbing inflation at the retail level through price setting. Some proposals in response to the high post-COVID inflation amount to government control of pricing for certain consumer goods. These are challenges to free markets and, in some cases to capitalism itself, coming from the left. There are also challenges to free markets from the right: for instance, the lawsuits brought by groups (and more recently the federal government) attacking private companies' diversity, equity, and inclusion practices or states' lawsuits against investment firms for integrating sustainability principles into their investment practices.

Transitional eras call for open-minded leaders willing to rethink what seemed like accepted or established frameworks. People like Professor Spar or PayPal's Dan Schulman, who are prepared to take meaningful risks to change embedded systems, in some cases reinventing them from the ground up—whether it's the definition of capitalism, as in Spar's case, or a firm's acceptable pay scale, in PayPal's. An era of profound transformation requires you to rethink some of your own values. Or at least to be certain of the ones you keep.

Do You Have to Be Selfish to Be a Capitalist?

Many scholars of economic markets and capitalist systems include the notion of self-interest in the description of the key pillars of capitalism. Adam Smith, the father of modern economics and author of *The Wealth of Nations*, proclaimed, "It is not from the benevolence of the butcher, the brewer, or the baker that we expect our dinner, but from their regard to their own interest."[6] This tantalizing notion of self-interest drove the embrace of Milton Friedman's work. Its acceptance was not surprising. It's a pleasant notion to think that when you act in your own self-interest, you benefit society as a whole. That philosophy took hold in political and corporate circles in the 1980s and 1990s. But is this correct?

The history of capitalism, and the comparison of the current US implementation of capitalism with other forms of capitalism, reveal that self-interest isn't as much of a force behind our capitalist political bargain as one might think, or that Friedman and others would have us believe. It is quite common for people in a free-market society to act in ways that aren't in their short-term self-interest. And what constitutes self-interest—monetary gain, social status, or the desire to live in a functioning community—is often not straightforward. Most people's self-interest falls somewhere on a spectrum, and they often make decisions with a broader purpose. This turns out to be an essential fact about our society. The norms that grew up around Milton Friedman's philosophy, and the laws and regulations that were established in the 1980s and 1990s, were predicated on the idea that human beings act rationally and mainly with a view toward short-term gain. In actuality, people frequently act emotionally and often make sacrifices for the long-term good of themselves and their communities.

Opportunities Amid Shifting Norms

Put bluntly, the idea that greed helps you succeed in business has been the norm for the past 50 years, so much so that the stories of people who succeeded by embracing a more nuanced approach to business have been subsumed by the more dominant narrative. The story of Vanguard and its founder, Jack Bogle, is a good example. Many people reading this book likely own a Vanguard index fund either directly or through a 401(k) or IRA, yet few know that Bogle is one of history's most successful social entrepreneurs. With more than $8 trillion in assets under management, the company is now one of the world's largest financial services businesses. Bogle is an example of a leader who tossed out a seemingly inviolable rule and invented a new reality of his own.

Vanguard was founded in 1975, born out of Bogle's disillusionment with the mutual fund industry. Funds of the day were all actively managed and, as a result, charged high fees, even if they often didn't achieve investor returns that beat the market. Bogle envisioned a low-cost style of investing that would be accessible to middle-class investors. But if Bogle wanted to sell these inexpensive index funds (i.e., structured to track specific aspects of the broader markets rather than hiring fund managers to pick individual stocks), he needed to eschew the typical ownership structure of finance firms, which face pressure from their shareholders to produce quarterly results.

So Bogle asked the federal government for permission to create a different kind of firm, one in which Vanguard's owners would be its customers. This incentivized Vanguard to drive costs down for its shareholders/investors because they were one and the same. Bogle's idea was groundbreaking, innovative, and ultimately transformational. Competition from Vanguard eventually reduced investing costs across the industry.

Bogle's decision to create a customer-owned structure meant he willingly gave up much of the wealth and immense power that other Wall Street titans wielded. He ended up with tens of millions of dollars that he made by saving and investing his salary as CEO, rather than the billions he might otherwise have made as the founder and principal shareholder of Vanguard had he structured it in the way of traditional finance firms. "It's hard to do the right thing," he told Elizabeth in an interview before he died. "We're just tiny specks in the universe. You don't know if anything you do will make a difference. But you still have to do the right thing. That's my philosophy if you want to call it that."[7]

We're not arguing that everyone should take Bogle's approach. People can and should have their own value systems, and our country is better off for that diversity of opinion. However, we can recognize that certain periods of history present more opportunities for people who are led by their values to create new measures of success—often those that go beyond profit or wealth.

Bogle grew up during a different era. He was a child during the Depression and launched his career just after World War II, influenced greatly by the economics of post-WWII society, which we'll talk about in more depth later. While we don't think we can return to that era (and there are a number of reasons why we shouldn't wish to), we can certainly learn from it. In researching this book, we found many examples of ways in which business leaders are struggling to revive a system that works better for the breadth of American society. What they're doing isn't particularly unusual when considered in the context of the long arc of the history of capitalism. They're building on the past, learning from the present, and evolving capitalism to fit the needs of a changing society.

This evolution includes important questions about the role of companies, corporate leaders, and the government in shaping our society and participating more actively in political, cultural, and societal debates. Those trying to hold onto the ideas of neoliberalism and Friedman-style shareholder capitalism use their belief that capitalism is solely an ordained economic system to both ignore and shut down debate on these issues. Their misunderstanding of capitalism conveniently allows them to avoid messy philosophical discussions about what it means to be "responsible" or to whom a company owes its loyalty. This black-and-white thinking makes for simpler talking points but falls far short of recognizing how capitalist ideas are actually implemented in the real world.

The Golden Age of Capitalism

During capitalism's Golden Age—1945 to 1973—labor benefited greatly from a rebalancing of the power dynamic between labor and capital, increased worker protections, the advent of the 40-hour work week, and the introduction of paid vacations. Safety standards for workers were greatly improved, and productivity increased on average by 3.3% per year during these decades, in contrast with the period after 1973, which saw productivity gains of half that amount.[8] Minimum wage and overtime pay were also established, both products of the Fair Labor Standards Act of 1938. These figures contrast sharply with the period from 1974 onward—the neoliberal era—when GDP growth averaged only 2.2% but unemployment averaged nearly 6%.[9]

Many factors contributed to the emergence of the Golden Age. The end of World War II led to a surge in demand for goods and services, which helped boost economic growth. The United States benefited from a favorable global economic environment, as many countries were rebuilding their economies after the war. The government played a significant role in promoting growth during this period, investing heavily in infrastructure such as roads, bridges, and airports. It was during this time, for example, that the federal government created the Interstate Highway System, which connected people and businesses across the country and enabled greater mobility of goods and commerce across our vast country (the Highway System also helped cement the dominance of cars; this was not an accident, and it's something we'll discuss later in the book as we uncover the linkage between fossil fuels and American-style capitalism). It was also a period when the government enacted or expanded policies and programs such as Medicare and Social Security to create a broad-based social safety net. Many such programs were born in the Great Depression but were solidified and scaled up in the postwar period.

Even more importantly, it was also a time of significant investment in education and research through programs such as the GI Bill, Head Start, and the founding of the Advanced Research Projects Agency, which would fund American technological research and innovation for decades. Some of this investment led to the creation of entire industries that now underpin the modern US economy. The most obvious, important, and impactful example of this was the creation of Silicon Valley and the internet itself, both initially funded largely by government dollars (importantly, dollars with relatively few strings attached). Indeed, research and development made up 10% of the entire US federal budget for the first half of the 1960s, with our government spending more on R&D than the rest of the world combined. It was this investment that led directly to the creation of the internet (initially described in 1962 by J. C. R. Licklider of MIT as a "galactic network") and the spawning of trillions of dollars of economic activity in the technology sector.[10]

The social contract of that time was strong; indeed, the foundation of American hegemony in the late 20th century was a delicate partnership between government, business, and labor. The Golden Age was also marked by a high degree of trust in government institutions. A 1958 Gallup poll found that 73% of Americans had a "great deal" or "quite a lot" of confidence in the federal government—the highest level since Gallup began tracking this question in 1935. Businesses also saw a great deal of trust from the general public; a 1966 Harris poll found that 67% of Americans had a "great deal" or "quite a lot" of confidence in big businesses.[11]

This degree of trust allowed the government to engage in society in ways that would seem nearly impossible today, and created the environment for policies that enabled broad economic development. During the early part of the Golden Age, many business leaders wanted to expand social programs with deliberate government policy, which was bolstered by a social norm around citizenship for individuals and companies. There was a common purpose to being an American that helped enable the policies that so dramatically affected our economic life. Communism, not the government, was the bogeyman, and many Americans felt a shared sense of ideals, regardless of their position in the social hierarchy. Interestingly, there was also an implicit pact between the cities and rural areas that cities would support their farming neighbors for what they felt was the benefit of society at large. Agricultural subsidies embodied this pact.

As for many economic periods, it's hard to define exactly what led to the end of the Golden Age, or for that matter, exactly when the United States exited it (in the declarative style that authors often adopt, we confidently stated 1973 a few paragraphs above, but in reality the end date is a bit fuzzier). The 1970s were a time of malaise in the stock market and high inflation for average Americans, partly due to fuel shocks as oil-producing countries moved to establish their power in the world economy. As the Vietnam War further divided America, trust in government significantly diminished, and the Watergate scandal and the resignation of President Richard Nixon put an exclamation point on this new low opinion. The Civil Rights Movement left some influential white Americans longing for a more rigid system that would keep wealth and power in the hands of people who already had it. Milton Friedman's 1970 treatise on shareholder capitalism was certainly another influence. It was after Friedman's essay that the neoliberal worldview he championed gained steam and, as the decade ended, found practitioners in Ronald Reagan, Margaret Thatcher, and the denizens of their administrations. That America continues to outpace much of the rest of the world in economic development and the creation of world-changing companies is not up for debate. How that success was shared across society—and the cost of embracing and implementing neoliberal ideology seen as fostering this success—certainly is.

Chapter 5

IS CAPITALISM EXPLOITATIVE BY NATURE?

One challenge of talking about capitalism is the question of whether it is fundamentally exploitative. Is the damage to our environment or the economic division that we're experiencing today inevitable because capitalism is hopelessly flawed? It's hard to engage in a debate with those who believe it is without hitting a wall somewhere in the discussion. If no form of capitalism is acceptable, why bother debating or arguing to change it? This strikes us as shortsighted. Many of the books and articles that have previously tried to tackle the subject of capitalism argue in favor of ripping it out completely or reshaping it in such a way as to make it unrecognizable. This may be interesting fodder for academic debates, but in the real world of the markets, few people are actually putting these ideas into practice.

Our best and clearest path forward is to lean into capitalism rather than abandon it, while rethinking certain aspects of the social bargain that underpins it. Throughout this book, we will introduce you to some of the leaders already succeeding in creating this new world. They are working within the system in an effort to make it work better for a broader portion of our population. This is the opportunity and the promise of Dynamic Capitalism—actions on the ground that provide opportunities for meaningful change and impact.

The question, as Kate Williams, CEO of 1% for the Planet, told us, is how to figure out the norms and rules of an economy that harnesses the speed and freedom of open markets, while distributing gains more broadly and moving away from the overconsumption of resources. The organization 1% for the Planet is a network of businesses—nearly 5,200 as of this writing—that commit to donating 1% of annual sales to environmental causes. Unlike the Business Roundtable pledge we introduced in chapter 1, businesses joining 1% for the Planet are subject to a rigorous certification and verification process. You may have seen the 1% blue-circle logo on products sold by member companies such as Cotopaxi, Boxed Water, and Patagonia. "Capitalism can be pushed to be a lot different," Williams told us. "Maybe not impact-free, but it could be very different than it is . . . for our planet to survive, ultimately, we need to figure out a new economic framework."[1]

Companies that have pledged to 1% for the Planet have donated more than $650 million to environmental causes since the network was founded in 2002. By building a brand of its own and providing a certification process to hold member organizations to their pledges, the organization also provides consumers with a way of differentiating the brands they interact with and buy from. A cynical view is that companies simply join for the branding and marketing value. An optimist's view is that these companies deeply care about environmental issues and want to take a stand about their values. Either way, the environment wins, and consumers can direct their dollars either toward or away from brands whose values they support. (For people who say this kind of norm shifting cannot work broadly enough to make a difference, consider the lessons of the Golden Age of Capitalism we talked about in the last chapter, when, for example, a large number of businesses operated under norms dictating that workers should be paid high wages.)

1% for the Planet's most significant impact—though one that is difficult to quantify—is the network's role in encouraging companies to consider how to replace more harmful modes of consumption with those that have less impact. Take the example of Boxed Water, which sells water in cartons made mostly from renewable plant materials that might otherwise have been packaged in plastic or aluminum. In a world without capitalism, we might all be drinking from our cupped hands at streams. Fortunately, companies came into existence to address peoples' need and desire for portable, clean water. The environmental downside to this is that companies worldwide now produce and sell an estimated 600 billion plastic bottles of water each year. Though attempts have been made to increase recycling or legislate against plastic bottles, they have made little difference (some people derisively label current recycling technologies "wishcycling"). One of the best ways to reduce the number of single-use plastic water bottles being consumed is for another company to figure out how to manufacture and distribute water without the plastic, leveraging ingenuity and the marketplace to change consumption patterns.

Enter Boxed Water, which, along with companies pursuing a similar goal, is responding to an evolving market demand for a different form for portable water. This is capitalism at work, but in this case with a nudge from 1% for the Planet, which helped push for the change in material. In this sense, 1% for the Planet (and other organizations like it) is an example of private regulation, not unlike professional organizations such as medical societies, which helped raise standards for doctors 100 years ago and now help the government police their actions. This private, market-driven regulation can be more powerful than traditional governmental regulation, in part because it helps reserve government regulation for more extreme cases where self-regulation either isn't working or is unlikely to be successful.

Capitalism supports innovation and scales it up via the dynamic of consumer demand. When those innovations are informed by entrepreneurs' desires to do more than just earn a profit, they can make a considerable difference faster than other approaches. When it comes to the environment, we need capitalists and innovators—from those who create boxed water to new thinkers of all stripes—to pursue the ideas that will ultimately reduce or reverse climate change and mitigate its impact. We'll discuss the path to correcting the economic framework that has led to ineffective environmental policies in more detail in chapter 8, highlighting further why capitalism will need to play a critical role if we are to effectively address the climate challenge.

Capitalism is far from irredeemable. In fact, it may be our best path to a more economically and environmentally sustainable future because it's the only system that works at the speed and scale required to create sustainable change. But before we dig deeper into the stories of the leaders at the forefront of Dynamic Capitalism, we need to address some of the critiques of capitalism and consider the other "ism" often talked about in debates of capitalism: socialism.

Critiques of Capitalism

Karl Marx most famously argued for capitalism's exploitative nature, first in his and Friedrich Engels's *Communist Manifesto* (1848) and later in *Das Kapital* (1867). Marx's view that capitalism was beyond redemption formed the basis of his argument for a completely different economic system—a form of socialism that became known as communism. Capitalist actors, in Marx's view, were so driven by self-interest that they were inherently biased toward the exploitation of workers. This bias, he argued, led to the concentration of capital in the hands of a small number of people who controlled the means of production (factories and the like), while the majority of the populace—the workers or proletariat—must sell their labor to earn a living. Marx's view of socialism grew out of this notion that people were inherently self-interested and, therefore, would exploit their fellow citizens, so much so that they couldn't be trusted to make decisions that would result in a sustainable society. Government's role, Marx observed, was to counter these impulses.

There is no shortage of more modern-day critics of capitalism as well, perhaps most notably Thomas Piketty, whose 2013 tome *Capital in the Twenty-First Century* topped the best-seller lists despite its nearly 700-page length. Piketty's fundamental argument is that returns to capital outstrip overall economic growth, leading to a flywheel of economic inequality. His is less an argument against capitalism itself versus a reading of history that suggests that aggressive taxation of the rich and generally broader redistributive policies are the antidote to laissez-faire capitalism with few guardrails. Because of the popularity of his writing, he has become in many ways the most vocal and well-known modern-day critic of our capitalist system.

Piketty and others argue for broader distribution of gains, by taxes or government programs, of both wealth and opportunity in a society that has become ever more polarized and unequal. Many of these ideas trend socialistic in nature. Indeed, socialism, which used to be seen as anathema to the US economic system and from which politicians tried to distance themselves, is now a concept that is thrown around freely, with mainstream politicians openly describing themselves as socialists, something that would have been unfathomable a decade ago.

But is socialism really the opposite of capitalism? And if it is, is it a realistic one? One of the challenges of today's debate is that capitalism is seen as static and unwavering. That's simply not the case. As we have already outlined, there is no single definition of capitalism, and the practice of capitalism is continually evolving. The framing of socialism as the only antidote to capitalism is expedient for both political parties but does an injustice to the complexities of the real world. It is a false choice.

The United States isn't on a path to socialism; if anything, more of the country's important infrastructure is in the hands of private companies than ever. Fifty years of neoliberal policies had the intended effect, and companies are now much more powerful, in most respects, than the government. Where there are guarantees and a social safety net for citizens, they are, in many cases, implemented by the private sector. Suggesting programs that reinvent capitalism or reshape it through a socialist lens is counterproductive—providing false hope on one hand and fodder for the irrationality of this thinking on the other. So, too, is the other extreme of completely unfettered markets. Friedman-style capitalism—with its emphasis on unchecked markets and limited government—isn't just an abstract concept, it's had real and terrible consequences, especially for our planet and for millions of middle-class Americans. The rise of America as a technological, economic, and military superpower hasn't solved these fundamental issues of how society consumes resources or distributes opportunities. The result has been an overreaction on both the left and the right to capitalism itself.

Rethinking the Debate

In *The Economics of Welfare*, published in 1920, Arthur Cecil Pigou worried about the negative consequences of "externalities"—the harm that companies may cause along the road to their pursuit of profit. Pigou was an English economist and professor at the University of Cambridge and was among the first notable economists to consider the overall economic system from the perspective of the good or harm done by individual actors, not just the effects of capitalism on the flow of goods and services. His concern was that capitalism incentivized short-term thinking and enabled individuals running corporations to maximize their own self-interest without considering the effects of their decisions on our society. Pigou saw these negative externalities all around him—pollution in London, as an obvious and, in his day, omnipresent example—and argued eloquently for the government's role in addressing what he saw as market failures. As a free-market economist, Pigou also worried about government overreach and the potential for governmental intervention to cause inefficiencies or unintended market consequences. Yet his argument for some level of government intervention in the economy was reasoned and based on real-world observations.

Pigou's views are compelling and are among the first modern examples of an economist arguing for what is essentially a more evolved view of capitalism—checked to some extent by government and with guardrails to ensure that it doesn't run to the extreme. And while we should debate what government interventions into capitalist society are appropriate and what form they should take (in fact, we'll do just that in chapter 10), no matter what capitalist society you live in around the world, it is at least partly held in check by government rules and regulations.

Marx argued that capitalism exploits workers. Pigou was concerned that capitalism exploits the environment.* Like most great philosophers, they have much to add to the conversation and debate. Unlike philosophers, though, we're not seeking a unified theory to explain how humans, the economy, and society interact. Dynamic Capitalism requires engaging with ideas like these to create what will, by definition, be an imperfect but new order; we can agree with some of their ideas, use what we like, and move on. This is key to our view of capitalism. We don't seek perfection—something simultaneously unrealistic and undefinable. We seek a realistic middle ground.

---

* We'll return to Pigou and his arguments about environmental externalities in chapter 9.

Short-Term Thinking/Long-Term Consequences

Beginning in the 1990s, biological research has given us a deeper understanding of the way humans are drawn to short-term rewards. Capitalism works so well, and results in so much growth, because it takes advantage of people's natural inclination toward the short term—both regarding immediate satisfaction (from a consumption point of view) and profits (from a business point of view). But capitalism can sometimes sacrifice too much of the long-term health of society in favor of either short-term growth or near-term satisfaction. We don't always resist eating the marshmallow in front of us for the promise of two marshmallows later, to paraphrase the famous experiment by Walter Mischel of Stanford University.[2] This short-term paradox is the most pernicious aspect of capitalism, especially the rigid form practiced in the United States for the last 50 years.

We don't view actors in our capitalist system simplistically. It's not that some are good and victims of the system, while others are bad and have power. We all behave in ways that are, at times, self-serving and narrow minded, while at other times, we embrace longer-term goals. However, as a society, we don't currently have the right balance of short-term versus long-term thinking. One of the most toxic aspects of Milton Friedman's worldview is its overemphasis on short-term decision-making. His philosophy produced incredible growth and efficiency in the near term, but after 50 years of acting largely for short-term benefits, our economy faces mounting problems and societal headwinds directly resulting from this myopic view. Eventually, as Marx predicted, a profoundly unequal society will explode. And as Pigou prophesied, externalities—damage to the environment, in particular—will catch up with us. Both are coming into sharp focus now.

However, a system based on free markets and private ownership of property includes the tools necessary to solve the problems that Marx and

Pigou laid out. For example, Edwin Gay, the first dean of Harvard Business School, challenged the school to help create business leaders who would "make a decent profit, decently."[3] Indeed, the idea that people in business may have stakeholders beyond shareholders was not controversial for much of the middle part of the 20th century. It can be again. In fact, it must be.

The Human Capital Crisis

With many scientists and scholars detailing the environmental crisis, millions of people are acting to create businesses and ways of life that are more sustainable, contributing to rather than detracting from the growth of the economy. But there's another crisis of similar magnitude that gets less attention. The middle class has now become yet another resource—a commons—that is being consumed in our current economic construct. With an ever-bigger share of profits going to owners and not to workers or communities, the middle class is being hollowed out and treated—much as the environment is—as a resource to be exploited and depleted.

This is no accident. Instead, it is the result of a deliberate redesign of our economic system. Proponents of neoliberalism tend to focus on growth and the costs of goods, with the idea that as owners invest more in innovation and scale, the cost of goods and services decreases. When this happens, companies need more workers and, at least in theory, pay them enough to afford these now cheaper products. It's this second step in particular where our economy has fallen short. Over the past 50 years, the cost of goods and services did indeed go down, but the combination of free trade and automation broadly reduced the need for American workers, raising the value of a select group of them while producing more profits for owners. As a consequence, inequality rose and the middle class suffered.

Inequality directly affects aspirations—if you don't think you can move up in life and you don't see others around you doing so, why believe that you can succeed where others haven't? Importantly, our education system, which in the United States is tied to local property values and community prosperity, has become more and more unequal. And because of this inequality, meritocracy and opportunity—once hallmarks of the American Dream—have suffered greatly.

Capital Evolution and the Middle Class

America still has the most potent market on the planet in the form of our middle class, struggling as they may be. Personal consumption accounts for nearly 70% of US GDP, and the middle class are critical consumers in our economy. In the early 1970s, about 126 million people were in the middle class, comprising 61% of the population. Today, the middle class consists of 171 million people, or about 50% of the population.[4] While the share of income going to the middle class has declined, the number of people in the middle class is still rising due to overall population growth, masking the realities of a middle class that is actually shrinking proportionately (see figures 2 and 3).

The United States sustains this middle class—whose spending in turn supports the economy—through the rising and widespread availability of credit. American household debt grew at four times the rate of income between 1950 and the financial crisis of 2008, according to a 2020 report from the Federal Reserve Bank of New York.[5] However, this debt load was not shared evenly across our society. "Middle-class households . . . account for most of the debt growth," the study reported. We're now facing the consequences of decades of debt-fueled consumption, as the middle class has become unable to keep up by simply piling on more debt to their balance sheets.

Share of Americans in the Middle Class (1971 and 2023)

☐ Lower Income ■ Middle Income ■ Upper Income

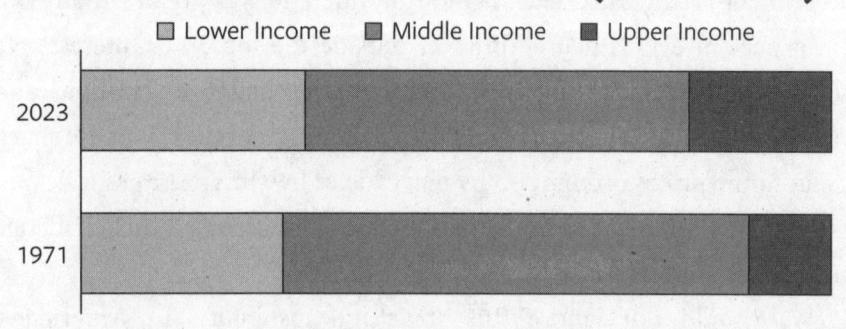

Figure 2. Source: Pew Trust.

Share of US Household Income by Class

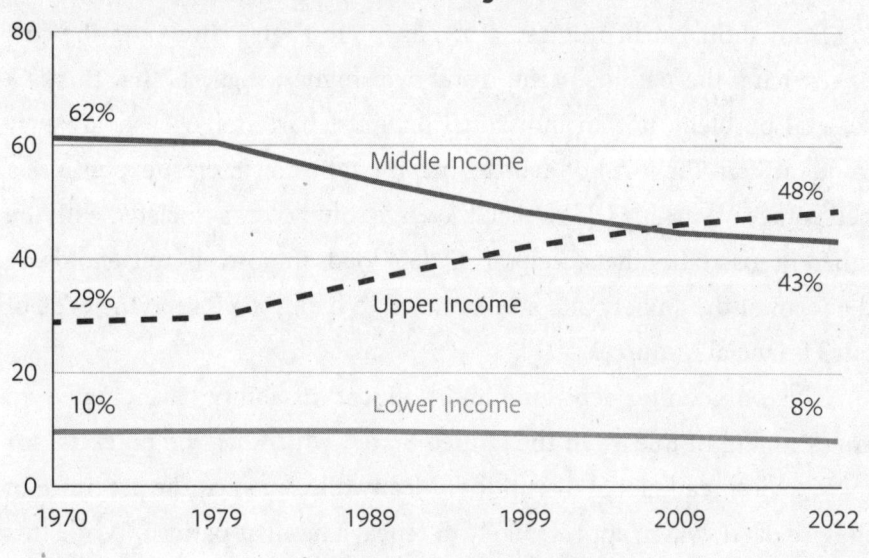

- Middle Income: 62% (1970) → 43% (2022)
- Upper Income: 29% (1970) → 48% (2022)
- Lower Income: 10% (1970) → 8% (2022)

Figure 3. Source: Pew Research.

It was easier to ignore this expanding debt load and its unequal toll on the middle class when interest rates were near zero. Neoliberals tend to focus on the cost of servicing debt and often fail to recognize how high debt levels create structural instability, especially among those outside the top of the income scale. Consider data on credit card debt as just one example. According to data published by the St. Louis Federal Reserve, the ratio of credit card debt to monthly income was greater than 50% for earners in every income bracket outside the top 30%. Interest rate increases at the Fed starting in 2022 have put the challenge of middle- and lower-income Americans' struggle with debt in stark relief. And the sharp rise in home prices brought on by a decade of low interest rates followed by the COVID-19-fueled housing bubble has exacerbated this challenge for younger Americans.

We should not ignore this structural instability. In Americans' never-ending quest to keep up with our neighbors, we've created a culture of consumption and debt accumulation that has nearly collapsed upon itself. That we've done the same with our government, which is suffering from similar debt-induced stress as interest rates climb and the cost of servicing the national debt grows ever higher, suggests that this is a societal problem, not an individual one. The hard dollar costs are easy to quantify in the form of debt-to-income ratios or interest expense as a percentage of earnings. However, there are softer costs associated with the inherent instability that accelerating debt loads impose on households, in the form of the anxiety and stress related to living so close to the edge of one's financial resources.

This burgeoning debt load and political instability have created an environment of unease in the United States, which has the potential for more widespread global disruption. Meanwhile, we sit at the precipice of the rise of AI, which appears likely to repeat a familiar pattern. While this new technology will create many innovations, any number of which will be likely to generate wealth for the capital class and increase the standard of living for people already advantaged, it may result in the same kinds of disruptions that the rise of offshore manufacturing and the deindustrialization of the economy did in the 1980s and 1990s. New AI companies will create jobs for workers with the skill sets required to leverage this technology, but it will disrupt many others. AI poses the significant risk of throwing our economic and political systems even further out of balance if companies use it to increase profits by automating jobs out of existence. However, the difference between the changes occurring today and the technological disruptions of the 1980s and 1990s is that the jobs now at risk are primarily those of white-collar professionals. This is already evident in the technology sector, where the rapid adoption of AI has led to job losses among software developers, marketers, finance and auditing staff, and sales development and prospecting professionals. These trends are only at their very early stages, but many—ourselves included—expect them to accelerate as AI technology matures.

Capitalism Needs a Refresh

It was partly because of the fight against the Soviets and communism that politicians moved to embrace neoliberalism. As Reagan famously stated in his 1981 inaugural address, "Government is not the solution to our problem; government *is* the problem" (emphasis added).[6] As George Monbiot, a columnist for *The Guardian*, described it, the Reagan administration's "massive tax cuts for the rich, the crushing of trade unions, deregulation, and privatization" marked the beginning of a new chapter of American capitalism.[7] His analysis continued:

> *Neoliberalism sees competition as the defining characteristic of human relations. It redefines citizens as consumers, whose democratic choices are best exercised by buying and selling, a process that rewards merit and punishes inefficiency. It maintains that "the market" delivers benefits that could never be achieved by [central] planning.*
>
> *Attempts to limit competition are treated as inimical to liberty. Tax and regulation should be minimised, public services should be privatised. The organisation of labour and collective bargaining by trade unions are portrayed as market distortions that impede the*

formation of a natural hierarchy of winners and losers. Inequality is recast as virtuous: a reward for utility and a generator of wealth, which trickles down to enrich everyone. Efforts to create a more equal society are both counterproductive and morally corrosive. The market ensures that everyone gets what they deserve.[8]

This neoliberal notion of capitalism has persisted, with the false notion that the "invisible hand" of the free market would guide us to the right balance between greed and altruism—between profit and good. Except it didn't. The very notion of the "invisible hand" was a flawed argument. Even its progenitor, Adam Smith, didn't describe it in the way he is often credited with. Smith was not a neoliberal. Instead, he took a more balanced view of capitalism. As the Nobel laureate Joseph Stiglitz described,

Adam Smith, the father of modern economics, is often cited as arguing for the "invisible hand" and free markets . . . But unlike his followers, Adam Smith was aware of some of the limitations of free markets, and research since then has further clarified why free markets, by themselves, often do not lead to what is best . . . the reason that the invisible hand often seems invisible is that it is often not there. Whenever there are "externalities"—where the actions of an individual have impacts on others for which they do not pay, or for which they are not compensated—markets will not work well.[9]

Implementing neoliberal ideals does not maximize our economy's overall health. Just as those who imagine jettisoning capitalism are living in a fantasy, those who believe a rising tide lifts all boats are ignoring reality too. These romanticized notions of business don't hold true in the real world. It's no wonder that one of the biggest proponents of the free-market world order is actually a writer of fiction. Ayn Rand, through her novels *Atlas Shrugged* and *The Fountainhead*, became the siren of the neoliberal and libertarian class. Lest you think that her views aren't widely popular, her ideas have been credited as foundational by former Federal Reserve Board Chair Alan Greenspan, the Tea Party, former Speaker of the House Paul Ryan, former Secretary of State Rex Tillerson, and President Donald Trump, among others. Her dismissal of the poor as "parasites" and her celebration of pure greed have been read by one-third of Americans.[10]

That *Atlas Shrugged* and *The Fountainhead* make for entertaining reading or pithy soundbites shouldn't be confused with their practical effects on our economy. It is appropriate that one finds Rand's works in the fiction section.

Capitalism is by far the best economic construct yet developed to promote economic growth. It is not fundamentally flawed, but it does need to evolve. American capitalism, which still leads the world, needs to shift in response to the new realities of the environmental crisis as well as the rise of populism—which is inextricably linked to growing inequality. We need leaders in the public and private sectors who recognize the ways capitalism is failing, see the need for a new system, and will work with others in imperfect coalitions to bring about real change.

Over the last few chapters, we've written a brief social history of American capitalism. The truth that emerges from this is not that capitalism is exploitative but that the social and economic arrangements people make, from capitalism to socialism to communism, are all exploitative in one way or another. In each case, they become more exploitative over time as power and money become concentrated. Eventually, the dynamics either shift or explode.

Section II

THE PREVIOUS CONSENSUS CANNOT HOLD

Chapter 6

CLASS MATTERS

Sam Reiman, the director of the $3.4 billion Pittsburgh-based Richard King Mellon Foundation, has given only two interviews about the circumstances of his childhood. The director of one of the world's 50 largest foundations, he is also a high school dropout and the son of a single mother.[1] In the fall of 2022, he told a story that goes to the heart of what it means to be poor in America, the lack of choices, the emotional toll visited on children and their caregivers, and the narrowing paths for climbing out of poverty.

As a child, he lived in Lancaster, Pennsylvania, in a down-at-the-heels apartment complex where his mother, Barbara, struggled to pay the rent. Reiman was 11 at the time and one of three children. His parents divorced when he was young. The only jobs Barbara could find were in fast food or retail, and they didn't pay enough to make ends meet. One day, she came across an advertisement for evening classes to earn a commercial driver's license. "She was 5'2" and 120 pounds," he recounted. He still marvels that his tiny mother found the courage to step into what was then (and still is) a male-dominated world of cross-country highways and truck stops.

The commercial license classes were offered at night, which allowed her to keep her fast-food job during the day (the family couldn't afford for her to be without pay, even for a week). She took the risk, took the classes, and got her license. The day she was to go on the road for the first time, 11-year-old Sam ran out to the parking lot, where she was sitting in the cab of her truck. All he knew at that moment was how much he was going to miss his mother and how ill equipped his older siblings were to take care of him—or themselves. He begged her not to go. She drove away anyway. "I still don't like to go back to that moment," he says. "I have an 11-year-old daughter myself now. I can only imagine what it was like for her to drive off."

It's taken Reiman a long time to be able to speak about these experiences. The memory of his childhood, combined with his now adult perspective of what it must have felt like for his mother, brings with it powerful pain. But the reason he kept silent has more to do with the taboo of talking about poverty and disadvantage, especially if you're a white man.

It's become normal to talk openly about the impact of race and, sometimes, of gender. But class has become a taboo topic, almost a matter of shame. Reiman quickly realized that if he wanted to get the jobs he aspired to, he needed to fit into upper-class cultures, which further reinforced the idea that he should stay silent about his experiences. "I never wanted to get a job because of my story," Reiman says. Most people don't have to even think about whether they should be open about their history.

Reiman's is an increasingly unusual case because he was able to climb out of his circumstances *and* has been willing to speak out about the experience. Many people comprising the working class, or even the middle class, hide their origin stories. Class has become an emotional box that traps you inside. The people who figure out how to get out of that box have insights into the systems that keep others from doing the same. The enduring damage of the illusion of American meritocracy is that if you don't rise above the economic circumstances of your birth, *it must be your fault.*

America Is No Longer a Functioning Meritocracy

The reality for almost anyone born into poverty or a debt-burdened middle-class family is that it's almost certainly *not* your fault. The statistics and the evidence show that it's now harder than it's been in generations to climb out of poverty or live a better life.[2] Americans like to think that we live in a meritocracy, and to some extent, our economy still rewards the very smartest and hardest-working people who weren't necessarily born into wealth—Reiman's story is an example of that. However, the statistics suggest that our economy isn't creating opportunities or security for millions of smart, diligent people who lack the connections or access of their wealthier peers. There simply aren't enough upwardly mobile or even secure jobs to go around. The loss of manufacturing jobs—which is the favorite bogeyman to explain the decline of the middle class, and which we'll discuss in more detail shortly—doesn't explain what's happening.

It used to be that an ambitious, hardworking person could use our public education system to pull themselves into the middle class or higher, and that a college education was nearly certain to lead to a secure middle-class life. However, researchers at the Brookings Institution, reviewing the past 40 years, found that this is less and less true. Even people living in households headed by a college-educated person—Black or white—are falling out of the middle class in rising numbers. Somewhat chillingly, the Brookings researchers described a constricted economy in which even families that can afford an ever-pricier college education find themselves competing for an anxiety-ridden toehold on the ladder of the American Dream. They recommended additional college aid, not for poor families or Black families, but for middle-class families.[3]

This was the populist pain that Donald Trump tapped into in 2016 and again in 2024, and that Hillary Clinton inflamed when she described portions of the Trump-voting American population as "deplorables." It is why the coalition of voters who swept Trump back into office in 2024 was the most diverse ever for a Republican candidate. America's economy is losing its dynamism and distributing more of its gains to people who are already wealthy.

While there are many ways to count the middle class, the Pew Charitable Trusts defines it as the middle third of Americans around the median income, which in 2023 was $80,610.[4] Those Americans are seeing the economy around them grow, but they are earning a declining share of total American income. In 1970, middle-income households accounted for 62% of the aggregate income of all US households. By 2022, this had fallen to 43%. At the same time, the share of overall income held by lower-income households edged down from 10% in 1970 to 8% in 2022. In 2019, the top 1% of Americans controlled 50% of the country's wealth.[5] Those at the top are taking an expanding share of America's prosperity.

The problems of the middle class have been hidden by the overall strength of our economy. Many economists, especially those who defend neoliberal capitalism, point to the American economy's strength compared to those of other countries and the rise in the income of the middle class. In actuality, those in the middle have largely stagnated. On six basic measures of financial security—a secure job, the ability to save money for the future, the ability to afford an emergency $1,000 expense without debt, the ability to pay all bills on time without worry, having health insurance, and the ability to retire comfortably—fewer and fewer Americans even qualify as middle class.[6] Interestingly, there are signs that people in the bottom quintile are also doing a little better, primarily due to improvements in America's social safety net (most notably Obamacare), stronger state minimum-wage laws, and the expansion of the earned-income child credit. A ray of hope in an otherwise disconcerting picture of America's economic reality.

There were, no doubt, some morally deplorable people among Donald Trump's supporters. We saw them turn out in 2017 at the Unite the Right rally in Charlottesville, Virginia, and when they besieged and invaded the

Capitol on January 6, 2021. But when Hillary Clinton made her "deplorable" remark, she was essentially saying to a world of people who were in pain and who had been struggling for decades that their experiences didn't matter. It's a mistake to simply marginalize these groups as either all racist or uneducated, as some on the left have described them. Most are neither. And the story the middle class is telling us may be the most important one in America today.

A Matter of Life and Death

The neoliberal answer to the questions about class mobility and the shrinking middle class used to be that a growing economy would increase everybody's standard of living. Inequality wasn't a big problem if everyone could afford houses, cars, and iPhones. But you have to question the role of the economy—and of businesses—in a nation where, after years of longevity gains, we're starting to die sooner. Beginning in the mid-1930s, when comprehensive US data began to be recorded, increases in Americans' life expectancy were the norm. By and large, American parents, like those of other developed countries, could welcome their children into the world expecting them to live longer, healthier, and more prosperous lives than they themselves had. America's size and great resources—from farmland to mineral wealth to an educated population—ensured that, on average, Americans of each succeeding generation were doing materially better than those who had come before.

However, that picture began to change in the late 20th and early 21st centuries—and just in the United States, not other developed economies across Europe and Asia. While there are many ways to measure the health of a society, America is failing on a half-dozen fundamental indicators—both against its own past and other countries' present.

Yet many people in the business world don't understand this, probably because of a combination of not seeing it (their social circles aren't struggling in this way) and not wanting to. For certain parts of the American population, things are *just fine*. This reluctance to address such fundamental questions of how their fellow Americans are faring goes far in explaining the rise of what many who are ignoring the problem would call, derisively, "populism," but would more aptly be described simply as people who feel rightly aggrieved and powerless to change their lives by giving voice to their frustration.

In the summer of 2014, economists Anne Case and Angus Deaton started researching the connection between happiness and suicide, especially among white middle-class Americans. But as they started to look at the statistics, they uncovered a more disturbing trend. Many more deaths than they had anticipated seemed linked to a deepening sense of hopelessness in the American population. Starting around 1999, these "deaths of despair," as they termed them (and titled a subsequent book that explored these trends), were becoming so numerous that they were shading the entire picture of American life. Whether from alcohol abuse, drug overdoses, or suicides, these deaths of despair were marching through rural areas, poor communities, and exurbs in state after state. Places like Helena, Arkansas, which had once been a small and thriving Mississippi port town, the home of a sawmill and a cottonseed oil company that evolved into ConocoPhillips; and Hazelwood, Pennsylvania, where the Hazelwood Coke Works had employed thousands before it shut down in 1998.[7]

The trend Case and Deaton highlighted had gone almost unnoticed in places like New York, Silicon Valley, and Washington, DC. But the enormous number of premature deaths were starting to show up in the statistics: Between 2013 and 2017, Americans' life expectancy declined for the first time since the Spanish flu pandemic of 1918–20.[8]

Case and Deaton trace these deaths to the opioid epidemic and then, one step further, to the globalization of manufacturing that began in the 1980s and 1990s, which decimated the economic prospects of people without a college degree. The damage was most acute among the working-class white population, with white men accounting for almost 70% of the 130 daily suicides in 2020, for example. This echoed what happened to Black communities in inner cities during the 1960s and 1970s. The 1950s post–World War II boom brought prosperity—and the Great Migration of Southern Blacks—to places like Buffalo, Detroit, and Kansas City. When manufacturing moved south from these cities to exploit cheaper, nonunionized labor, poverty moved in. This created a vacuum of jobs in these once more prosperous middle-class communities—and sparked a crisis in the Black community.

At the time, Black Americans didn't receive sympathy or economic support. They were sent to jail. By 2010, one-third of all Black male high-school dropouts under the age of 40 were in prison or jail, primarily for drug-related offenses—which, in turn, are mostly economic crimes. Today, the incarceration rate in the United States is about 810 people per 100,000. That puts us on par with China, which imprisons a million Uyghur Muslims, according to Pew Research.[9] Compare that to the rates of peer nations, which are closer to 100 inmates per 100,000 adults.

It's fair to see the difference between the response to the opioid epidemic and the crack epidemic as an example of America's endemic racism. It is. But turning this into an argument about race skips over the economic pattern that we are trying to trace, which is about not just race but class.

Death rates among young people are also pushing down life expectancy. One in 25 American five-year-olds now won't live to see 40, a death rate about four times as high as in other wealthy nations. This increase in deaths by the end of adolescence and young adulthood is being driven primarily by homicides, suicides, car crashes, and accidental drug overdoses.

Some commentators used this new set of statistics to argue that Case and Deaton were wrong. Instead of focusing on older white Americans, they argued, we ought to be focusing on young Black Americans. But for us, the real message of these premature deaths is different: Our economy isn't working for large swaths of our population, regardless of race. The result is an epidemic of despair and violence that is both deepening and widening. Since its publication, the *Deaths of Despair* narrative has actually become somewhat out of date, but not in the way one would hope. It turns out that deaths due to alcohol, suicide, opioids, and other similar causes are no longer a white American problem. Black Americans are dying of deaths of despair in growing numbers as well. In 2022, data suggested that these deaths among Black Americans actually exceeded those of white Americans.[10] A sobering example of the power of class to supersede race.

Why Aren't We Talking About Class?

In April 2023, a young writer and podcaster named Coleman Hughes gave a TED Talk making the case for "color blindness." He defined the term as a devotion to the principle that we should try to treat people without regard to race. In his telling, focusing solely on race (or gender) penalizes people for an immutable quality—their skin color (or sex).

"Eliminating race-based policies does not mean ending policies meant to reduce inequality," he told the TED audience, but "class is almost always a better proxy for true disadvantage." He gave the example of the COVID-19 pandemic-era Restaurant Revitalization program, which allocated $29 billion for restaurants owned by people of color, women, and veterans. The policy was challenged successfully in the courts by white male restaurant owners, and white applicants who were initially rejected were moved to the front of the line. As a result, the program ran out of money, and people in both groups who had been promised funding did not receive it. "There are people who lost their restaurant in both camps because of their skin color," Hughes said.

As podcasters and young writers often do, he framed his ideas in a controversial way, but his speech was respectful and generally grounded in facts and history. Dr. Martin Luther King Jr. had advocated for including "the forgotten white poor" alongside people of color in government programs, Hughes pointed out. But Hughes's title for the talk, "Color Blindness," put him in direct rhetorical conflict with influential people on America's political left.

The backlash was strong and swift. After pressure from a Black employee group within TED, the company at first refused to post his speech online (the TED website receives millions of monthly visitors, and their most popular videos have been viewed nearly 100 million times).[11] Then, under duress, TED posted his talk but refused to promote it as it does other videos on the site, which meant few people saw it. Sociologist, author, and media personality Adam Grant got involved, throwing some of his views about the ineffectiveness of past colorblind policies into the mix, which further inflamed the controversy.

We don't have a fully formed view on the right way to run affirmative action programs or on Hughes's work, but we are certain that it's impossible to legislate or dictate the end of racism. We believe that the conversation about race is important—we argued extensively for measures to help women and people of color who own small businesses in our last book, *The New Builders: Face to Face with the True Future of Business*. Racism is America's original sin and a topic our country continues to grapple with. However, Hughes wasn't arguing that race isn't important but rather that class differences are a better way to create new government programs. Whether he is right or not is a matter of opinion. Apparently, it is an opinion that some didn't want to see discussed.

Hughes eventually went public with the censorship he was experiencing. After he waged a high-profile fight with TED, the company relented (somewhat) and allowed the video of his talk to be more easily found on their website. Ultimately, more than a million people watched (although not before TED appended a "debate" about the questions Hughes raised to the end of the video).[12]

Hughes, who himself is Black, argues that because race and identity are such visceral issues—and so easily weaponized—they obscure some of what has been happening in our economy. We think he's right. It's easy to see poor white people in competition with poor Black people for limited government resources. And that narrative has been readily exploited by politicians of both parties, not to mention agents of foreign governments looking to sow divisions across American society.

The reality is much more complicated and nuanced. We see the story of poor Blacks as a bellwether, starting in the 1960s, for what has been happening to all kinds of vulnerable people in the United States. Without question, race continues to be a critical factor in American society and a topic we shouldn't stop talking about. But we need to start talking about class as well. The inflamed conversation about race prevents us from seeing that, as economic mobility in America has significantly decreased in the past 50 years, people of all races struggle to climb the economic ladder.

It's the Economy

Sam Reiman's and Coleman Hughes's stories are important. Reiman has begun talking about his history because he wants to remove the stigma around poverty, especially around being white and poor. "There are a lot of people who need to hear that story," he says. "There's an assumption that there's only one path."

Hughes, who was raised in an upper-middle-class family in New Jersey, wrote a book about his experiences. "Even though a majority of Americans believe that color-blind policies are the right approach to governing a racially diverse society, we live in a strange moment in which many of our elite believe that color blindness is, in fact, a Trojan horse for white supremacy," he wrote on his blog.[13]

A productive conversation about the benefits and limits of capitalism necessarily includes fair, open conversations and empathy. You don't have to agree with everyone. But we won't get anywhere if people on all sides of the debate won't listen. That's the place to start. As one listens, one's point of view on many topics, political issues, and even business decisions will widen. "As a society, we need to rediscover the meaning of empathy," Reiman told us. "We must believe in the potential of every person, regardless of their race, gender, or zip code. And we must acknowledge that economic success is only one metric in our lives and that achieving it or not doesn't define us. Our legacy is in how we support each other."

Refocusing on the Middle Class Without Defocusing on Race

The leaders who thrive in the new America will be those who recognize the importance of economic dynamism and a thriving middle class. But that's not enough. We need to go a step further to recognize why we haven't been talking about class.

As most people intrinsically understand, the power of any solution is in the details of how it is executed. A colorblind selection process run by kind people in a community that genuinely cares about citizens will do more good than a rigid race-based program in which frontline managers have little power. But the opposite is also the case: A race-based program in a community that genuinely cares about citizens will do more good than a rigid colorblind program. The program's rules are critical, but they are not the only important element. As a society, we focus and fight over the rules because we can more easily control them. This myopic focus on rules overshadows more important factors of how a program is run and whether the human beings who implement it can determine how to make it effective. Progress often depends on getting the balance between rules and humanity right, more than on the details of the exact rules that govern it. This is a theme—individual power and leadership in balance with policy—that we have returned to often in long careers that between us span journalism, business, finance, philanthropy, and government.

There are many examples of people working on issues of poverty and declining economic mobility. Their work, which crosses boundaries of race and class, stretches our imaginations. They help frame the idea, which has existed since the beginning of America, that you can work with one foot inside the system and one foot outside—to be part of building a new system.

The best advice for people who want to play an active role in Dynamic Capitalism is to begin by looking outside your own bubble, without judgment, at the stories you might not be hearing. There are likely to be many. One of the best ways to do this is to put yourself into proximity with people struggling economically. Whether you chose to become personally involved, it's important to recognize that the health of the middle class, and the question of whether America's economy is mobile enough to reward work and aspiration, are both crucial. Statistics about the lack of social mobility and the decline in life expectancy are signs that our system—despite its headlines of strong economic growth—is sick on the inside. America cannot function optimally without rewarding aspiration, as we have done for centuries. To fully usher in the era of Dynamic Capitalism, our economic ladder must work reasonably well for more people.

Chapter 7

MID-CENTURY MIRRORS

There was an era in living memory when our economic ladder worked, and gains from economic growth were widely shared. American economists and politicians tend to romanticize this era, but even the United Nations calls the period after World War II through the early 1970s the "Golden Age of Capitalism." While it wasn't golden for everyone, it was an era in which more of capitalism's promises seemed to hold true.

So we examined that era in more detail, with an eye to the question of the right mix of incentives, corporate freedoms, regulations, and government action (or inaction in some cases) to create broad, sustained prosperity. We also discovered an explanation for the divisiveness of our own time. Understanding the story of the Golden Age, and our own, requires untangling two dynamics—one light, one dark—that have been intertwined through 20th-century American history. One is a sense of personal responsibility. The other is oil.

Black Gold

Most Americans today think of oil in the context of the Middle East. However, oil refining was discovered in the United States—in Pennsylvania, after the Civil War—and the US remains at the center of the oil economy. Oil became the power source for the machines of the Industrial Revolution and supplanted coal as the primary fuel for a growing nation. Between the 1930s and 1950s—the period when the foundation for the Golden Age of Capitalism was laid—fossil fuels became the basis both for the domestic economy and America's international economic expansion. And it may surprise many readers to learn that the United States, today, remains a major oil-producing nation.[1] Perhaps more importantly, the United States continues to be the world's top oil consumer, using over 20% of global production (see figure 4).[2]

Fossil Fuel Consumption

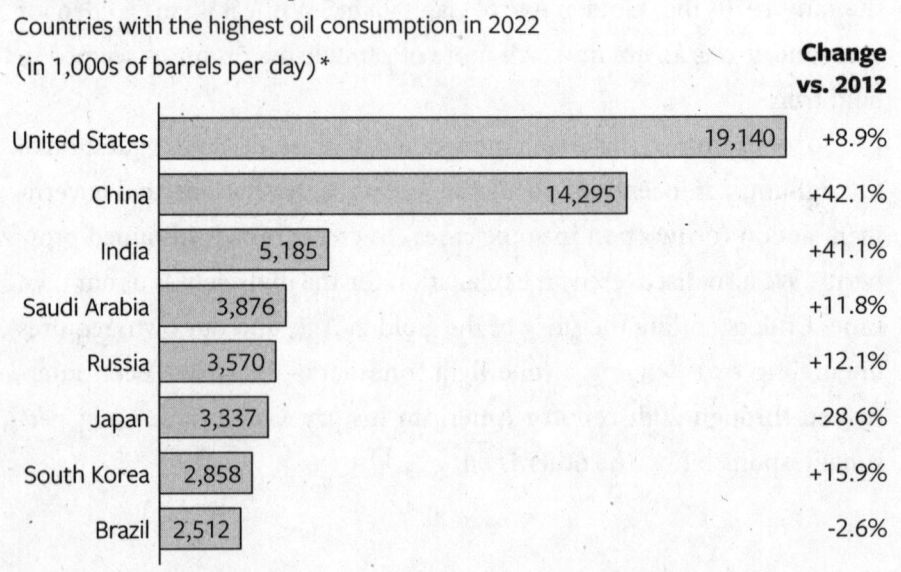

Countries with the highest oil consumption in 2022 (in 1,000s of barrels per day)*

Country	Consumption	Change vs. 2012
United States	19,140	+8.9%
China	14,295	+42.1%
India	5,185	+41.1%
Saudi Arabia	3,876	+11.8%
Russia	3,570	+12.1%
Japan	3,337	-28.6%
South Korea	2,858	+15.9%
Brazil	2,512	-2.6%

* Including derivatives of coal and natural gas, excluding biogasoline and biodiesel

Figure 4. Source: Statista.

Oil has been deeply woven into America's sense of self. Historian Darren Dochuk described this eloquently in his 2019 book, *Anointed with Oil*:

> *Americans could rightly assume that their nation enjoyed sovereignty over the black stuff and that this dominion placed it in an advantageous, even hegemonic, position on an international stage. However, that power, real and imagined, was not simply a natural outgrowth of America's fortuitous proximity to oil or prowess in its handling. It was also generated by the U.S. oil industry's ideological prerogatives and self-interests, as well as by its fierce internal clashes, all of which blended religious, economic, and political concerns into one combustible fuel.*[3]

The climate crisis compels the United States and the world to move away from a fossil-fuel-dependent economy. Given how deeply fossil fuels have been part of American history and how fundamental they have been to the economy for the past 150 years, it is not surprising that we are in a moment of deep division in the United States. The social compacts, underpinned by fossil fuels, that underwrote both the Golden Age and neoliberalism are being rewritten.

The Roaring Twenties

Every era has roots in history, and picking where to start any particular story is always a challenge. For expedience, we'll start our detailed understanding of the last Golden Age in the 1920s, an era with eerie echoes of our own. America's economy was enjoying an unprecedented boom, partly because of the industrial strength that grew out of oil but also due to a liberalizing society and the increasing participation of women in the economy. The decade is known as the Roaring Twenties because they were a time of exuberance, opportunity, and growth (though they only roared for some). Following World War I and the Spanish flu pandemic of 1918–20, the US economy boomed. In urban areas, irrational exuberance reigned. The modern stock markets were evolving, with the power to distribute ownership and wealth more widely while allowing some to make wild fortunes extremely quickly and in new ways that were dissociated from hard assets. Meanwhile, the Industrial Revolution of the previous century had created faith in the productive power of American business, the first sense of industrial, scalable business structures, and a generation of unimaginable fortunes. Many of those fortunes, with their ties to the fossil fuel economy, still exist today.

As we examine the social compacts that comprise capitalism, it's important to remember that the oil industry—like today's tech sector—produced mind-boggling wealth during the period leading up to the Golden Age. John D. Rockefeller Sr. is the most obvious example, but other great American fortunes have been born out of oil (both in the Golden Age and more recently). In many cases, their creators' names are well known, even if we've forgotten the source of their wealth. These include the Mellons, the Pews, the Kaisers, the Hunts, and the Koch brothers. The oil fortunes of these families continue to exert a profound influence on many aspects of our society today, especially our politics.

A Disrupted Era

Back to the Roaring Twenties. The United States and the world were recovering from the war and the flu pandemic, with all the trauma that accompanies the sudden severing of social encounters and normal work. The 1920s were also a period of international isolationism, racial and labor strife, and greater disconnect between urban and rural communities. The population of the time was also uniquely conscious of race, both because of the proximity of the Civil War (adults of the 1920s and 1930s—or their parents—had lived through it) and because of rising immigration in the early part of the 20th century. The 1919 Elaine Massacre, in which several hundred Black sharecroppers were killed by their white neighbors, took place in the Arkansas Delta. Labor violence was common, including the 1914 Ludlow Massacre, when, during a strike at a Colorado mine co-owned by John. D. Rockefeller Jr., as many as 199 miners and their families were killed by hired strikebreakers and National Guardsmen.[4] Though some federal safety measures had been implemented, the divisions between urban intellectuals (what we now term "elites" in our more polarized nomenclature) and the working, rural, and urban poor were stark and, to anyone who cared to look, horrifying. In rural communities, and for working people and many people of color, the 1920s were dangerous and sometimes deadly.

Surely that time must have felt as strange and confusing as our own. In such environments, people often turn inward to their communities, their class, and their families. When trust in institutions is declining, it's easy to lose faith in the idea of institutions at all. Humans can start to believe that individuals can't make a difference. A form of self-absolution or resignation can set in: If you don't believe you can make a difference, why try? And yet, starting in the 1920s, the Progressive Movement began to reshape society, with a focus on ending corruption as well as expanding equality and justice in the economy. The 1920s also saw the birth of the widespread idea that hard and social sciences could and should be used for the benefit of communities. Public health systems, along with sewer and clean-water systems, grew out of that belief. Communication systems of the time were local in nature and, despite often being relatively slow and deliberate, promoted a sense of community. Local newspapers were the main source of information, with radio starting to become more widespread in the late 1920s and 1930s, and most Americans' view of the world outside their local towns was limited to information shared through these concentrated media choke points.

Marion Folsom and the Rochester Plan

As we were thinking about Dynamic Capitalism, we went looking for the people who, in the 1920s and 1930s, were instrumental in building the Golden Age. Most histories of this period have focused on the role of Progressives working in government, but this view is in itself a product of the present. Our experience in the business world tells us the private sector drives most innovation, sometimes with the help of government, but rarely the latter acting alone. These innovations occasionally make their way into government, where they scale and become institutionalized.

The story of Marion Folsom, an executive at Eastman Kodak in Rochester, New York, is illustrative. Folsom's life was largely insulated from the challenges of the working class around him. He was born in a Georgia cotton town to a wealthy family, and it seems likely, based on that history, that his family prospered because of the work of enslaved laborers. He was bright academically and attended Harvard University, where he trained as a statistician. Shortly after graduating, George Eastman, the founder of Kodak, lured him to upstate New York to work for his company.[5]

Almost as soon as he arrived in Rochester, Folsom was troubled by the conditions he observed for workers as well as the risks labor unrest posed for the company. Though jobs were plentiful, pay was low and working conditions were extraordinarily harsh. The typical industrial worker put in 12-hour days, often with just one day off every two weeks. With worker safety an afterthought at best, accidents were common. One of the worst injustices of this era was widespread industrial layoffs. When economic conditions dictated that a company pull back production or shut down completely, men were thrown out of work and their families went without. The birth control pill wasn't invented until the 1950s, and abortion was illegal, so a typical American family had three or four children. Marion Folsom must have witnessed many hungry children on the streets of Rochester as he made his way through town. Labor unions were weak, and most corporate executives had no need or desire to pay them much attention.

Folsom looked for ways to improve working conditions and workers' day-to-day lives while lowering the risks of strife for Kodak and Rochester. He eventually hypothesized that if enough companies banded together, they could establish a fund that would pay limited benefits to furloughed employees, a sort of insurance scheme for workers. In 1931, after a full decade of lobbying other senior executives, he won an unlikely victory. Folsom convinced Kodak to set up a private unemployment fund to pay workers if the company laid them off. He recruited 13 other companies to take part in what became known as the Rochester Plan.

The plan ultimately failed, overwhelmed by the economic catastrophe of the Great Depression. But Folsom—and others advocating for workers in similar ways—didn't give up. He recognized the flaw in implementing his idea: The fund had been too small to bear the risk it was taking on. As the Depression deepened, Folsom continued arguing in magazine articles and, undoubtedly, into the ears of many people who didn't want to listen, that the plan shouldn't be abandoned but, rather, expanded. His writings show he deeply believed that the federal government could not stand by while the economic security of millions of Americans turned to personal despair.

Meanwhile, one of the wealthiest men of all time had been undergoing a change of heart. John D. Rockefeller Jr., whose practices in his inherited businesses had been exposed by activists and investigated by the federal government, had taken a different path than his father and was funding research and policy organizations focused on how to help elevate working-class Americans. Rockefeller biographer Ron Chernow points to the Ludlow Massacre as John Jr.'s turning point. Beset by negative press and a hostile country, Rockefeller, who had become a symbol of the moral bankruptcy of the wealthy, traveled to southern Colorado following the massacre. "He betrayed the feverish urgency of a man on a spiritual quest," Chernow wrote.[6] It was the first time Rockefeller spent time with the laborers working in his mines as well as their families. He emerged from his trip with an altered perspective, newly prepared to stand up to his purely business-minded father. John Jr. ultimately became a prophet for better working conditions and the communal good.

Importantly, the Rockefeller Foundation became the largest donor to the Institute for Government Research, the forerunner of the Brookings Institution, and a key policy organization that would later support Folsom's ideas.[7] Folsom eventually worked with a coalition of people espousing worker security. He took his message to both parties, working for Democratic and Republican presidents, first as an advisor to Franklin D. Roosevelt and then as a cabinet secretary in the Eisenhower administration. He is remembered today, when he is remembered at all, as the architect of Social Security. By bridging the worlds of business and government, he and others kept millions of people from slipping into poverty and helped lay the foundation for the Golden Age.

The point of recounting this history is not to turn Folsom into a hero, though we see a certain white-collar heroism in trying to explain actuarial tables to Congress. Rather, we recount his story as an example of the powerful role individuals, particularly business leaders, can play in shaping critical economic policy and, therefore, society.

Meanwhile, the important role the oil economy plays in this story should also be clear to attuned readers. Oil drove the economic boom that produced both the injustices of the Industrial Revolution and the resources necessary to alleviate some of the suffering. It was an oil fortune—Rockefeller's—that helped establish the social norms that governed the business community and the actions and obligations of the elites. This history also stands as a powerful example of how people can change over their lifetimes, as was the case for the younger Rockefeller.

The Foundation of the Golden Age of Capitalism

The pattern for how Social Security was founded was repeated many times in the 1930s, 1940s, and 1950s, when working coalitions between the government, labor leaders, and business leaders were common. Together, these coalitions reached a series of informal and formal agreements that distributed the income generated by the oil-driven industrial economy through wages, profits, and government benefits.

Here, we return to our practical definition of capitalism—a working consensus between different elements of society that ultimately creates the conditions for broader and more sustained economic growth. The creation of Social Security is an example of the consensus-building that took place during the 1920s and 1930s. But it's only one of a series of compacts that developed during these decades, many of which are now so entrenched that we do not recognize them. Coalitions between government, labor, and business helped create important legislation, tax structures, and institutions between 1932 and 1950. The Agricultural Adjustment Act, for instance, provided farmers with higher prices for crops, kept prices steadier for consumers, and was funded by a tax on food processing companies. It was essentially a money transfer from city dwellers to people living in rural areas. With the benefit of history, we can look back and label some of the policies as mistakes—like the one that offered welfare only to families where a father *wasn't* present—but also successes, such as the introduction of Social Security.[8]

The point is that they happened.

Agreements in the auto and steel industries were among the most important. In 1950, the United Auto Workers and General Motors signed the Treaty of Detroit, which gave two generations of manufacturing workers a stepping stone into the middle class. Economist Mark Blyth of Brown University has pointed out that these coalitions pulled together the Midwest, East, and South; the financial and industrial sectors; and, most importantly, capital and labor. "This broadly inclusive distributive coalition, in turn, softened the sectional and partisan divisions that had roiled US politics almost continuously since the 1890s," Blyth wrote.[9] This does not mean that we see these days as uniformly halcyon. They were golden for some people but not for plenty of others, especially if you were Black, an immigrant, or in other marginalized communities. But in many ways, that period's society and economy functioned better and for the benefit of many more people than those of today. It's not surprising, Blyth points out, that as the environmental crisis has made it clearer that America needs to end its reliance on fossil fuels, the disruptions and breakdowns in old compacts created during the Golden Age are contributing to today's political storms.

By the end of World War II, national mobilization and economic evolution had helped create a massive, consumer-oriented, and optimistic middle class. Even those who had been historically excluded from the nation's burgeoning prosperity—especially Black Americans—found opportunities via the insatiable demand for workers at factories throughout New England and the Midwest.

Taxes on top income earners were also very high during this time, though we're not suggesting the return of tax policies that mimic those of the 1950s through the 1970s. Tax rates as high as those of that era—with the highest marginal rate topping 90%—simply aren't politically palatable, nor are they economically logical. After decades of lobbying by special interests, the US tax code is so complex that major changes must be carefully calibrated. We highlight the Golden Age tax rates instead to show the degree of alignment between and among segments of society. The doctrine of the free market has taken such a hold over our mindset that many believe that individuals play no role in shaping the distribution systems of our economy and that inequality is inevitable. Yet we have examples in living memory of leaders forming coalitions to develop systems and rules that created social safety nets and deliberately distributed economic gains more widely.

The End of the Golden Age

The alignment began to erode in the 1970s. The Golden Age was built on the oil economy represented by the Rockefeller family and the large oil companies—ExxonMobil (still separate companies at this time), Chevron, and BP America—which resulted from the breakup of Rockefeller's Standard Oil. They represented not just an industry but a way of looking at the world, which centered American capitalism as a force for progress. For individuals, that translated into the idea that the wealthy owed something back. Tycoons were expected to give away substantial fortunes by establishing large foundations (in their names, of course).

As the Rockefellers' Golden Age influence on politics faded, a new group of oilmen who had made their fortunes in the West and Southwest stepped in. These more independent-minded men generally took a pessimistic view of the role of the federal government, which they felt had only served to reinforce Standard Oil's power. In the mid-20th century, the most prominent among them were the Pew brothers. More recently, the Koch brothers took up the anti-government mantle.

Darren Dochuk calls this branch of the oil industry the "wildcatters": "That kind of wildcat spirit is this fiercely independent, kind of more highly speculative, risk-taking kind of spirit of capitalism that lines up quite organically with a more evangelical Protestant kind of theology and worldview. So what we see basically is a clash between these two spirits of capitalism, two kinds of religions, and then also the politics," he told us.[10]

"We so often think of oil as big oil, as monolithic, when, in fact, it's always been highly segmented," he added. "Of course, there have been the majors, which really come out of the Rockefeller legacy . . . But then, on the other side, is what I call wildcat Christianity. That's these fiercely independent oil men who, you know, were driven out of the business by the Rockefellers in Pennsylvania. Then they just got lucky and happened to be in the Southwest when oil exploded there."[11]

The new oilmen's rise to power coincided with the rise of neoliberal capitalism. In both politics and business, a new generation of leaders was coming into power: politicians and statesmen who had been shaped not by the 1920s and the Great Depression but by World War II and ideas of American hegemony. Moving away from the idea of individual responsibility, they instead embraced individual freedom. These new norms extended to politics, taking the form of libertarianism and a distaste for large government programs and the social safety net. It is not surprising that this era saw the rise of both the gun owners' rights movement and the feminist movement—both sharing an underpinning of individual liberty, despite their political differences.

These new business leaders enthusiastically embraced the theories that Milton Friedman promoted and that, a little later, Ronald Reagan found politically expedient to embrace as a stark contrast to the Soviet Union and communism. Once again, fossil fuels were the backbone of the social compact. Oil and oil money were essential components of both the Golden Age and the rise of neoliberalism. It's this centrality that we are grappling with today as the current generation of business and political leaders form new coalitions and begin to embrace new ideas about the future, a future we see defined by Dynamic Capitalism.

Individual and Collective Power

For hundreds of years, the discipline of history has mostly focused on the actions of great leaders, often in a war-and-peace context. Hardly anybody makes a name writing economic history by investigating the mundane decisions of business leaders, or describing the day-to-day actions of consumers. Data science is changing this picture. Applying data science to a historical database comprising many different data sources, from parish records to environmental records to anthropological studies of human remains, a scientist named Peter Turchin developed a theory of what leads to violence and revolution. His book, *End Times: Elites, Counter-elites and the Path of Political Disintegration*, outlines some of the factors he identified. In particular, he names the "growing immiseration" of a large swath of the population (via falling incomes and declining life expectancies) and an oversupply of people vying for a spot in an "elite class" of growing power. Alarmingly, he shows that those factors, worsening in the United States since the 1970s, were also present in other societies that erupted in revolution or war, including the pre–Civil War United States and Russia before the Communist Revolution.

By studying counterexamples, including the Golden Age of Capitalism, Turchin finds that, yes, individuals of course make a difference in history if they are in the right place at the right time. But he also argues, very much in alignment with our thinking, that groups of people, acting together, can change the course of society that otherwise shows all signs of disintegration or dysfunction. That's where the United States was in the 1920s—increasingly isolationist, with racial tensions and divides that sometimes turned violent, markets that seemed ungovernable, and rising inequality. That's where we are today.

We need leadership, bankrolls, and a greater acceptance of change. But we also need the commitment of other members of society who are willing to engage and rebuild—or build anew—a different set of institutions. As the son of a wealthy, white, well-educated family from a cotton plantation town in Georgia, Marion Folsom grew up privileged. He went to Harvard and stepped into a role at one of the country's most important companies. But what he did with that privilege is important. He could have spent his time, no doubt very happily, being with his family and amassing wealth, protected from the stress of life experienced by people in lower economic strata. He had no incentive to risk the displeasure of his bosses, engage in uncomfortable conversations around country club tables, or spend meaningful portions of his career laboring in Washington, DC. It is the little-sung decisions of people like Folsom to live lives of purpose that ultimately create ages of peace and broad-based economic expansion.

Obstacles to Change

When liberal academics scoffed at the Business Roundtable's redefinition of a corporation, and right-wing activists turned it into a fundraising bonanza, were they giving up the chance to build meaningful coalitions? Our reading of history suggests they were. At the same time, partly because businesses are still functioning where other institutions are not (though big businesses are certainly not very trusted in today's hyperpolarized landscape), academics and nonprofits are pinning too many of their hopes on the business sector *owning* change. That's not going to happen.

Few give up power lightly. The structures of the old economy, some dating back to Marion Folsom's time and some newer, are shifting. Indeed, the consensus that created the Golden Age of Capitalism was based on profits from carbon-intensive industries: the coal mines of Appalachia, the agriculture of the South, and the steel and auto industries of the North. Neoliberal capitalism was also largely built to align with the attitudes of the next generation of the fossil fuel economy. In the 1970s and 1980s, as the environmental consequences of extractive energy sources became clearer, shareholder capitalism and libertarianism became central to that era's ideal of capitalism.

Today, the environmental crisis has become so clear that there is little choice but to shift to a less damaging energy supply. Companies, including the old fossil fuel firms, are moving in that direction, albeit more slowly than they arguably should. The backlash against Dynamic Capitalism and efforts by business leaders to build new, forward-looking coalitions is significant. When big companies such as BlackRock or PayPal make changes that undermine the existing economic or political order, they risk facing boycotts—and their leaders face death threats. Powerful forces are fighting against the tides of change.

Chapter 8

A NEW NARRATIVE

From the beginning, some people didn't buy into the black-and-white thinking that was a hallmark of neoliberal capitalism, especially its chief tenet, shareholder primacy. There have always been leaders who succeeded by adopting principles that ran counter to neoliberal ideals and who operated more in the vein of Dynamic Capitalism. Some succeeded in building large companies and climbed high in their professional fields, even as they deliberately broke the rules of what businesses were supposed to do and be at the time. Working in different spheres, often over decades, they have consistently argued for a new direction, enacting ideas about how to combine building profitable businesses with other values. Where the dominant narratives of the last 50 years were built around the ideas of completely free markets, shareholder primacy, and limited government, Dynamic Capitalism's consensus and narratives lie elsewhere.

Lisa Green Hall, an impact-investing pioneer who was eventually recruited by Apollo Global Management (one of the world's largest asset managers), reminded us that all forms of capitalism are ultimately the product of their implementation *by people*.* And people are never entirely driven either by ideology or by profits. One of the Achilles' heels of neoliberal capitalism was its rigidity. Over the past 50 years, researchers have discovered just how much human emotions drive decision-making. A group from Stanford University estimates that emotions drive somewhere between 90% and 95% of decisions, despite most people considering themselves rational rather than emotional decision makers.[1] The world is full of people who think and act with empathy and who are willing to consider complex factors as they make decisions. They're the employees, consumers, and, in many cases, the business leaders of today. In reality, no manager bases any decision solely on maximizing profits for shareholders, even though the dominant narrative of shareholder-based capitalism tells them that's what they ought to be doing. "One of the things we often want to divorce but that we *can't* separate is that real people run these companies," Hall told us. "Often, these people are driven by values . . . They are quite motivated to do things because they believe they are the 'right' things to do . . . At the same time, they have a responsibility to deliver returns to investors. And that's what investors are demanding because they are values-driven people too."[2]

While still raw and unpolished, this is the new way of thinking that is taking form as neoliberal capitalism retreats and Dynamic Capitalism takes its place. It may not have the advantage neoliberalism had of being simplistic, but it benefits from a dose of reality that neoliberal thinking was never able to embrace or even meaningfully consider.

During our research and through our interviews, we identified a surprising number of people we consider economic pragmatists. These are business leaders who long ago recognized the limitations of shareholder primacy and instead have been formulating the new thinking and ideas that

---

* Lisa Green Hall died in March 2025. She was a groundbreaking figure in the impact world, responsible for bringing billions of dollars into communities nationwide. We're honored to have been able to include her story.

have underpinned the early days of Dynamic Capitalism. Often, their work has gone unrecognized. In other cases—notably impact investing—their ideas have been demonized in today's overly politicized environment.

The history of this new consensus reveals how firmly rooted it remains in the idea of markets. Dynamic Capitalism is not an attempt to morph capitalism into something else but rather an effort to leverage free markets in ways that are more sustainable for the long term and lead to broader prosperity and less inequality. When you examine the underpinnings of Dynamic Capitalism, you can more clearly see where politically motivated, divisive myths have grown up. Clearly, many feel threatened by any changes to the existing neoliberal orthodoxy or their own individual business interests and are prepared to leverage or co-opt the current culture wars to selfish ends.

Despite these headwinds, some businesspeople have been carving out space to meld corporate values into corporate operations, better reflecting a broader set of beliefs in operating a business both profitably and justly. These ideas—mini-movements themselves—are coalescing to form the shape of Dynamic Capitalism. No longer sitting at the fringes of the capitalist-values debate, they are now front and center. The Business Roundtable didn't suddenly come up with the idea of stakeholder capitalism in 2019. They were following in the footsteps of leaders across the business landscape who had been thinking about market-based evolutions to a system they could see wasn't working. Dynamic Capitalism has always had its proponents, even if, for a time, they were largely ignored or overshadowed by their neoliberal peers.

Success Is Not Measured in Dollars Alone

The ideology of shareholder primacy led, at its extreme, to the idea that success was measured by share price alone. The 1980s were the era of "greed is good," conspicuous consumption, and *The Art of the Deal*. It is not a coincidence that many of the most vocal and ardent supporters of neoliberal tradition and policies came into young adulthood in the 1980s.

Ronald Reagan, an early and fervent proponent of neoliberal policies, correctly identified the special role that Silicon Valley plays in promoting new thinking and new ideas. Reagan witnessed the rise of Silicon Valley when he was governor of California and deftly wove its narrative into a powerful message, bringing entrepreneurship, technology, and neoliberal capitalism together in a way that formed the basis of his economic platform. In Reagan's eyes, Silicon Valley–style entrepreneurship was the perfect example of American exceptionalism. And neoliberalism was the ideal conduit for taking full advantage of it.

But by the 1990s, some of that rigid view of the world was wearing thin. With the growing tech sector's unique culture, and its mantra of "moving fast and breaking things," it's not surprising that as thinking started to shift in the 1990s about the role of corporations and the value (many would say the reality) of purpose beyond the simplistic thinking of shareholder primacy, Silicon Valley became an incubator of something its proponents call "social entrepreneurship." The idea started small but has now become part of the mainstream business world, if often under different names. Strict social entrepreneurs put purpose on par with, or even ahead of, profit. Profit-making potential, or ability to scale, is the vehicle for the broader impact they hope to have. These entrepreneurs didn't give up the idea of scale or profits but instead redefined success to mean more than simply returning value to owners. In a study of the sector, the Schwab Foundation found that there are about 10 million of these strict social enterprises worldwide, comprising about 3% of all businesses. Half are led by women.[3]

Some social enterprises grow to be big companies, belying one of the myths surrounding Dynamic Capitalism—that you can't grow a large business if you're not strictly devoted to profits. These include Me to We, a millennial-focused company that places goods produced by global artisans in retail stores (over 12,000 at the time of this writing) and sends volunteers on aid-related trips; Kiva, which has provided small loans to millions of small businesses; and Goodwill, a social enterprise that uses profits from its thrift stores to train people with disabilities. Ben and Jerry's, the ice cream company, was born out of ideals from the realm of social entrepreneurship, though when such firms are acquired by larger companies (as Ben and Jerry's was, by Unilever) or raise money in the public markets (which was the case for Etsy, for example), they tend to run into the complexities of our corporate governance laws, which enforce the neoliberal doctrine of shareholder primacy. And, perhaps most notably, there is Patagonia—a company we return to a number of times in this book as one of the largest and most successful businesses founded with a mission-based focus.

You can argue the extent to which these companies serve their stated purpose, whether they pay their executives too much or have a business model that really does good. But that is to miss the point. We've shifted out of a world where success is measured in dollars alone.

Strict social entrepreneurs aren't unique in thinking innovatively about purpose and impact. There are entrepreneurs across the country and the globe who are pushing the ideas of capitalism further and reckoning with the shortcomings of neoliberalism by redefining their role in the system and, in so doing, pushing it to work for a larger number of people. For many forward-thinking entrepreneurs, capitalism is a tool to a greater end.

Entrepreneurship, More Broadly Defined

In the 1990s, at Stanford and Harvard, small groups of students and a few professors began advocating for this different approach to business.

"That wasn't a recognized, respected way of pursuing your business career at that time," Melinda Tuan, a consultant who was teaching at Stanford during this period, told us.[4]

In San Francisco, George Roberts, one of the founders of the global private equity firm that bears his name, Kohlberg Kravis Roberts (KKR), funded a nonprofit called REDF, the Roberts Enterprise Development Fund, which he launched in 1997. KKR had been excoriated as an example of American capitalism gone bad in *Barbarians at the Gate* (the book and HBO movie that detailed KKR's role in the leveraged buyout of RJR Nabisco), which perhaps led to Roberts's shift, though he has not acknowledged that publicly.

REDF's initial aim was to expand job development programs for people striving to overcome serious employment barriers. REDF invested in social enterprises that created jobs and reinvested profits in training and services for employees to help them improve their prospects. In doing this, REDF quickly became one of the centers of the nationwide social entrepreneurship movement, which now exists in many locations and is supported by prominent philanthropic foundations.

Steadily through the early 2000s, a growing number of companies began weaving missions into their profit making, taking the "social" caveat out of the name and redefining entrepreneurship to include constituents beyond the bottom line. Some examples of companies founded during this time are Toms, which donated a pair of shoes for each one sold, and Warby Parker, which developed a similar model for eyeglasses. Both were economically successful, and both leveraged their social mission as part of their marketing and brand. They succeeded at least partly *because* of their social stances, not in spite of them. Today, following the example of these and several other businesses that blend mission with profits, many companies pursue broader callings. This kind of social consciousness is becoming table stakes for all businesses.

Jed Emerson, one of the first leaders of REDF and CEO of the organization for more than a decade, described their early efforts to us. "We were trying to figure out how to take capital and put it to use in a way that used business skills, practices, and acumen to drive community change and other outcomes. Not instead of profits—in addition to them."[5] Like many innovators, Emerson's and Roberts's ideas were initially not taken seriously, despite the weight that Roberts's business career brought to their efforts. But slowly, over time, others started to take notice. Roberts and Emerson didn't invent social entrepreneurship, nor did their specific implementation of these ideas become *the* standard for socially conscious investing. They were among a handful of influential people working during that time, trying to rethink the role of corporations in our society. As is often the case, it was the work of a number of organizations, often relatively disconnected from each other, that laid the foundation for the broader changes that we're seeing take hold more widely now.

Today, many companies have woven the idea of performing a social good into their identities, even if just for marketing or employee retention. Many of the biggest companies in the United States submit to examination and reporting by an organization called Just Capital, which ranks American businesses on their commitment to local communities, how they treat employees, and their environmental stewardship. Just Capital's top companies in 2024 were Hewlett-Packard, Bank of America, Accenture, Intel, and Citigroup. You can dismiss the list as greenwashing, and undoubtedly, you would find some egregious examples of corporate behavior among those on the list. But the fact that Just Capital even exists, not to mention is backed by a group of well-known individuals and foundations, including the hedge fund billionaire Paul Tudor Jones II, the Robert Wood Johnson Foundation, the Ford Foundation, and the Nathan Cummings Foundation, is a sign of just how far public sentiment has changed about the responsibility of business over the past few decades. Just Capital creates its criteria through surveys of some 10,000 people each year. By tracking consumer sentiment and behavior, the organization attempts to capture what attributes Americans believe are most important in corporations and their leaders. Americans want the businesses they interact with to be active members of their communities, to treat their employees well, and to not pollute the environment.[6]

Mainstreaming Purpose

At the same time that the norms were gradually shifting among company founders and executives, another movement was gaining traction in the financial world. Free-thinking business leaders were experimenting with new investment ideas in banking and publicly traded funds. Interestingly, this was at least partly spurred by a government requirement. The Community Redevelopment Act (CRA), passed in 1977, required banks to invest in the communities in which they worked. That meant they had to find ways to work in low-income neighborhoods, long overlooked formally and informally by banking institutions. The history of systemic racism in America meant that many low-income communities had populations that were majority non-white, which added a racial-equity dimension to the CRA. Spurred by this initial requirement and paying attention to other ways to drive profit from what by the late 1980s and early 1990s had become a small but vocal area of interest for certain investors, banks sought other ways to combine profit with "impact."

In 1991, Dick Parsons became CEO of Dime Savings Bank in New York City. Founded in 1859, the bank was struggling. Parsons turned it around, eventually guiding it to merge with another bank in the mid-1990s. A central part of his strategy was embracing the communities around the bank's offices. Shortly after he became CEO, he went on a tour of the bank's 60 branches to better understand the operations of the business he had just taken over. In Coney Island, what he saw at one of the city's most famous beachfront destinations dismayed him. "I was excited to go because I had grown up on Coney Island as a kid. We lived in Brooklyn, and my father would take us all the time," he said. "But it had slipped off the radar. The city wasn't investing in it. It had put a lot of public housing out there. It [still] had some things on the boardwalk, and the rest of it was just trashed," he told us. "So there was this grand old [bank] building in the middle of this despair and debris. And you realize that if you're a part of the community and the community goes down, well, you go down with it."[7]

From that time, Parsons adopted what was then an unpopular position: that companies should invest some of their profits in the long-term health of their communities. At Dime, that meant donating to local organizations working on cleaning up Coney Island and lending to small businesses located around the bank. He took that philosophy with him as he rose to increasingly influential positions in corporate America, eventually becoming chairman of AOL Time Warner and Citigroup, and interim CEO of the Los Angeles Clippers.

"I got a certain amount of shareholder pushback both there [Dime] and at Time Warner because I carried that perspective forward," Parsons recalled. "People would say a CEO's job is to look after the shareholders, to create value for them, and then let them take that value and decide what they want to do with it," he said. "I used to get criticized because we also had a pretty active charitable program within the bank. And I remember having conversations with people telling me, 'It's not your job to decide what to do with the company's profits.' Then you have to make the case that we're a citizen of this country and community, and we have an obligation not just to look after shareholders and employees."[8]

"I think that big giant wheel on which we hang our cultural values is turning. It's not gotten quite to the place it needs to get to within corporate America. But it's much closer," Parsons said. "The Larry Finks of the world and others have jumped on the bandwagon and sort of said corporations have a responsibility beyond just to shareholders but to communities and to employees and other stakeholders. Not only is this a good thing, it's something I've been advocating for for decades."*

Long-Term Thinking Yields Higher Returns

Environmental, Social, and Governance investing, which turned into a political controversy in the early 2020s and resulted in people like Larry Fink publicly eschewing the term in the exchange at the Aspen Ideas Festival we described in chapter 3, grew out of these ideas. The roots of ESG investing reveal another myth about Dynamic Capitalism: that ESG investing is "woke" or politically motivated. Rather, it was a meeting of the minds, not an overarching political statement. On one hand, serious thinkers like Hall and Parsons were in positions of power, with ideas about companies' responsibilities. On the other hand, consumers wanted products they felt good about buying. Some sophisticated investors, who understood how markets work, wanted their money to do more than just earn returns.

As consumers began demanding more financial products that incorporated the idea of social good, many large mutual funds offered by big firms whose names you'll be familiar with, such as Vanguard, Schwab, and BlackRock, started marketing funds targeted at "social good." The exact criteria that define "good" continues to be a topic of debate. For instance, some funds don't invest in weapons manufacturers or oil companies. Others invest in projects that reduce emissions or companies that promise to pay their suppliers fairly. These funds are typically fairly high priced (it costs a lot to do the required research), but how much social benefit the underlying companies actually provide is an open question and the

---

* Dick Parsons died in late December 2024. It was truly a privilege to have had the chance to speak to him about these ideas he held so deeply, and we feel honored to have been among the last formal interviews he gave before his death.

subject of scrutiny by both proponents and skeptics of socially conscious investing. How do you measure the worth of paying cotton growers in India at fair market rates versus the good of producing organic cotton in the American South—or for that matter, sourcing clothing from wool? There are entire industries, now aided by AI and other software, focused on making these fine calculations and searching out the best investments to match particular investors' values.

Companies across the financial sector have begun offering investors these values-driven approaches. To many, Goldman Sachs's acquisition of Imprint Capital in 2015 marked a turning point for impact investing's move into the mainstream. Viewed through the lens of this evolution, BlackRock's Larry Fink was actually late to the party when he made headlines with his 2019 shareholder letter. The ideas he talked about then had been taking shape for decades.

Lisa Green Hall eventually went to work for Apollo. In an attempt to turn a new page, senior leaders at Apollo were considering different ideas to move beyond the problems of their past. Hearing from investors that they wanted opportunities to benefit people and the planet, they turned to Hall and the emerging category of impact investing.

Surprisingly, over time, ESG returns haven't been much lower or higher than other kinds of investments (despite all the political drama surrounding them). And as of 2025, consumer demand for these kinds of investments remained high. While money was flowing out of the stock market overall into 2023, for example, it was still flowing into ESG funds: By year end, ESG fund holdings had reached $3.4 trillion.[9]

These two facts are related. With so much money flowing into "impact" categories, it's certainly possible that impact investing has become somewhat of its own asset bubble (too many dollars chasing too few investment opportunities). We think a different force is at work, however. With the industry greatly expanding the definition of impact to accommodate accelerating investment in the category, vast swaths of the market have now been labeled as "impact." It's no wonder their returns mimic the broader markets—they essentially *are* the market today.

Whatever your view of impact or socially motivated investing, one thing is clear: Impact investors, who, like social entrepreneurs, began as renegades within the business community, have become mainstream.

Diverse Coalitions and Complex Problems

It's not a coincidence that women and people of color were disproportionately represented among the early leaders of values-driven capitalism. People who are aware of the failings of the prevailing system are often more open to taking a stand against it. That turned out to be a considerable advantage as businesses in the United States became more diverse, and it illustrates another myth about Dynamic Capitalism—that diversity is a drag on business. Diversity initiatives shouldn't be rigid, especially in a country of so many races, where disadvantage isn't obvious and can arise from class as well as race. However, most people responsible for growing revenue or profits understand that finding new markets and making long-term bets on those markets is part of their responsibility. And new research suggests what executives like Hall and Parsons knew all along: Economic growth comes from inclusion.

In one recent study, researchers from a group of top universities observed that in 1960, 94% of doctors were white men. By 2010, the fraction had fallen to 60% as barriers against women and people of color fell. By studying these dynamics over time, the researchers estimated that 20% to 40% of US growth in GDP can be explained by the improved allocation of talent. Diversification of our workforce—allowing more qualified people to have broader opportunities—has paid huge economic dividends, despite the rhetoric that accompanied Donald Trump's return to office in 2025 that suggested otherwise. These same researchers also cited the example of Sandra Day O'Connor, the Supreme Court justice who graduated third in her law school class in 1952 but could only find a job as a legal secretary.[10] If you're a business leader, it pays to be aware of the allocation of talent.

The Third Rail of Neoliberalism: Fossil Fuels

One of the symbolic turning points in the long shift toward Dynamic Capitalism came in 2014, when the Rockefeller Foundation, funded by the family that had helped lay the foundation for the Golden Age of Capitalism, took a step toward creating a new economy that wasn't based on fossil fuels. That fall, the Rockefeller Brothers Fund announced that it would sell the fossil fuel investments held by its $1 billion endowment over the following five years. While other philanthropies and university endowments had done the same, the action of the Rockefeller Brothers Fund carried much greater symbolic significance. Their divestment marked the end of an era and a complete departure from the extractive past that created the Rockefeller endowment in the first place. For much of the 20th century, fossil fuels had been seen almost as synonymous with capitalism as the energy source that drove economies. Now, the family that had benefited more than almost any other from the oil industry was saying that it believed finding a path forward would require a hard turn away from fossil fuels.

In hindsight, we can see the significance of the moment. Today, environmentalists and impact investors are working in a powerful, pragmatic coalition to change the financial system and steer money away from fossil fuels. That movement and coalition have triggered some of the strongest backlash against the rise of Dynamic Capitalism. Yet Rockefeller Brothers was willing to weather the political backlash of their decision. Joined a few years later by the larger Rockefeller Foundation, they were part of a coalition of some 150 foundations, universities, and municipalities that have announced divestment from fossil fuel investments. "We see this as both a moral imperative and an economic opportunity," the president of the fund, Stephen Heintz, said at the 2014 press conference, where Justin Rockefeller, the great-great-grandson of John D. Rockefeller Sr., was also present.[11]

The shift by the Rockefeller foundations away from fossil fuels turned out to be too large to ignore. Pragmatists and long-term thinkers operating in different corners of the American economy took notice. They were finally coalescing into a force to be reckoned with.

This Isn't "Woke" Capitalism

Narrowly defining the changes taking place in how businesses, individuals, foundations, and others are practicing capitalism as something akin to a culture war misses the point. That framing only serves to undermine the meaningful changes that are taking shape across the American and global business landscape. Not every issue needs to be construed as a "to-the-death" fight. As with every issue involving people and their opinions, there is a spectrum of behavior, with the center point in constant flux. As they tend to, the fringes exert a certain gravitational pull on mainstream opinion, pulling it in one direction or another. Focusing on the endpoints often misses the actual change taking shape. We see it in the new attitude of businesses toward government. We see it in the rising power of consumers. We see it in social entrepreneurship. We see it in organizations like Just Capital. We see it in how businesses market their products and position their brands. And we are seeing it—finally—in the shape of a new energy system that will underpin Dynamic Capitalism.

Chapter 9

THE CLIMATE FALLACY

While climate change poses a threat to human life on our planet, we must recognize that energy underpins and enables our global economy. Shifting away from fossil fuels, the energy source that drove the last 100 years of our economy, has become incredibly contentious, precisely because energy is so integral to our existence. Yet this is a critical topic to address as we describe the shift to Dynamic Capitalism. All the politics in the world cannot change the reality that forward-looking companies, communities, and countries are moving away from these extractive power sources toward cleaner sources of energy, as well as advances in technology that will make burning fossil fuels more sustainable and environmentally friendly. Dynamic Capitalism compels us to find new energy sources if we are to ensure that the planet does not become inhospitable to human life.

Climate change was once widely acknowledged as a critical issue facing humanity, even if there wasn't anything close to a consensus for how to address it. But in our overly politicized environment, it has become a flashpoint for identity politics. Neither free markets nor government regulation alone can adequately address our climate challenges. We need solutions that encompass both the speed of the free market and the power of governmental laws and guardrails.

Some of the solution must come from consensus within our fractious political system. Despite seemingly endless disagreement, there are reasons to be hopeful. Environmental causes have always given rise to strange bedfellows and interesting coalitions. We all share an interest in a healthy planet, clean drinking water, and a sustainable future. And environmentalism wasn't always such a partisan issue. Some of the foundational legislation dealing with environmental stewardship, such as the Wilderness Act, the Clean Air Act, and the Clean Water Act, passed during the 1960s and early 1970s with broad bipartisan support. An unlikely lobbying coalition of hunters and hippies came together to back them. We may see unlikely bedfellows do the same now. Hunters in the American West are some of the earliest environmentalists and can be surprisingly pro-government in certain circumstances (for example, they rely on the Forest Service, the Post Office, and other government entities regularly; they're also face to face with the effects of climate change, including the growing number of forest fires).[1]

But the climate crisis isn't just about environmental protection in the form of governmental action. As we shift away from environmentally damaging energy sources, the most consequential changes are likely to come from within companies. The United States owned the last energy revolution. It's not a foregone conclusion that American companies will lead the way to the next. More global CEOs are grappling with the environmental and climate crisis by using the powerful tools at their disposal. For instance, Mitsui, a Japanese company with more than 46,000 global employees, has identified the global energy transition as one of its key opportunities. An interview with CEO Kenichi Hori gave us a window into the decision-making processes of this giant operation. The decisions Mitsui is making aren't about giving up profits to pursue a social good. Instead, they're about balancing the short-term profits against more significant long-term opportunities.

The day-to-day work of finding profitable business prospects in the energy economy while still helping reduce carbon emissions means engaging in complex analysis. "The complex problem solving becomes a business opportunity," Hori told us. "This is the time when you talk about what is at stake here. Does this short-term profit really mean a lot for us? How are we going to balance the short-term issue and the long-term rewards that we are aiming for? I think the most important part of this is that you can never go into the game late in the stage. You have to be in the game today for future projects."

The company relies on the values-based decision-making of the people who work there. "One more thing I would add is I want our people, Mitsui's employees, to line up their own individual aspirations with these types of activities. I think that's very important," Hori said.[2]

This view of the realities of life inside companies makes us hopeful about the role that the business community writ large can have. But we're also pragmatic about how far corporate actions can take us without some governmental intervention. If fossil fuel companies have so much at stake in the short term—they need to deliver profits to shareholders based on their existing capital investments—they are unlikely to transition quickly to cleaner business models without significant government pressure and incentives. With just 100 companies responsible for 71% of the greenhouse gas emissions since 1988, providing these incentives to the right businesses and in the right way is critically important.[3]

As the United States has bounced back and forth between Democratic and Republican administrations, we failed to create the stability and consistency that businesses need to make decisions about their environmental footprint, let alone invest in longer-term climate mitigation. While we are wary of government oversight and are natural skeptics when it comes to the role of governments broadly in the economy, we believe government's greatest and best use is often in defining the rules of the game and providing appropriate incentives to guide corporate action. Some people take skepticism of government action to the extreme and, as a result, struggle to address large societal issues. With its emphasis on individual action over collectivism, this might even be seen as a feature, rather than a bug, of the neoliberal worldview, conveniently allowing its proponents to ignore climate externalities that otherwise would have been costly to mitigate and have the potential to slow economic growth. Because the impact of human activities on climate is so widespread and, at the same time, so diffuse, the neoliberals have it wrong. Governments must set incentives and guardrails that allow markets to address climate challenges. Solving the climate problem is a whole-of-society challenge. Ideas such as carbon credits and cap and trade fit into this mold, and we especially lean toward models that combine government intervention with the ability to leverage market dynamics to create sustainable solutions. If the US federal government cannot act, state governments and international organizations must step up.

Arthur Cecil Pigou, the early-20th-century French economist whose ideas we talked about in chapter 5, wrote passionately about what we now call the "Tragedy of the Commons"—the propensity for individuals and companies to act in ways that benefit themselves but to the detriment of their communities by depleting natural resources and harming the environment. It turns out that the Tragedy of the Commons doesn't always hold, especially for communities with shared values and connections. Elinor Ostrom, the first woman to win the Nobel Prize for Economics, did groundbreaking work in this area. Living through the Great Depression, she witnessed how her community banded together to survive, which informed her ideas and approach. Rather than observing from afar, she preferred to be in the field and the trenches, spending thousands of hours in communities around the globe. This makes her theories all the more meaningful—she observed them firsthand, almost in the style of an anthropologist rather than that of a traditional economist. Using this methodology, she discovered that connected communities with a shared sense of values don't exploit their resources in the way that the Tragedy of the Commons theory predicts. Shared bonds drive community-minded thinking and action.

Similarly, we are observing a sea change in behavior by corporate leaders as more come to realize that while no single company or country acting alone can solve climate change, each has a responsibility to act in ways that make them better stewards of the environment—both for the good of society and also for the good of their long-term bottom line.

A Practical Imperative

It may be counterintuitive to consider the role oil and gas companies can play in solving our climate crisis. After all, fossil fuels account for an enormous share of greenhouse gas emissions globally.[4] But they're also closest to the problem and, in many respects, are in the best position to invest in solutions to our dire march toward climate instability—if they can take the long view.

Occidental Petroleum, a Houston-based oil and gas consortium, is an interesting case study. With a market capitalization of nearly $60 billion, it is one of the world's 30 largest oil and gas companies. Its size and reach give it clout in the industry and also make the actions it takes meaningful in the broader context of climate action. Some people argue that looking to the polluters for solutions to our pollution issues is counterproductive or gives extractive industries a pass for their complicity in leading to our current climate instability. We don't agree. The challenges that climate change poses to our planet are so great that we must embrace ideas from all sectors of society. Every human on the planet has a climate footprint. Pretending that the only bad actors in the climate debate are those responding to the world's demand for cheap and reliable energy is counterproductive.

While other oil and gas companies have made strides toward investing in green technologies, Occidental's stance on climate change stands out. It was the first US-based oil and gas company to commit to net-zero emissions goals for their operations and products—aligning these goals with the Paris Climate Accords—and has been a leader in taking a holistic approach to climate goals and initiatives.[5] Occidental aims to be a net-zero carbon producer by the year 2050—not a small feat for a company whose main line of business is to pull carbon-producing substances from the ground. Much of the company's effort focuses on carbon capture, which has been the focus of criticism of their plans. However, we believe that a transition to a green economy will necessarily require us to find solutions to mitigate the impact of what will certainly continue to be the large-scale burning of fossil fuels. These technologies can and should be deployed in combination with a greater push for cleaner energy sources. Indeed, one of the world's most long-term-oriented investors, Warren Buffett, recognized the potential of the carbon capture market when he made a significant investment in Occidental in 2019.

Other oil and gas producers are also involved in this transition, albeit slowly. British Petroleum has made a similar net-zero pledge to Occidental's and has invested heavily in solar, wind, and other renewable energy projects. Royal Dutch Shell has done work around its climate footprint and has organized a division called Shell New Energies to catalyze efforts in this area. Total Energy, Chevron, and others have also been making substantial investments in renewables, as have many of the member states of OPEC. For these global companies, renewable energy is a good long-term bet. Of course, there are many examples of oil and gas companies either failing to take action or making grand proclamations and failing to live up to them. For example, in 2013, after pressure from an investor group called Ceres, Exxon issued a report about the risks of climate change.[6]

However, the report resulted in only modest actions, and in 2017, Exxon was forced to write down reserves as "stranded assets" because they were no longer viable in a carbon-constrained world.[7] Even when the business case was clear, the company couldn't act fast enough.

We can't rely solely on the actions of companies themselves to address climate challenges. Nor will shareholder pressure alone be enough to force change fast enough to address these issues, if at all. The managers of these businesses don't have enough incentive to bow to the pressure. It's a clear failure of the markets and a flaw in the shareholder primacy model. And our current politics is only making change harder.

Climate simply won't be addressed without the help of larger forces. Government must be involved. In fact, it already is involved in ways that some Americans—both those who dismiss capitalism as a vehicle for change and those who demonize the government—conveniently forget. For instance, Tesla—now one of the most valuable companies in the world—was propped up by a $465 million Department of Energy loan as the global recession nearly caused it to go out of business. Tesla repaid this money (and did so nine years before the loan was due), but the cash came at a critical time for the business, when it was unclear whether the company could stay afloat. These were smart investments by almost any measure, and our point isn't to take anything away from the thousands of companies that have benefited from government support (such as its early role in developing what became the internet), nor from Tesla, which has greatly affected the pace of development of electric vehicles across the automotive industry. Instead, we use them to highlight the potential for relatively modest government interventions that can result in massive economic gains (instead of going out of business, Tesla went on to be worth more than $1 trillion and is driving the rapid electrification of the auto industry).

Governments Are Being Forced to Act

While some political rhetoric suggests governments are overly keen to intervene—in their view, often forcing economic changes on unwilling citizens—this is often not the case in reality. Instead, citizens globally are turning to the courts to *force* their governments to take action. While market-based climate solutions will likely lead to faster and more scalable interventions, governments must provide the ground rules, including specific laws and regulations from which companies can make economically motivated decisions.

The US regulatory and government landscape around climate change is fractious, almost to an extreme. Look no further than the seesaw of rules and regulations that have been enacted, rescinded, and enacted again, only to be rescinded once more across the last decade of American leadership. Despite this—perhaps because of it—citizens are taking matters into their own hands and trying to force government action. In one high-profile case, a group of Montana youth sued the state over its failure to consider climate when approving fossil fuel projects. The plaintiffs, aged 5 to 22, argued successfully that the state had failed to follow the Montana Constitution's provision that guarantees Montanans "the right to a clean and healthful environment" and requires the state to maintain the environment "for present and future generations." A handful of other states have similar constitutional requirements, and several have also seen legal challenges to state environmental practices. While this ruling was an interpretation of the Montana Constitution, not the US Constitution, it shows the potential for legal challenges related to climate while highlighting challenges to action in the United States, which has a multi-tiered and often conflicting set of rules between federal, state, and local municipalities.[8]

A recent court case in the European Union went even further. In 2024, the European Court of Human Rights ruled in favor of a group of Swiss women who argued that nations must better protect their citizens from climate change impacts.[9] This landmark decision established a precedent within the Council of Europe's 46 states and may go down as a turning point for future climate litigation—at least in the countries that are members of the Council (the United States is an "observer state" and is not subject to the court's rulings). The ruling stated that Switzerland had "failed to comply with its duties" to combat climate change. Although the court required no specific action, and the effect of the ruling on Swiss policies and practices won't be clear for some time, it does serve as a good example of the growing call for governments to address climate.

Climate Denial

One of the biggest and most obvious reasons that action on climate change has been so slow is related to the powerful lobbies that exist to reinforce the status quo. Not surprisingly, many with entrenched economic interests—especially those who lack the ability or vision to adapt—are digging their heels in, seeing any change as a threat to their power base, their wallets, and—harkening back to the wildcat oil culture that's embedded in neoliberalism—their God-given right to live the lives they want on a planet they consider theirs to use. The issue has become politicized as these embedded interests use the bully pulpit of politics to stall climate action. They frame their rationale in terms of economics, but ultimately their argument is cultural, not economic. The broad coalitions that once existed to address climate challenges either have been dismantled or severely hampered in their effectiveness due to these political divisions. If you are against change, these divisions are the perfect recipe for slowing it. Or stopping it altogether.

Shortly after the Business Roundtable declared that the purpose of a business extended beyond its shareholders, a man named Leonard Leo stepped into the business arena. A stalwart conservative political and judicial activist, best known for his decades-long effort to shift the Supreme Court rightward as the longtime vice chairman of the conservative legal group the Federalist Society, Leo has become one of the most recognizable figures—and main financial backers—defending a libertarian worldview that helped form the basis of the neoliberal system.[10] Leo leads a network of for-profit and nonprofit organizations that have spent more than $500 billion establishing what they describe as an "anti-woke" movement. "I spent close to 30 years, if not more, helping to build the conservative legal movement," Leo proclaims in a video he recorded for the Teneo Network, a sort of Federalist Society for business interests. "And at some point or another, I just said to myself, 'If this can work for law, why can't it work for lots of other areas of American culture and American life?'"[11]

There is ample reason to believe Leo when he says this. Over 40 years of patient and methodical work, the Federalist Society has reshaped the American judicial landscape. Leo now sits at the helm of a series of lobbying groups with an aim to fight what he sees as the leftward lurch of American business and its encroachment into areas of political and personal life that he, and others in his movement, see as overreaching and dangerous to American capitalism. Included in this fight against "woke" capitalism is a deeply held skepticism around climate change as well as the role of government in combating it. He and his funding networks, including Teneo, provided significant financial support to Project 2025—the effort to jump-start conservative initiatives and prepare for the Republican return to political power. The Trump administration has already implemented some of Project 2025's goals, including significant cuts to the Department of Energy and the Environmental Protection Agency.[12] Leo and his disciples have also called for an end to ESG, with a particular focus on how they believe environmental politics—from both companies and governments—are harmful to consumers and to the economy as a whole.[13]

There's an obvious contradiction between neoliberals and their current movement against ESG and other innovations designed to produce a cleaner energy system, which is more evidence that their arguments aren't rational or economic but cultural. After all, neoliberal capitalists purport to believe in limited government and the power of the free markets. Asking the courts to intervene in the way investment managers run their funds is an obvious interference in the free market, and using the power of free speech to ignite a culture war on businesspeople seems counterproductive to American enterprise.

To understand what's going on, consider the history of neoliberalism and the fossil fuel economy, which we discussed in chapter 7. Neoliberalism emerged in an era when the wildcat oil families of the West were gaining influence in Washington, DC, replacing the earlier generation of oil wealth that had seen oil as a gift. The wildcatters brought with them a form of evangelical Protestantism that enshrined a right to use the earth's resources. Along with other ideas rooted in these faiths, including the right to life and gun rights, climate denial is now an entrenched part of the right-wing approach to the culture wars. These tenets place people—usually white men—atop the natural order and see hierarchies as the most efficient and productive ways to organize both the world and the economy.

Leo and the Teneo Network are not alone in their opposition to climate policy among neoliberal groups. Both he and his organizations are striving to unite others with similar views to fight back. The Heritage Foundation, the Heartland Institute, and Consumers' Research, among many others, are all examples of mainstream neoliberal think tanks actively working against changes to US laws and policies that support the move to a new energy economy. A number of these groups have direct ties to, and financial backing from, the fossil fuel industry and their executives.[14] These groups gained powerful influence with the reelection of Donald Trump in 2024 and are positioning to pull back many of the environmental gains that have been achieved over the previous years.

Liberals and Climate Extremism

The political right isn't alone in pushing its agenda on climate change. Some on the left are arguing for what many believe to be equally unrealistic goals, even if their aims (reducing carbon emissions and mitigating the rapid changes to our environment) are, in our view, directionally correct. The Green New Deal—more political marketing than realistic policy reform—is just one example. A sweeping set of climate actions whose consequences would be quite stark for the economy, it nevertheless has many hardcore environmentalists calling for its adoption.[15] Others have argued for a ban on all fossil fuels by the year 2030 or the implementation of massive taxes on carbon emissions. To bring attention to their cause, environmental protesters have created near riots in the streets of major US cities, sabotaged equipment, thrown soup on priceless paintings, vandalized Stonehenge, and blocked critical infrastructure.[16] There is plenty of room for extremism from both sides.

Consumer Power

Consumers are beginning to pay attention to climate change, and this attention is starting to affect corporate actions. Study after study has shown that Americans as a whole—particularly younger Americans—view climate change as an existential threat. Yet only an estimated 3% of charitable contributions go toward environmental causes.[17] Brands are picking up on these greener trends. Environmental concerns used to be considered "nice to have" rather than a necessity. But this appears to be changing. As Ashley Reichheld, John Peto, and Cory Ritthaler recently described in the *Harvard Business Review*: "We're on the brink of a major shift in consumption patterns, where truly sustainable brands—those that make good on their promises to people and the planet—will seize the advantage from brands that make flimsy claims or that have not invested sufficiently in sustainability. We're fast approaching this tipping point where sustainability will be considered a baseline requirement for purchase, and companies should prepare now."[18] Consumers are willing to pay more—often quite a bit more—for products produced by brands that align with their environmental goals. To businesses, consumers matter even more than government policies. That suggests to us that even though some actions companies take to go "green" may get quieter during the Trump administration, these changes will ultimately continue.

We explored these trends with Kate Williams, CEO of 1% for the Planet, whom we first introduced in chapter 5. She's been helping drive companies to pay more attention to the shifting consumer sentiment toward sustainability and environmental causes. In addition to raising money for environmental aims, 1% for the Planet also helps guide member organizations to lessen the environmental impact of their businesses—from packaging to supply chains to materials. While we suspect most companies become members because they and their executives deeply believe in being better stewards of the planet, member companies also have the option of using the 1% logo on their websites and products, signaling to consumers that the brand takes some level of environmental responsibility.

As with sentiment around environmental causes more broadly, the 1% movement is growing. "We've seen really significant growth year over year since 2018, and it has really accelerated," Williams told us. She described consumer trends—particularly among younger generations—similar to those we've cited earlier. For brands, "we solve real business problems, create real brand value, create new ways of connecting to customers . . . aligning with their marketing and business growth goals."[19]

People who advocate for harnessing the power of markets to slow climate change are sometimes accused of enabling "greenwashing." And companies do sometimes oversell the importance of their actions or don an environmental activist's mantle without earning it. But when asked about the potential for greenwashing, Williams's response was surprisingly nondefensive and practical. "I think we gained so much more by thousands of companies making meaningful, incremental changes than by saying nothing counts until people are 100%," she said in response to our probing. It's a lesson that could be more widely adopted, especially for problems as large and complicated as climate change. Incremental progress is still progress, and while we should push companies and governments to be better stewards of our planet, we must also recognize that change often comes in fits and starts. Penalizing small steps because we think they're not bold enough will only discourage companies from acting at all. Incremental steps, as long as they're real, should be applauded, even while we push for more progress.

What Is the Climate Fallacy?

There are companies making practical long-term bets on new energy systems. There are consumers doing their part to advocate for change. And there are climate deniers and climate advocates pushing or protecting cultural and political agendas. What's missing is powerful political leadership—a rhetorical figure or Great Communicator, to pull America or the world around the goal. Today's broken information environment makes that harder than ever.

In the meantime, if you believe, as we do, that we face an existential climate risk, consider embracing capitalism and government as parts of the solution, while recognizing that companies will be the most consequential actors (especially in the current political environment). Climate deniers have tricked many people in the environmental movement into seeing capitalism as the enemy of climate. In doing so, they've created much larger obstacles to change. If tackling climate policy isn't big enough, consider trying to do so while redesigning capitalism into something completely different. It is an unrealistic and unfathomable lift.

For too long, the knee-jerk reaction of neoliberal capitalists was to fight against any form of government regulation or oversight. Over the decades, the fossil fuel companies embraced this ideology and either denied climate change altogether or dragged their heels on any meaningful progress during a time when it would have been easier to act. It was simpler for them to create division and doubt while maintaining their short-term profits than to shift to a long-term vision of the future. There is a direct line from that way of thinking to the political divisions of today. But if we're going to shift to Dynamic Capitalism successfully, we must untangle the concept of capitalism from fossil fuels. Fossil fuel companies are deeply part of the Milton Friedman firmament in people's minds because they've been so intertwined for so long. The fallacy at the heart of the neoliberal argument about climate change is that we can't have capitalism without fossil fuels. But we can. In fact, we have to.

Is a Shared Future the Enemy?

The right wing's ability to take the long view of their work is remarkable. This has allowed them to work slowly and methodically over decades. Certainly this has been Leo's playbook for the Federalist Society, which has been one of the most dominant forces shaping the American legal profession over the past 30 years. Foundational to Teneo's operating principles is identifying and recruiting influential members to serve as catalysts for the change the organization seeks. ProPublica notes that the network already counts numerous powerful allies, including members of Congress and leaders across the conservative business landscape.[20] It fancies itself the "Silicon Valley of conservative ideas" and is guided by libertarian entrepreneurial principles that pervade certain parts of Silicon

Valley culture (Evan Baehr, the cofounder of Teneo, worked for Silicon Valley billionaire and noted libertarian Peter Thiel; Thiel is also the key mentor to and proponent of Vice President JD Vance). Culture wars run deep in society today, which makes the opacity of groups on the right (and the left) troubling. Debating the role of companies in society and talking about the edges of corporate influence are important discussions that we believe will result in more alignment across society, government, and business. It's hard to engage in that debate when major players pushing back on these questions fancy themselves puppet masters in the background rather than true participants in the discussion.

There is some reason to be hopeful. On a 2023 Teneo podcast, former House speaker and current Teneo vice president Paul Ryan addressed this when he talked about the challenges of an increasingly polarized society. "Am I worried that identity politics is being played by the right and the left . . . yes I am . . . I think we need to do everything we can to try to get rid of identity politics, which both sides have been playing."[21]

Notably, in the spring of 2025, a group called the New Civil Liberties Alliance, backed by Leo and others, filed a lawsuit against the Trump tariffs, alleging executive overreach. Perhaps there is more common ground to be staked out than is apparent at first. It's a reminder that even within organizations that are seemingly at odds, some people, perhaps, will be open to a more collaborative approach.

Section III

THE MESSY MIDDLE

Chapter 10

GOVERNMENT IS NOT THE PROBLEM (BUT IT'S NOT THE SOLUTION EITHER)

The neoliberal worldview generally holds that government regulation stifles innovation and serves as a drag on the economy. The call for smaller government and nearly blind allegiance to reducing regulation and government intervention in the economy has become a near-religion across the neoliberal movement. But even a cursory reading of history shows that this view is misguided. What started as an easy shorthand for a group that likely understood in more subtle terms the reality on the ground (Milton Friedman's work, after all, was at least partially funded by government grants, and he served on any number of government commissions) was co-opted by subsequent adherents to neoliberal ideology who lacked this nuance. That many of today's most ardent neoliberals are the beneficiaries of financial and technology industries that, in large part, owe their existence to government subsidies and defense spending adds to the irony of this position.

Unfettered, free-market competition works fine in the abstract, but the real world is much more complicated. Recognizing this complexity, Dynamic Capitalism isn't just about a change in the corporate sector; a new role for government is also emerging. While Dynamic Capitalism involves the consideration of stakeholders beyond just shareholders, there's a limit to what is reasonable to expect from businesses acting alone. More importantly, it's simply not true that the "market" solves all problems. If capitalism is a *political bargain*, we believe that government's role in that bargain is to provide a framework for implementing a shared (or at least somewhat shared) set of values and goals—whether those goals relate to product safety, the environment, or worker rights. Instead of allowing the government to shirk its responsibility, we believe we should hold government accountable for the role it can and should play in shaping some aspects of our society, limited as we believe those should be.

New eras of history often appear to unfold quickly, but in retrospect, you can see their underpinnings forming over longer periods. In the case of Dynamic Capitalism, three related crises are propelling change: deepening economic challenges, especially from China; rising inequality and the decline of the middle class; and the climate crisis. There is a role for government in each of these areas, but one that we believe should be approached with skepticism and caution, lest it overstep.

Regulation and Industrial Policy

The instinct of governments to "control" (or, more likely, attempt to control) is a strong one, especially in the case of emerging technologies, but we think it's important to allow for new ideas to develop before they are constrained. A current case in point is regulation related to AI. China, the European Union, and the United States are all experimenting to find regulatory approaches that maintain national security while giving their respective business communities an innovation edge. In China—where the state and the business community are deeply intertwined and the government, in many respects, controls the economy—the approach has included concrete, wide-ranging regulations on synthetic content and generative AI. The regulations also protect workers' rights and require conspicuous labels on synthetic or generative content. The United States appears to be taking a different and, we believe, unfortunate approach, instead looking to regulate the size and specifics of AI models. It's impossible for regulations of this kind to keep pace with innovation, and this approach is unlikely to drive the outcomes regulators seek. Instead, these regulations showcase many regulators' lack of understanding of emerging technologies.

US technology executives have been asking Congress for regulation. They want to better understand the rules by which their technology will be governed—or, more cynically, the large tech companies, with their armies of lawyers and compliance staffers, are happy to leverage an uninformed United States government to create barriers to others entering this fast-moving and promising area. This "regulatory capture" is often misunderstood by both those in power and the broader population. Instead, we have an opportunity to consider more reasonable frameworks that don't stifle innovation. But to date, thoughtful regulation has not been forthcoming.

While AI is the emerging technology most talked about at the time of this writing, other new technologies are catching regulators' eye, most notably quantum computing. Here, again, there is an opportunity to be judicious in establishing regulatory frameworks, lest we quash innovation before these new technologies really take hold. The lack of certainty in regulation makes it harder for companies to invest the large sums required for deep tech research. But regulating inputs in a fast-moving industry is a fool's errand. Any emerging technology is, almost by definition, moving too quickly for regulators to fully comprehend, let alone anticipate. The answer is a deliberate and likely slower approach to setting rules, not the knee-jerk government desire to control or use regulatory power as a political wedge. We need balance and thoughtfulness while staying open to the idea that regulation should follow innovation, not attempt to be ahead of it.

Government as a Partner

Anybody who has ever had to deal with the workers' compensation system, file taxes in multiple states, or cope with a corrupt regulator can attest to the Kafka-esque quality of some federal, state, and local government systems across the United States. If you've had to wrangle with a state unemployment-compensation office, had your land taken by eminent domain, or suddenly had to pay unexpected regulatory levies, you might also have a chip on your shoulder about government. In its enforcement capacity, the government is unfriendly, and this power can certainly be abused. In fact, it is more likely to be abused if we don't restore democratic accountability.

One of the more destructive mindsets that grew out of the adherence to free-market, shareholder-only policies was the idea that government wasn't just an irritant or a detriment—it was the enemy. Some think tanks and executives have propagated this idea, a sort of Ayn Rand libertarianism run amok. Ronald Reagan's quip that "government *is* the problem" perfectly sums up this way of thinking. In the early months of the second Trump administration, we saw this mindset morph into the cruelty of Elon Musk's seemingly indiscriminate cuts to the federal workforce. Instead of taking advantage of a unique opportunity to consider areas of government waste, he and his team took a wrecking ball to entire government departments and functions. This "government is evil" mentality is the kind of strictly binary thinking American businesses need to shed in the world of Dynamic Capitalism. At the same time, there are also those who see the government as our ultimate savior. In their worldview, there is no problem that the government can't or shouldn't try to tackle. This line of thought also suffers from absolutism and needs to be abandoned. Fortunately, we see both extremes changing. America at the end of the Cold War, whose dominance was unquestioned, could afford black-and-white thinking. Today, things are quite different.

One of the most prominent economists of the neoliberal order, Columbia University's Glenn Hubbard, has given a mea culpa of sorts. But rather than advocating an evolution in government regulation or acknowledging that not everyone plays by fair, free-market rules, he and others propose to double down on the idea of unfettered free markets. Instead of confronting the complicated reality in which smart regulation or government funding of deep science research is necessary, the old guard of neoliberal capitalism continues to embrace worker retraining and other small changes to the status quo that are too modest and don't actually address root problems.

"Economists could have done more to talk about how labor-market interventions could have prepared people more for change," Hubbard said in interviews about his book, *The Wall and the Bride,* which centers on Youngstown, Ohio, and attempts to address the state of the workforce in today's economy. "The bigger political error economists made is not coming up with more in terms of tangible programs to help workers and communities: place-based aid, worker aid, and so on."[1]

Youngstown, which had been a post–World War II manufacturing center, lost 60% of its population between the 1970s and the 2000s. Ohio, one of America's largest manufacturing states, is experiencing a death rate from the opioid epidemic that is twice the national average.[2] To us, Hubbard's view reflects fanciful thinking. As anyone around during the 1990s remembers, retraining programs that tried to turn manufacturing workers who had been making middle-class wages into entry-level coders were little more than absurdities. The economy was moving too fast. And it gets harder to change as you get older. Many workers in Youngstown—and around the country—couldn't adapt quickly enough. Access to retraining and educational opportunities for displaced workers is a perfectly acceptable policy goal, but it can't be the only way we blunt the impact of rapid change across our economy.

One of the American business community's greatest strengths is its optimism about operating through chaos. The most powerful forms of innovation require freedom of speech as well as universities, private-sector institutions, and markets that are free from too much government control.* Free markets, decentralization, and less regulation will always be hallmarks of the American approach to governance. But America makes progress when businesses work *with* the government, not always seamlessly but at least steadily, in various partnerships and at different levels. This new era requires fluidity and nimble action, not doctrine. Simplicity is rarely tenable in a complex world.

Many of the most promising shifts in the arena of public–private cooperation are happening at the state and local levels. Take, for instance, Ford Motors' billion-dollar investment to restore Detroit's former Michigan Central Station and its 18-story office tower. This development will serve as space for innovators—including entrepreneurs and researchers—working on new energy innovations as well as electric vehicles. The automaker cooperated with the city and state in planning the project, which included rebuilding a section of the adjacent roadway to prototype a system that could permit battery-electric vehicles to charge while driving.[3] Or consider Pittsburgh's Innovation District, which encompasses a densely populated area in the city's Oakland neighborhood that includes Carnegie Mellon University, the University of Pittsburgh, the University of Pittsburgh Medical Center, and a number of tech

---

* It's worth noting in this regard the massive break from traditional norms around free speech that is taking place in the second Trump administration, targeting universities, law firms, and others whose speech or actions it disagrees with.

startups and research organizations. The creation of this district, designed to bring new jobs and new industries to this once heavily industrialized city, has been funded through a series of federal, state, and local grants and tax incentives, working in partnership with private companies.

There are examples of these sorts of public–private partnerships across the United States. But they are also the kind of developments that most Americans never hear about. In our highly polarized media and political environment, stories of successful partnerships between government and the private sector don't serve the aims of either side of the political debate. Those on the left side of the political spectrum, who favor more significant government intervention, often criticize a greater role for private businesses and prefer the idea that government should simply step in and fill what they perceive to be gaps in society. For those on the right, where almost any government program outside of defense spending is viewed as wasteful, such partnerships fly in the face of their antigovernment narrative. The problem, of course, isn't the government itself. It's the application of government resources and the lens through which we view how and where the government intervenes in our economy.

Economic Diplomacy

One of the flaws of neoliberalism was its assumption that the world inevitably would come around to the American way of thinking and converge on a similar set of neoliberal policies and ideals. This was naive and failed to recognize the extent to which direct government action boosted key industries in the United States. The United States emerged as the dominant world economy in the late 1980s due to a number of factors, including its ability to rapidly commercialize technical innovations and military prowess. These gave it the ability to outmaneuver its main rivals—the USSR, militarily, and Japan, economically. None of this occurred in a vacuum; instead it was the result of meaningful collaboration between government and industry, which partnered more than many neoliberals would choose to admit.

Throughout the past 50 years, the US government has made meaningful investments in industries across the manufacturing and agricultural sectors to prop up US firms, fund new technologies, and protect key industries. The US Department of Defense and related agencies were key funders of both research and early products developed by emerging US industries that would later serve as the backbone of economic growth and progress. This was especially true of semiconductor technologies, which would eventually spawn not just an entire global industry but also foster the environment from which the US startup ecosystem—by far the most powerful and innovative in the world—would emerge. While the transistor was developed by a private company, Bell Labs (then a part of AT&T), when that technology was eventually commercialized into the early semiconductors that replaced vacuum tubes in the computers of the day, it was the Department of Defense that became their largest and most important customer. Fairchild Semiconductor, considered the first Silicon Valley startup, derived nearly half of its revenue from government contracts and was particularly reliant on military contracts during its early years, and Intel's first customer likewise was the US government.

This history sometimes seems lost amid the rising pressure to reduce the size of government. However, the government can and should play an important role as an early investor in innovative technologies and set goals and guardrails to ensure that certain key technologies remain onshore. We lost this bearing toward the end of the neoliberal era, which allowed for dangerous bottlenecks in critical supply chains and an overreliance on a small number of key trading partners, often in unstable parts of the world—both politically and environmentally. The COVID-19 pandemic served as a stark reminder of this as countries shut down production and the world learned the pitfalls of "just in time" manufacturing, where only small inventories of key components are kept on hand and the free flow of parts is necessary to keep production lines running. These disruptions resulted in delays in the manufacturing of personal protective equipment and other key medical supplies. Oil and gas became more volatile as global shipments were halted. And interruptions in the semiconductor industries in Taiwan and South Korea resulted in delays for goods ranging from automobiles to refrigerators to gaming consoles.

Neoliberal capitalism was founded on the idea that government interventions into the economy were negative. If government was the problem, less government was the solution. This mindset infected how politicians and practitioners reacted to world events for decades. The resulting economy turned out to be overly reliant on a small number of big companies and thus remarkably brittle. Dynamic Capitalism takes a more pragmatic view of governmental impositions, recognizing that in some cases, the government can aid, not harm, our broader societal goals.

Rethinking Safety Nets

Despite the prowess of the overall US economy, the increasing economic disparity that was the inevitable result of neoliberal policies has weakened key underlying antecedents to future economic growth. America may have the largest GDP in the world—in 2024, this measure of total economic output was more than 50% higher than that of our nearest rival, China—but by a number of other measures, we are starting to fall behind.[4] While the inequality we've documented throughout this book is becoming harder to ignore, it also has real consequences for our economic vibrancy.

Economic disparity and uncertainty are reducing risk-taking in the United States, resulting in fewer people starting new businesses and impairing overall job mobility. The Global Entrepreneurship Monitor tracks attitudes toward failure across various countries, including the United States, which has historically had a relatively high acceptance of failure (without question contributing to our entrepreneurial success).[5] However, there are signs that America's comfort with and acceptance of failure are starting to wane. We see a growing national narrative around failure that is disconcerting when considered in the context of the importance of embracing failure in fueling our entrepreneurial economy. America appears to be grooming its next generation from an early age to not differentiate between success and failure, more often rewarding them for simply showing up or participating. This may seem egalitarian, but it's causing us to rear generations of children who don't understand the difference between them or the work required to improve. Through this, we risk losing not only some of the grit and resilience that results from healthy competition but also the edge that comes from embracing the learnings from failure.

Meanwhile, just as that resilience is declining in the overall population, the practical consequences of failure, which earlier generations sought to mitigate, are rising. A middle-class American who loses their job or whose small business closes incurs a much higher cost than a generation ago. The economic realities today are harsher than they have been for decades as years of slow but steady decisions across the political divide have slowly chipped away at the social safety net established in the mid-20th century. Consider a 2024 Bankrate survey showing that most Americans (56%) would be unable to pay an unexpected $1,000 expense.[6] American households' median savings are just $8,000. And to give you a sense of how skewed this is to the top end of the wealth scale, the *average* savings across American households is just over $62,000.[7] The net result is that the cost of failure for the average American is significant. Dan Schulman of PayPal realized this after company surveys showed a surprising number of employees were living paycheck to paycheck. As the Bankrate data suggests, this is not uncommon, even among the relatively well employed.

Recognizing this, and understanding the importance of enabling both stability and risk-taking across our economy, Dynamic Capitalism argues for a reasonable social safety net, including broad access to health care, as a critical ingredient for supporting our changing economy. In our push toward neoliberalism, we've forgotten some of the key factors that enable the risk-taking and personal responsibility that neoliberals so cherish. The United States was founded on the principles of shared destiny and collective responsibility. Through this communal ethos, our early cities and towns were built, and the infrastructure that enabled our modern-day economy was forged. This isn't a political argument for access to healthcare and a basic social safety net, it's an economic one. Tying healthcare to employment (and, most typically, to large-company employment) is one of the biggest impediments to entrepreneurial activity and economic mobility. The same is true for a reasonable level of social safeguards, including protections for workers who lose their jobs, and meaningful and real workforce-retraining programs.

Dynamic economies, as the United States seeks to continue to be, are marked by a certain degree of disruption and change. Both are good for society as a whole, but we need to recognize the havoc they can wreak on communities and individuals. This occurred in the 1990s and 2000s as globalization swept across the manufacturing heartland, paying little heed to the people and towns it dislocated. As more automation washes over the business world, we risk displacing another generation of workers.

This isn't an argument for a socialist-style society. On the contrary, it's a recognition that to maintain our entrepreneurial and capitalist edge, we need to consider exactly who constitutes the next generation of entrepreneurs in our country and create policies that enable and encourage their entrepreneurial spirit rather than stifle it.

Federal, state, and local governments may be poised to repeat the mistakes of the 1990s and 2000s if they don't consider that the disruptions we face today have the potential to be even larger than those we experienced during the industrial shift abroad. Existing social safety net programs are underfunded and under threat. Now is a time to rethink how best to offer economic security and, in doing so, how we can potentially shape those programs to be empowering rather than paternalistic—all the while keeping them in check to ensure they don't overwhelm the economy.

Dynamic Capitalism better balances the needs of capital and labor, and because of that offers workers and families greater stability. However, that balance should be further steadied with basic protections around healthcare and economic security. A foundational principle of Dynamic Capitalism regarding government intervention is for that intervention to be the minimum required to achieve the intended outcome. What that looks like for social safety nets is too lengthy a subject for this book, but there are some experiments taking place with approaches that could streamline government aid that are worth considering.

Though there are many reasons to take care with how government benefits are designed, we have some evidence from the COVID-19 pandemic of what happens when workers aren't forced into training programs but are instead handed cash. Indeed, the surge of no-strings-attached unemployment benefits and other government aid, which amounted to a few hundred or thousand extra dollars a month for many American families, resulted in one of the largest surges in entrepreneurship of the past several decades. Household wealth increased 36% between 2019 and 2023, according to the Federal Reserve. Despite the fears of some, most Americans didn't blow their stimulus money on drugs or binge-watching Netflix—a surprising number started companies or looked for ways to learn new skills to take to a different job.

Universal Basic Income?

Many of these ideas could fall under the definition of Universal Basic Income, or UBI. UBI has become popular among a broad set of proponents, from technology executives such as Elon Musk, Mark Zuckerberg, and Sam Altman, to former Service Employees International Union President Andrew Stern, to the late Pope Francis. UBI could build upon these pandemic-era benefits and establish a basic level of support for all Americans. Exactly what its proponents believe it entails varies, and it's important to consider the underlying motivations of its advocates before jumping fully on the UBI bandwagon. From the perspective of Dynamic Capitalism, some of the concepts behind UBI are interesting to explore, especially as they relate to reducing government bureaucracy and boosting individual agency. Existing social programs were established in an era that considered the government's role as that of caretaker, not enabler. There are better ways to offer assistance than those that were a product of our grandparents' or great-grandparents' day.

Many of UBI's most vocal proponents—especially in the tech sector—approach the topic from the perspective of fending off critiques of fast-moving technologies: UBI is their answer to questions about their disruptive potential. "The growth of income and wealth inequalities, the precariousness of labor, and the persistence of abject poverty have all been important drivers of renewed interest in UBI in the United States. But it is without a doubt the fear that automation may displace workers from the labor market at unprecedented rates that primarily explains the revival of the policy, including by many in or around Silicon Valley," reported the Stanford Basic Income Lab.[8]

Streamlining existing programs to allow them to be easier to administer will create more direct benefits to program recipients—more money that can be allocated to benefits instead of bureaucracy. And fewer strings attached to benefits will allow more Americans to use funds in ways that more directly benefit them. This is different from what some UBI proponents argue, which is essentially a perpetual government salary. Some level of safeguards will be important, but the goal of most government assistance programs should be to enable their recipients to get to a point where they no longer need the assistance.

Ironically, UBI was supported back in the 1960s and 1970s by Milton Friedman himself, as well as Dr. Martin Luther King Jr. (not people one typically thinks of as agreeing on much). It's another reminder that neoliberal capitalism—a construct of society, politics, and business—took on its harder edges only when it became politicized. Indeed, most economists recognize that a developed society needs to create a dignified solution for people who can't find work. We failed profoundly at that in the 1990s, and American society has paid the price since.

Universal Basic Income is far from a viable federal benefit, but the experiments underway are important. They are an example of the kind of cross-spectrum thinking from governments, business, and labor leaders that can help restore America. UBI is also an example of an attempt to reshape the relationship between government and the citizenry and allow for more trust and individual liberty. It also may be a pathway to much-needed changes to US social safety net programs that were designed and implemented some 80 years ago and desperately need updating and a more sustainable economic model.

See Yourself in Others

Humans have a natural tendency to project their own experiences onto others. This can, at times, make us extremely unempathetic as a species—we struggle to see others' lives for what they really are. This phenomenon has been labeled the "empathy gap" and applies equally to our ability to predict our own future reactions as it does to our inability to see the world through the lens of others.[9] It's hard to understand a situation if you haven't lived through it, even if that situation involves your future self.

In one light but common example, people consistently believe they would perform better under pressure than, say, the game show contestant they are watching on television or the person struggling to speak extemporaneously in front of a group. More consequentially, it affects our ability to relate to people from different circumstances and backgrounds.

The empathy gap is a feature of neoliberalism, which tends to see humans as largely interchangeable economic units. This libertarian view suggests that we are what we make of ourselves and, having all started with some base level of opportunity, our differences in circumstances are largely due to individual factors such as drive and desire. Neoliberals apply a natural extension of this way of thinking to governing and legislating, leading them to favor policies that are both narrow in scope and often paternalistic in nature. If we are what we make of ourselves, then government programs should be limited in size and duration and should come with guardrails that protect against the assumption that those who haven't already taken advantage of the opportunities the US economy has to offer should be closely watched, lest what left them in a circumstance to need help makes them unreliable stewards of that assistance.

This is not to say that we shouldn't have reasonable expectations of our fellow citizens or that government programming should solve all, or even many, problems that our society faces. As in many things in life, carrots work better than sticks. But to do this effectively, we challenge ourselves and our readers to take a more empathetic approach. As the economist Joseph Stiglitz wrote, we "often fail to recognize that one person's freedom is another's unfreedom."[10] Freedom to choose not to be vaccinated might mean that others lose the freedom to live. Freedom from unreasonable surveillance might mean that more criminals go undetected. Freedom in the form of lower taxes (so people are free to spend more of their money the way they wish) means less funding for programs like schools, welfare, and infrastructure.

That we have different views of these topics across our economy can be a frustration for those with deeply held beliefs, but is a feature, not a bug, of the diversity of thought that exists in our country. The political bargain that comprises modern capitalism involves all manner of these sorts of trade-offs. It is easy to identify trade-offs that benefit you, but it is harder to understand what that same trade-off might look like for others. We will have to make compromises to get ourselves on a path to a more sustainable future. Existing in the messy middle is something we should embrace rather than retreating to the comfort of our increasingly polarized camps. Most importantly, we need to get comfortable engaging people with whom we don't agree, especially those who feel that the current system is not working for them.

Finding Balance

All of this leads us back to the overarching theme of this book, which is that the answer, as it so often is, can be found in the middle ground. In the balance of how the government applies its authority and resources. In a more nuanced view of the relationship between government and business.

We believe in a streamlined government that largely stays out of the way. At the same time, we also believe in a government that protects basic rights and provides a framework for a reasonably level playing field upon which businesses can compete and thrive. In many respects, consistent government frameworks are a requirement for capitalist systems to function properly. Thoughtful minds may differ on what constitutes "reasonable" or, for that matter, what "out of the way" means. But our discourse is missing a thoughtful debate of these and other ideas by those who are open to listening to differing viewpoints. We can and should look to corporate leaders to help us through these debates, which is exactly what we did as we were working on this book. You'll find their stories in the upcoming pages.

Chapter 11

THE HEART OF FINANCE

Thirty years after its founding, Apollo Global Management—one of the largest asset managers in the country with over $750 billion under management, and the employer of Lisa Green Hall, whom we met in chapter 8—was ready to embrace ideas around investing for impact more seriously.[1] The firm recognized mission-driven practices that were already taking place across its various funds. Apollo also was reacting to clients' demand for "impact" investment products. Either way, for this top 25 global asset manager, it marked an important change that served as a harbinger for others in the industry.[2]

"We launched Apollo Impact Mission in 2020 as our first impact-focused fund. That coincided with my joining the firm," Hall told us when we spoke with her about the changes taking shape across the asset management landscape.[3] Hiring Hall in a newly created role with the title of "Impact Chair" changed Apollo, likely in ways it didn't anticipate at the time. "Impact investing as an approach to investing was new for the firm," she told us. "We were hearing from investors this demand for funds and investment opportunities that were benefiting people and the planet. Asset managers are responding to investor demand and appetite for stakeholder capitalism."

"Impact" investing has become an expanding segment of these funds: Total assets managed with an impact orientation exceed $1 trillion.[4] If we broaden this to include funds applying some form of ESG lens to their investment practice, the numbers are an order of magnitude larger. According to the US Sustainable Investment Forum, which has been tracking investor activity since the mid-1980s, nearly one in eight dollars invested in funds in the United States—a total of more than $8 trillion—is invested in what they term "sustainable investment strategies."[5] The practice of considering a broader set of factors when making investment decisions is becoming more popular. As the report notes, "Our 2014 Trends report was the first time we saw ESG integration emerge as a significant strategy." The past decade has seen rapid change in the importance and growth of what can generally be termed "impact investing." There is clearly greater consumer demand for impact-related investment products.

However, the industry lacks any real standards around what constitutes an impact fund or what "impact" means and how it should be measured, and critics have rightly pointed out that many so-called impact funds are simply funds looking to market to a certain investor group but lack any real investment discipline. For example, in the latest Sustainable Investment Forum report, the authors changed their methodology for considering what funds qualified as using sustainable investment practices by removing those that claimed to be employing ESG filters but that failed to define what those filters were. One of the respondents highlighted in the Sustainable Investment Forum report summed it up nicely: "The industry is being forced to mature as regulators begin to pay attention. There will be a shakeout . . . Asset levels will likely move lower to a truer base of real sustainable investing, and managers will have to be clear about the underlying approaches they employ."[6] In other words, because there is neither a standard for what constitutes an impact fund nor any regulatory watchdog providing oversight to the marketing practices of these funds, far more of them claim the "impact" moniker than should. And of course, one person's version of what constitutes impact can vary significantly from another's. As long as the industry uses subjective terms and vague concepts to measure itself, we should carefully scrutinize the actual practices behind it.

Follow the Money

As we think about the next iteration of capitalism, we can't overstate the importance of the US financial sector. Though other centers of financial power are rising, most obviously in Singapore and the Middle East, the United States remains the epicenter of global finance. A handful of giant financial firms, primarily US based, are the most powerful owners of large public companies, and the biggest technology businesses in the world are largely all from the United States. America is home to large private equity firms, like Apollo, which buy and sell stakes in big private companies. And even as China's technology industry is on the rise, the US early-stage venture investment system still finances an outsized share of the technological innovation in the world.

But it's the asset managers working in the public markets that have become the nexus of control in our current system of neoliberal capitalism. In 2018, the late Vanguard founder and index fund pioneer Jack Bogle warned of the growing concentration of power in the hands of money managers, stating, "A handful of giant institutional investors will one day hold voting control of virtually every large US corporation."[7] As just one example, asset management firm BlackRock (whose founder and CEO, Larry Fink, has appeared a few times already in this book) owns more than 5% of nearly every company in the S&P 500 index. Collectively, the largest three asset managers in the United States hold approximately

25% of the voting power in the companies comprising that index.[8] This power is fueled by fewer investors directly owning stocks and instead using intermediaries—from index funds to ETFs to actively managed funds—to invest on their behalf. From 1950 to 2017, the percentage of stock held by institutions increased from 6.1% to 65%. In many respects, institutional investors don't dictate the market; they *are* the market. And the asset management business itself is becoming concentrated too. BlackRock, Vanguard, and State Street Global Advisors account for nearly 80% of capital inflows to funds over the past decade, and while exact data aren't available, these three firms comprise a meaningful portion of the entire asset management business. What they say and do around investing will, quite literally, move markets.

That's why when these asset managers began to openly consider somewhat intangible "values," in the mid-2010s, people started paying attention. Larry Fink's 2018 letter to CEOs, saying that BlackRock wanted to see clear evidence that they were considering stakeholders, not just shareholders, was sent to the corporate chiefs of nearly every important company traded on public exchanges. BlackRock owns part of all of them.

Vivek Ramaswamy, the former biotech CEO and one-time 2024 Republican presidential hopeful, called asset managers the "most powerful cartel in human history." Hyperbolic language from a political candidate, but indicative of a genuine concern—and the lightning rod that these large asset managers have become—about the power that sits with a small number of massive institutional investors.

And the truth is that impact or ESG investing, especially in the United States, which lags Europe in this area, should become more rigorous. "I think ESG is table stakes," Lisa Green Hall told us. "It's kind of the bare minimum. And the challenge with ESG approaches is that they typically are about checklists or scorecards and not about integrating E, S, and G factors into their operations."[9] Without clear definitions about what constitutes ESG in the first place and its weaponization in our culture wars and politics, it is no surprise that business leaders like Larry Fink are shying away from the label. But that doesn't mean that they are oblivious to the benefits that thinking about a broader set of constituencies could bring to investment returns.

That investment managers believe they will see better returns in companies that employ the principles of Dynamic Capitalism isn't surprising. After years of short-term thinking and plenty of lessons for how and why that way of managing businesses can lead to decreased overall returns, it's not surprising that money managers—who view themselves in the long-term capital accumulation game—would look to companies that are employing practices likely to benefit them for a longer period of time. This is a natural and positive by-product of a functioning market economy.

However, the question of the power asset managers should have over how companies operate is an important one that needs fuller consideration. Certainly, the economic model of asset managers is sensitive to the whims of their customers. But those investors mostly aren't paying close attention. They may simply not care in the same way that those complaining from one political perspective or another seem to. Or they may not recognize that their investments are providing a powerful platform to a small group of investment firms. This rising concentration of power in a small number of firms is a threat to the overall progress of Dynamic Capitalism. Ultimately, we need more experiments, more competition, and more ways to turn consumers into investors and owners.

That a handful of firms—more precisely, a handful of key executives at these firms—can drive corporate practices across a wide segment of the global economy should catch our attention, if not raise alarm. The concentration among asset managers suggests that consumers are not taking a critical look at the firms they are placing their money with. Yet the influence these managers have over corporate practice is enormous. And while it's easy for those who are in general agreement with the direction they're heading to feel like these firms have the right intentions, we need to acknowledge that it's complicated. Most people making investment decisions are purchasers of goods, services, and products that don't fit an impact or ESG label. Yet more and more of us are directing our investment capital away from those businesses. Many Americans may not want to invest in oil and gas companies, but as we were told by the CEO of a coal mining business, "If you want to stop pulling coal and gas out of the ground, I suggest you turn your lights off."[10]

Everyone Is a Shareholder

One of the basic concepts of neoliberal capitalism, dating back to the 1970s and 1980s, is that stocks would be broadly held. If everyone were a shareholder of public companies, the theory went, then what benefited "shareholders" would extend to benefiting society as a whole. In 1970, when Milton Friedman penned his treatise on the virtues of promoting shareholder value to the exclusion of other stakeholders, he had an eye toward the idea that greater numbers of Americans would be direct owners of company stock. In this sense, he likely felt that by focusing on shareholders, companies would, in fact, be supporting many more citizens, including the company's employees.

While personal ownership of stock was still quite low in 1970—just 5%—it was soon to increase significantly, as Friedman believed it would. The concept of individual retirement accounts (IRAs) came into existence in 1974 through the Employee Retirement Income Security Act, creating the platform through which most Americans now own stock. The first index funds were introduced in 1976. Through the 1980s and 1990s, stock ownership rose steadily, and it appeared that our economy was on its way to nearly universal ownership of stock and, to some Friedman adherents, toward a blending of shareholder and citizen in a way that conveniently allowed Friedmanites to argue that benefits to shareholders necessarily meant benefits to all.

However, stock ownership initially peaked around the financial crisis of 2008 and 2009 at just above 60% and thereafter backed off into the mid-50% range. Likely driven by the advent of free and easy online trading platforms, led by the tech startup Robinhood, this number ticked back up to 61% in 2023 according to Gallup, although even at these numbers, stock ownership remains out of reach for a large segment of our population.[11] While the idea of more democratized stock ownership fits nicely into the neoliberal worldview, even this 61% ownership number is somewhat misleading. Within that figure, the concentration of stock ownership largely mirrors the concentration of wealth in the United States. The wealthiest 10% own 92.5% of all the stocks owned by Americans, and the richest 1% comprise more than half of that, owning 54% of total stock (up from 77% and 40% 20 years ago, respectively).[12] To us, this feels like a desired outcome rather than a nuisance of neoliberal capitalism—as inevitable as it is inconvenient for neoliberals to defend. It is a prime example of something that Dynamic Capitalism looks to change.

Important Questions

Why are rising numbers of large asset managers discussing factors other than shareholder value creation? Presumably there is at least a baseline belief that focusing more broadly will lead to better long-term investment results. For example, BlackRock's Larry Fink has talked at length in many of his recent annual shareholder letters about the importance of the transition to a clean energy economy: "Over the long run, investors also need to consider how the energy transition, among other factors, will impact the economy, asset prices, and investment performance. For years now, we have viewed climate risk as an investment risk. That's still the case."[13]

But often there is a sense of the need to play a part in something broader than simply making money and, while not explicit, an understanding that some level of trade-off between investment returns and a wider set of societal goals is, especially in the short term, not just acceptable but necessary. In Apollo Global's 2022 Annual Sustainability Report, CEO Marc Rowan wrote, "At Apollo, *we're in the business of making things better*. Every action and every day, we are focused on making things better for our investors, shareholders, communities, employees, and the environment. This approach is embedded in our business, culture, and operations" (emphasis added).[14] We have no doubt that Rowan means this sincerely and that he, Lisa Green Hall, and the other investment professionals at Apollo believe that their work is creating impact beyond just the bottom line for their investors. But what "better" actually means is worth at least stopping to consider, along with who gets to define that term in the first place.

Larry Fink's proclamation that "as minority shareholders, it's not our place to be telling companies what to do" may make for a good soundbite, but it isn't how the markets operate in the real world, nor is it consistent with his sending an annual letter to CEOs with his prescriptions for success.[15] BlackRock and others exert immense market influence, both directly and indirectly. Even if their motivations are pure, we should question the sustainability of a system that allows such a small number of individuals and entities to exert this much power over companies across the financial markets. At a minimum, we should demand transparency and accountability for what these business practices aim to achieve. But our current financial system actually inhibits that transparency while encouraging companies to skirt the laws governing corporate action.

In an attempt to address this imbalance, moves have been made to place greater decision-making power in the hands of fund investors rather than in fund managers. Not surprisingly, given its history, Vanguard is a leader in this area, launching an initiative called Investor Choice that allows individual investors to determine the voting positions of the funds in which they have invested. This gives voice to these investors and better reflects the sentiments of the fund's customers rather than the fund's managers. Investors Choice is just a pilot, and there is more work to be done at Vanguard and more broadly in the financial services industry to allow for a more impactful consumer voice in corporate voting. Just as Dynamic Capitalism seeks better balance between the power of capital and labor, it also seeks to provide balance and voice to individual investors.

Legal Frameworks

While investing for "impact" often includes investing in sectors or companies considered positive for the environment or society, it can be harder to understand what statements like "investing for purpose," "considering a broad set of stakeholders," or, as in the quote from Apollo's Marc Rowan just earlier, "making things better," actually mean. In fact, the legal framework that most companies fall under in the United States doesn't give much leeway to management teams and boards of directors regarding the ultimate goals of their businesses. As Skadden, Arps, Slate, Meagher & Flom LLP and Affiliates, one of the country's largest law firms, wrote in a 2019 thought piece for their clients:

> In Delaware [where most companies in the United States are incorporated, and from which most other states mirror their corporate legal frameworks], court decisions have clearly established that the shareholder primacy rule applies. In short, directors have a fiduciary duty to make their decisions looking solely to the best interests of shareholders. In other words, enhancing and protecting value for shareholders is the ultimate interest to be served. Delaware Supreme Court Chief Justice Leo E. Strine, Jr. has made clear where

Delaware law stands on the subject: [A] clear-eyed look at the law of corporations in Delaware reveals that, within the limits of their discretion, directors must make stockholder welfare their sole end, and that other interests may be taken into consideration only as a means of promoting stockholder welfare.[16]

So what do investors like Fink, Rowan, and others mean when they talk about "shareholders, communities, employees, and the environment"? Yes, corporate boards are generally given broad leeway to determine what actions best support shareholder interests and over what period those interests might be measured. And certainly, legitimate arguments can and have been made about the benefits of considering the interests of other business stakeholders—especially employees, but also suppliers and others in a company's orbit—contributing to a company's long-term success and, therefore, longer-term shareholder value. But ultimately, all of these good intentions eventually run into the directive to create value for shareholders, which is a fundamental underpinning of corporate law in the United States and around the world. Simply put, the fiduciary standard—a Roosevelt-era product of the Investment Advisers Act of 1940, which essentially directs corporate executives and boards to act narrowly and only for the benefit of shareholders—is an obstacle to Dynamic Capitalism and needs to be addressed. Shareholders should remain a key consideration for any corporate action, but companies should be given more latitude to make decisions with a broader set of constituencies in mind.

Important efforts are being made to change the fiduciary standard—most notably the B Corporation movement—and to rewrite corporate law to allow companies and their boards to consider other stakeholders when making decisions. As of this writing, 40 states have enacted some sort of legal framework around "benefit corporations," which enable those businesses to designate other stakeholders to which the business will be accountable.[17] It brings the kind of transparency to the markets that we referred to just earlier. According to B Lab, the creator of the benefit corporation and B Certification movements, more than 8,000 companies are designated benefit corporations or are B-Certified.[18] These include businesses such as Room and Board, San Pellegrino, Danone, Aveda, Unilever, Nespresso, and Patagonia.

The B Corp movement looks to address challenges with existing corporate law and to broaden the scope of responsibilities for companies, providing a legal framework for them to do so. There have always been plenty of companies who sought to act in ways that benefited stakeholders beyond just shareholders. But the legal framework to more fully support this way of operating is still novel and has not been broadly adopted. For perspective, the B Corp movement was only founded in 2006.

The concepts behind benefit corporations fit nicely into the Dynamic Capitalism framework. Perhaps counterintuitively, they are also very much market-driven. Andrew Kassoy, one of the founders of B Lab, explained to us, "We believed in the power of business and the capital markets to create scale in a way no other sector can, but we were also clear that 'purpose' wasn't built into that growth, and that required a new legal structure and new standards."*[19]

The current legal frameworks across the United States, as well as most of the rest of the world, simply don't allow that—certainly not at scale or without meaningful risk to companies and their boards. At its core, the B Corp movement is trying to change this by allowing companies to leverage market principles of growth and scale for purposes beyond just making more money for shareholders. Whether you agree or disagree with what a company outlines as its purpose beyond shareholder profit, shareholders (and the public) benefit from the additional level of transparency.

---

* Andrew Kassoy died in June 2025. An inspirational leader, he encouraged thousands of businesses to focus on more than just profits.

Efficient capital markets can and will allow investors who are most aligned with the purpose delineated by a corporation to make better capital allocation decisions. In this sense, B Corporations are often misunderstood. Far from being anticapitalist, their added layer of transparency enables the free markets to make better decisions. If you don't like that a company's charter includes mention of specific stakeholders, don't invest in that company. If you're not interested in businesses that consider themselves stewards for stakeholders beyond shareholders, don't put your money behind them. This is fundamental to Dynamic Capitalism—the ability of companies to recognize stakeholders beyond shareholders and, just as importantly, the ability of the capital markets to make investment decisions informed by that understanding.

Before we leave the topic of benefit corporations, it's important to touch on the intersection of B Corporations and AI. When it announced its intention to transition from a nonprofit to a for-profit business, artificial intelligence leader OpenAI tried to assuage fears that it was moving away from its founding purpose of building software to "benefit all of humanity" by stating that it would become a public benefit corporation. OpenAI's chief rival, Anthropic Corporation, is also a public benefit corporation with a similarly lofty goal: "to ensure transformative AI helps people and society flourish." Plenty of public debate can be had about what benefiting humanity or ensuring a flourishing society actually means; and some, including Kassoy, have publicly expressed concerns about just how these businesses will be held to account for their stated public benefit. But it's meaningful that businesses on the cutting edge of technology are concerned that traditional corporate structures don't provide the legal protections they feel are needed to operate their businesses effectively and provide the public with assurances that their technology won't be developed in ways that threaten humanity.[20]

A Middle Ground?

It's telling that BlackRock's Larry Fink, who has become a leading voice in the movement to test traditional thinking around the role of companies and their investors, feels trapped in the debate. "I don't use the word ESG anymore because it's been entirely weaponized . . . by the far left and weaponized by the far right," he said in 2023.[21] The only consensus around impact investing and ESG seems to be that the paradigm we're in today isn't working. As Fink correctly points out, people on both sides of the political spectrum continue to express concern about how standards around ESG are implemented—or whether they are implemented at all. While disagreement from both sides of the aisle can be a sign that we are close to finding the appropriate middle ground, in this case that disagreement feels both more fundamental and exacerbated by the nascency of the work in this area. That makes for dangerous ground for Fink and others like him who are working to push changes. The SEC acknowledged this challenge when it postponed the implementation of rules related to ESG disclosures that it first outlined in early 2022, after receiving pushback from both those in favor of the reporting but who felt that the SEC rules didn't go far enough, and those opposed who thought that the SEC was overstepping its authority. The European Union, while ahead of the United States in adopting reporting rules around ESG, is similarly pushing implementation dates back.

Conversations about the role of companies in today's society have become divisive, even more so because of the presence of social media. Never before have consumers had such a direct way to engage with brands. The same can be said of shareholders, who, after all, are consumers as well. And what they want isn't solely the greatest return on their investment. Other factors—the environment, social issues, alignment with religious beliefs, among others—drive their decision-making and belief structures. These factors often conflict with each other, and viewpoints vary about how a company should act. In a recent National Bureau of Economic Research working paper, "What Do Shareholders Want? Consumer Welfare and the Objective of the Firm," Keith Marzilli Erickson reports that only 7% of consumers would opt for pure profit maximization.[22] What the other 93% want is neither uniform nor particularly clear. This is at the heart of Fink's struggle and, ultimately, a challenge for every professional investor and corporate manager.

We certainly don't pretend to have all the answers. But we know the solution lies in being willing to engage in messy conversations and believe that undoing the rigid approaches of neoliberal capitalism, including adapting or letting go of the fiduciary standard, is part of the solution. So, too, is a better and clearer definition of how investment companies can use the impact label to market their wares, along with the realization that fund investors must be given a greater voice in the decisions made on their behalf. As in most things, Dynamic Capitalism seeks a middle ground that better reflects the long-term best interests of investors and consumers, as well as a transparent and clear framework that allows them to make informed decisions.

Chapter 12

VALUES

At first look, Patagonia and Hobby Lobby seem like wildly different organizations. Patagonia, founded by the free-spirited climber turned eco-businessman Yvon Chouinard, is an active and forceful advocate for environmental causes. The business spawned the environmental organization 1% for the Planet, and more recently, the Chouinard family placed the entire business in a trust dedicated to fighting climate change—a multibillion-dollar commitment. Hobby Lobby, on the other hand, is a conservative organization whose values stem from the religious views of its founders, David and Barbara Green. The company's core values feature religion prominently, starting with "honoring the Lord in all we do by operating in a manner consistent with Biblical principles." The ultimate goal of the organization includes "providing a return on the family's investment, sharing the Lord's blessings with our employees, and investing in our community."[1] Hobby Lobby is a vehicle for the Green family to show their faith and, especially, to share that faith with the employees and customers of Hobby Lobby. The family's interpretation of their religious values essentially becomes the values of the organization as a whole.

In a way that might be uncomfortable for some to accept, these organizations, as well as other companies who have deeply held values such as Chick-fil-A, are kindred spirits. That those values don't necessarily align with each other doesn't change the fact that the driving force behind these businesses shares a common ancestry. As private businesses, each can put these values ahead of profits. And sometimes, those values turn overtly political.

But it's not only private companies that are publicly embracing "values." The leaders of publicly held companies are doing so too. Jamie Dimon, CEO of JPMorgan Chase, was among the most forceful CEOs we spoke with in advocating for the distinction between a company's expressed values and the politics behind them. Dimon calls himself an unabashed capitalist. This isn't surprising, given that he is the CEO of America's largest bank. But he also described to us how he is driven by a clear set of values and purpose.

People on the political left often decry the words of business leaders as window dressing, and people on the right use them as weapons to inflame today's populist rage about the dangers of "woke" leaders. But both sides are missing the point. It's not necessarily what the companies and their leaders stand for; it's that today's business leaders—public and private—have been pressing for the platforms and regulatory structures that give them more ways to exercise their power. The current environment, in which consumers demand more corporate responsibility and the power of government is waning, requires them to do so.

As economic pragmatists, we see this as a mixed bag. On one hand, the incredible power of today's corporations seems to be the inevitable development of neoliberal capitalism. On the other hand, the leaders of companies—especially private companies—are less accountable than elected officials, and because of this have few real checks on their actions. We believe that the government needs to reassert itself, but only to a limited extent. We also need corporate leaders who see themselves as responsible to their communities and other stakeholders, while also being skilled at expressing values without being drawn overtly into politics. Most of all, we need to create a new social norm that supports values-driven business decisions without infusing the business sector with the toxicity of our politics.

The Declining Power of Government

As capitalism continues this evolution, the power of the various players in our capitalist system is changing. Corporations have emerged as the most important institutions, arguably surpassing nation-states in influence. As they've done so, global corporate leaders have become more influential than all but a small number of world leaders in their impact on the lives of most of the world's citizens.

Companies, particularly large multinational corporations, wield enormous economic power. Their influence on global financial markets, trade, and economic development has increased to such an extent over the past 50 years that their reach is almost unrecognizable when compared to the largest companies of previous generations. Tech giants like Apple, Amazon, Nvidia, and Google's parent company, Alphabet, have market capitalizations exceeding a trillion dollars each, rivaling the domestic output of most countries. Likewise, revenue generated by large corporations surpasses the GDP of many nations. In 2024, for instance, Walmart, the American retail giant, reported revenues of more than $648 billion, exceeding the GDP of countries like Sweden and Switzerland. These companies' financial might allows them to shape economic policies, attract top talent, and invest in future development on a scale once thought solely achievable by nation-states. And as some countries pull back on research and development spending, companies are becoming more important actors not just in near-term technical advancements but also in longer-term research initiatives.

The globalization of production and distribution has made companies central players in international trade and economic diplomacy, which can put them at odds with the governments of the countries where they are headquartered. These global supply chains grant both cost savings and access to specialized expertise and resources. Such interdependence between companies and nations has given corporations significant leverage in negotiations and trade disputes.

Additionally, multinational corporations can influence policies and regulations on a global scale. This power dynamic is especially evident in the technology sector, where companies like TikTok, Facebook, and Google face international scrutiny over issues such as data privacy and anticompetitive practices. Governments have the power to regulate, but in today's landscape, the private sector often outpaces their efforts.

In one example of companies' rising power, in spring 2024 the Department of Homeland Security asked CEOs to serve on a federal advisory safety panel for AI. As it struggled to understand the implications of this new technology, the government had to turn to the biggest source of power in our economy—corporations. OpenAI, Microsoft, Starlink, Google, and other firms are now being called on to supplement our military capabilities, traditionally the sole purview and responsibility of the government.[2] However, placing too much power in the hands of large technology companies to develop the frameworks for regulating emerging technologies runs the risk of the kind of regulatory capture that we warned about in chapter 10—promulgating a set of rules that work to the benefit of incumbents and stifle innovation.

Importantly, companies and individual executives—Elon Musk's role in the Trump administration is a case in point—exert significant and accelerating influence on government policies and regulations, both at home and abroad. Their lobbying efforts, campaign contributions, and ability to mobilize public opinion make them formidable actors in shaping the legislative landscape. The energy sector provides an illustrative example. Oil and gas companies have long played a central role in shaping energy policies in many countries. Their financial resources and lobbying efforts have influenced decisions on drilling permits, environmental regulations, and subsidies. Technology companies are involved in shaping regulatory frameworks, including ongoing debates about data privacy and antitrust issues. Especially after the US Supreme Court decision in *Citizens United v. Federal Election Commission,* which ruled that the First Amendment of the US Constitution protected the right of corporations, nonprofits, and labor unions to donate to political causes, corporations have increased their efforts to influence policy outcomes. Companies are not just the subject of regulations but are more actively engaged than ever in advocating for their preferred regulatory outcomes.

Corporate Values

It's in this context of rising corporate power that we need to consider the growing number of companies seeking to establish "values" as a part of their brand identity. The smartest business leaders realize that they need to differentiate their companies and use values to attract customers and employees. Of course, this runs the real risk of further exposing rifts in our society. Companies are being branded as "blue" or "red," depending on their perceived political leaning, often derived from something as simple as whether they have an executive in charge of diversity or marketing campaigns targeting LGBTQ+ communities.* Depending on your political persuasion and, consequently, what media sources you tend to pay attention to, you'll likely hear about only a subset of these businesses. There are CEOs from across the political spectrum speaking out about topics that, viewed through yesterday's lens, are far afield from their day

---

* And as we write this, in 2025, the Trump administration is actively targeting companies for their DEI practices.

jobs running corporations. But as more corporate leaders address cultural issues, the pressure to not stay silent mounts.

Just as the economy is the mutual creation of the people acting within it, corporations also are shaped by the individuals who inhabit them. Corporate CEOs have never had so much clout in our society or occupied so much mind share. With trust in the media and government at all-time lows, more people look to corporate executives for the kind of steady leadership and guidance that was once the purview of elected officials or national news anchors.

This is a lot to ask, and CEOs we interviewed told us that navigating today's hyperpolarized political and social environment on behalf of their businesses has become more complicated. Many spoke about the importance of forming and maintaining a set of corporate values that transcended politics—values that can serve as a larger framework for decision-making. Most of the corporate leaders we spoke with said that straying into political waters was dangerous. But as the line between values and politics further blurs, CEOs face a nearly impossible balancing act.

As social media continues to upset the traditional media landscape, corporate leaders have direct access to an audience through platforms like X (formerly Twitter) or Instagram. Whether because of ego, perceived necessity, or desire, many CEOs take to these platforms to share their thoughts and ideas on a wide-ranging set of topics, often entirely unrelated to their businesses. They've done this at their own peril and to mixed results, as measured by public backlash and, in some cases, their stock price.

One common theme that emerged from our discussions with corporate leaders is the idea of "values-based" leadership. Many CEOs and executives we spoke with attempted to draw a distinction between "values" and "politics." Perhaps values are best described as the underlying principles and beliefs that drive an organization, while politics refers to how these values are put into action from a policy perspective. However, it strikes us that there is often no clear line between a specific value and policies supporting it. Or put another way, many political views—often conflicting in nature—can flow from any given set of values. Perhaps this lack of clarity is what is causing some companies and their CEOs to stumble in the market of public ideas.

Skirting the Line

Jamie Dimon, for one, does not see these two ideas—being a capitalist and running a values-based business—as being in conflict. In fact, he says he can't separate himself from the values with which he leads the company. "I was raised that you take care of others . . . to make Earth a better place for it," he told us, just after he provided a vociferous and compelling defense of American exceptionalism and the capitalist system. He also declared forcefully, "I am a full-throated, red-blooded, American patriotic free-market capitalist." His annual letters to shareholders, written in the style of Warren Buffett's letters to Berkshire Hathaway shareholders, outline JPMorgan's policies that put these beliefs into practice. "We've always had—and published—principles to guide how we do business, with values embedded within them," he said in his 2022 letter. "These tenets unite our company across the globe. To complement these guidelines, we recently developed a clearly stated purpose—*Make dreams possible for everyone, everywhere, every day*—to knit together our values with our everyday business principles and explain how we have done business for years" (emphasis in original source).[3]

But in Dimon's telling, he stops short of having these values push him, or JPMorgan, into politics. This is debatable given the stances he's taken on politically charged issues ranging from education reform to racial equality to the need for greater government investment in infrastructure. But Dimon does seem to find a way to walk the line between supporting the issues he and JPMorgan care about and becoming overtly political. This is what he was referring to when telling other corporate leaders, "Don't let yourself be weaponized," as we recounted earlier.

Other CEOs are more willing to take overtly political stances. When Dan Schulman was the CEO of PayPal, he led a very public effort against the 2016 North Carolina law known as House Bill 2 (HB2), which required individuals to use the restroom for the gender assigned to them at birth. Schulman and PayPal publicly opposed the law (along with a number of other tech and business leaders) and backed out of plans to open a large operations center in the state. "Becoming an employer in North Carolina, where members of our teams will not have equal rights under the law, is simply untenable," he said in a statement at the time. "The new law perpetuates discrimination, and it violates the values and principles that are at the core of PayPal's mission and culture."[4]

Taking such a public stance was not without its challenges, including death threats. And perhaps because of that, it stands out as a particularly bold move, especially for the CEO of a public company, in a sea of more equivocating statements on a variety of issues from corporate leaders that fail to make much of an impact—values based, political, or otherwise. There was purpose and forethought behind the decision, however. Corporate leaders drawn into politics often ascribe it to a decision-making process within their companies, one that holds themselves accountable to employees.

"We have a set of values [at PayPal] around inclusivity and broad access to the financial system. We saw a number of things happening in the country that we thought were anathema to those values. North Carolina was an example of that," Schulman told us. But the power of the backlash was surprising and strong. "I don't think I realized how divided our country was until [we made that announcement]. I was inundated with all sorts of threats, including death threats . . . It showed me just how difficult it can be to make these decisions . . . they involve threats, including threats to your family... But I always felt like we were just doing the right thing."[5]

Organizations such as the NBA, NCAA, American Airlines, Apple, IBM, and Microsoft all eventually followed PayPal's lead and came out in one way or another against the bill, adding to the pressure—both political and economic—for the law to be overturned.[6] Ultimately, North Carolina repealed HB2 in 2017. That said, the fight over HB2 stands out as a harbinger of the sharply politicized environment that defines our current economy. The backlash against the bill and the strong reaction by those who supported it were a bellwether for the broader cultural fights that continue to define our society and into which companies risk being drawn. There are no easy decisions in hyperpoliticized situations, where even staying silent is seen as a political statement.*

For any business, particularly public companies, engaging in political speech carries significant risks. This suggests that most of the movement among corporate leaders to take values-based stands is emerging because they feel they have no other choice. The combination of the decline in the effectiveness of governments and the growing demand from customers for companies that do "good" is creating a pressure cooker for public CEOs. As some companies speak out, more feel compelled to do so. And in our view, the politicization of business on this scale isn't beneficial to society. That's not to say that standing up for core values isn't the role of companies or their leaders. On the contrary, we believe the most effective corporate speech does exactly that while not getting weaponized, to use Jamie Dimon's term. But as values cross the line into the overtly political, we run the risk of creating not just two political Americas, but two economic ones as well.

Leaders of private businesses have much greater leeway to speak out on issues that matter to them—whether or not they affect the businesses

---

* As Disney found out, in just one example of this trend, in its fight against Florida's "Don't Say Gay" bill, which we described in more detail in chapter 3.

they run—than public company CEOs, for whom broad investor perception is both more important and more easily measured in the form of a company's stock price. Because of that, it's not surprising to see some of the greatest levels of activism coming from large, closely held private companies. And while most companies, public or private, have opted to stay focused on their core operations, a few are speaking out in potentially challenging ways for their peers.

Competing Values

To grapple with these changes in the business world, consider the examples of Patagonia and Hobby Lobby. They both offer some clues to business leaders—indeed, leaders in general—about how to navigate the changing landscape.

Since nearly its founding, Patagonia's commitment to the environment has meant lobbying on behalf of environmental and other causes. This has included taking positions on issues that occasionally put the business in the public eye, including a high-profile lawsuit it filed objecting to the 2017 decision by the Trump administration to reduce the size of the Bears Ears and Grand Staircase–Escalante National Monuments in Utah. For Hobby Lobby, taking a stand for its values meant pursuing a landmark lawsuit against the US government over a clause in the Affordable Care Act that requires companies to provide insurance coverage to their employees, including for contraception. Both are examples of values-driven corporate activism, even if those who agree with one are unlikely to agree with the other.

In 1970, David and Barbara Green, funded by a $600 loan, started Hobby Lobby, making picture frames in their living room. Two years later, they opened their first retail store—a 300-square-foot operation in Oklahoma City. David Green's father was a preacher, and the couple incorporated their religious beliefs into their business from the start. The influence of these beliefs magnified as the company grew, at first slowly—Hobby Lobby opened several stores in Oklahoma but didn't expand outside of the state until the mid-1980s—and then more rapidly. Today, the business operates some 1,000 stores in 48 states with an employee base of more than 46,000. It is the largest privately owned arts-and-crafts retailer in the world.

In its lawsuit, the company argued that the Free Exercise Clause of the Constitution's First Amendment and the Religious Freedom Restoration Act exempted it from the mandate to provide contraceptive coverage as part of its health plan. The US Supreme Court eventually issued a 5–4 decision in favor of that position. The ruling allowed Hobby Lobby to exclude certain forms of contraception from its health insurance plan and, more importantly, formed the basis for a precedent that has influenced how religious freedom is weighed against federal mandates. The ruling has empowered companies in ways that many businesses simply had not considered.

Patagonia also started as a passion project more than a business and, from the beginning, took on its founder's persona, values, and, ultimately, his politics. Yvon Chouinard started making and selling climbing hardware to pay for his outdoor obsessions. However, the hardware damaged fragile rock, so he experimented with different ways of constructing climbing gear that would be less destructive. He shifted to aluminum, and over time, his side hobby turned into a full-fledged business. Patagonia expanded into clothing, backpacks, and countless other items sought by customers seeking (or appearing to seek) adventure. Along the way, it pioneered new business practices, put the environment at the center of its principles, and sought to increase the role of employees in decision-making at the firm. The company often takes stances that are in direct opposition to short-term profits, even when it's impossible to say that there will be a long-term benefit. That mission-driven, long-term approach has worked. As of 2021,

Patagonia had $1.2 billion in revenue, operating 70 stores worldwide and employing a workforce of more than 3,000.

In 2022, the Chouinard family took another detour from the route followed by most founding families of successful businesses. Instead of the traditional model, used since the time of the Gilded Age billionaires, that sees business owners charter a philanthropic foundation to steward their business earnings toward causes the owner champions, the Chouinard family transferred the entire company into a trust-nonprofit structure designed to move all profits toward efforts to protect the environment. This was an almost unheard-of move. "As of now, the Earth is our only shareholder," Chouinard said.[7]

Purpose or Profits?

It's unusual to see businesses go as far as filing lawsuits to advocate for political positions they care deeply about, and it's unrealistic to expect—or even to want—businesses writ large to do so. But we respect both Patagonia and Hobby Lobby, even though our personal belief is that women should have access to reproductive care. Each of these companies charted a path in keeping with the key values upon which they were founded. That they are relatively extreme versions of this and bookend the political spectrum only highlights the challenges of balancing profit and purpose in a business.

Finding the right balance between corporate values and shareholder returns wasn't important for these companies. Perhaps that was because each was successful enough not to worry about their decisions' impact on what was, in both cases, a highly profitable business. Or perhaps they subconsciously felt that their actions only served to bolster their standing with their core constituencies. Both argue that, while they explicitly gave up short-term profits, their advocacy created more long-term opportunities. And both would likely also say that if they did sacrifice profits to live their values, it was a worthwhile trade-off.

Their examples suggest a few lessons we can draw upon as this new version of capitalism emerges. Importantly, we must become comfortable with a certain messiness as businesses flex their voices. That said, companies—especially public companies—need to consider the boundaries of their actions, not to mention how their corporate policies affect those who may disagree with the implementation of their values.

We can disagree with either company's stances, but we must acknowledge that they come from the same place. Recognizing leaders' sincere commitment to a set of values—even if they are values you don't share—is an exercise in the pluralism we need. Indeed, the most likely and lasting compromises happen when people who are deeply rooted in a clear set of values come to the table.

A second lesson is that we need to recognize that the growing power of companies and their newly public embrace of values, to some extent, reflects a failure of government. This isn't necessarily merely an American failure, though we're most familiar with it here. In most regions of the world, governments are struggling to cope with the rapid pace of technological change and the climate crisis. We believe finding the right balance of corporate power, or taking the burden off of companies, will require governments at multiple levels—national, state, and local—to step up in partnership.

We also believe that one of the measurable outcomes of a successful transition to Dynamic Capitalism will be increased economic mobility and the reemergence of a healthy and educated middle class, which benefits not just our economy but also our democracy. Corporate actions that support these outcomes ultimately, in our view, support broader economic development and are in the best interests of both individual companies and our economy as a whole, especially in the medium and long terms.

In embracing these ideas, we absolutely cannot lose the concept of free markets (which even Friedmanites remind us require some amount of government enforcement). In fact, we argue that the more open companies are about how their values drive their decision-making, the more the free market economy will serve to embrace the best of these ideas and spread their practices, and the more consumers will be empowered to make investments of capital, time, and dollars to support the work they most care about. The US Constitution and the Bill of Rights give us some guidelines for commerce in a pluralistic society—that is, one where not everyone shares the same values but where we unite around a handful of key tenets. One of the most important—but not often remembered—benefits of these founding documents was creating the very large, cross-boundary market that comprises the United States. While Americans like to talk about exceptionalism, freedom, and our capacity for innovation, none of those things would exist if it weren't for the size of the American market and the free trade that exists *within* our borders, despite political differences across states and localities. For more than two centuries, we've managed to keep the bigger picture in mind even as we've navigated any number of different opinions and perspectives, often strongly held and many of which deeply divided our nation. We have faith that this will continue to be the case.

Chapter 13

GLOBAL BLIND SPOTS

On July 24, 2007, Steve Tritch, the CEO of Westinghouse Electric Co., walked into China's Great Hall of the People in Beijing to sign a $7 billion agreement committing his company to build four nuclear reactors in China.[1] Westinghouse was to work with Chinese state-owned enterprises in what was described as a "win-win deal" that promised to expand Westinghouse's reach into the energy-hungry country. Back in Westinghouse's home city of Pittsburgh, newspapers were celebrating the thousands of highly skilled new jobs the deal would create.[2]

At the time, Westinghouse was a leader in the nuclear energy business. The 150-year-old company, partly owned by Japan's Toshiba Corporation, had spent 15 years designing its AP1000 nuclear reactor, which was proving wildly successful. In 2007, the reactor was powering about half the globe's nuclear power plants. But at the same time the partnership was announced, a Chinese hacking group called APT1 was infiltrating Westinghouse's servers. Eventually, the group stole 700,000 pages of emails and documents, including those detailing the design of the reactors. Just 10 years later, in 2017, Westinghouse declared bankruptcy, ceding market leadership to Chinese firms that had benefited from APT1's industrial espionage. Toshiba sold its ownership stake in the business and Westinghouse's payroll, which peaked at 50,000 employees, fell to just 10,000.[3]

The effect of China's entry into the World Trade Organization in 2007 and the subsequent embrace of China, not just by Westinghouse but across the US business landscape, was mixed. Job losses, predicted by many, did come to pass, due largely to the outsourcing of manufacturing jobs to China and other low-cost countries.[4] At the same time, American consumers benefited from lower prices, as decreased production costs led many products to become significantly less expensive. To some extent, US companies found new markets in China, although the balance of trade continued to be significantly in China's favor. Importantly, Chinese politics did not, in fact, reform. If anything, the state's control over its people, including the business community, is tighter today than it was 20 years ago. And the Westinghouse cyberattack and subsequent raiding of its IP turned out not to be an isolated case. Though not all attacks by Chinese state-affiliated companies are public, a number have been reported, including the attacks on several US steel companies and their labor unions by hackers affiliated with the Chinese government. Beijing has also accused the United States government of cyberattacks, and US companies have been found in violation of human rights standards.[5]

Unfettered, free-market competition works fine in the abstract, but the real world turns out to be more complicated. Dynamic Capitalism recognizes that the "market" doesn't solve all problems. It can't, for instance, solve the problem of cyberattacks enabled by government money, nation-states that don't abide by international trade rules, or military enemies that use media systems to steadily weaken another state's institutions. Russia is the most notable example of this last point, but other rising powers have also taken aggressive tacks against the United States, most notably Iran. In the run-up to the 2016 election, for instance, the Russian government was steadily pouring misinformation into America's social media platforms. The misinformation wasn't specifically designed to elevate one party but rather to sow more general division and chaos. Foreshadowing today's AI-driven fountains of misinformation, Russian bots released memes and posts centered on gun control and gun rights, the dangers of Muslim immigrants, and other topics that reliably drive polarizing opinions.

The United States' open-armed approach to new technology allowed TikTok to gain widespread adoption, especially among America's youth. All Chinese companies are ultimately controlled by the Chinese government, via its investments in private businesses and threats against senior executives who refuse its demands. This has led countries worldwide, including India and several European nations, to impose various restrictions on TikTok and other apps. China does the same. It both censors foreign-owned social media companies and imposes limits on the use of Chinese social media companies, restricting the amount of time young people can spend on apps, for instance. The United States is late to the game in considering the influence of these platforms—and their owners—on the health and safety of its citizens. Only after TikTok gained widespread adoption did the government start to consider the security implications of having an app controlled by the Chinese government installed on hundreds of millions of phones across the country. Our unthinking and un-nuanced pro-business policies left us open to national security threats while jeopardizing the mental health of American youth.[6]

Judged with the benefit of hindsight, some of the global free-trade and pro-business policies that were hallmarks of neoliberal capitalism seem naive and simplistic. While we are generally proponents of limited restrictions on trade and the greater global flow of goods and services, we recognize that both state and business actors will readily take advantage of global systems set up to govern trade—or skirt them entirely. The idea behind free trade was that free markets fostered innovation and that this unfettered innovation would naturally lead to the dominance of American ideas. The thought was that companies, through these avenues of trade, would transmit American freedom and democracy around the world. The attitude in Washington, DC—at least in public—could be summed up as, "Who wouldn't want to be like us?" The Washington Consensus, as economists called the US approach to capitalism during this period, envisioned steadily less-fettered markets as the best economic progenitor of a free society.

In retrospect, it was a mistake to see the world as if the other players in it would respond only in the way the United States wanted them to. Policymakers will inevitably make mistakes, but there are clear dangers in the monolithic thinking of an insular group of decision makers, which is yet another hallmark of neoliberal capitalism. The dominant inner circle of business and political leaders in the United States saw the world as they wanted to see it, not as it was.

The media tends to treat business news as a sideshow to politics, a holdover from the birth of journalism as a profession during the time of World War II when government, political, and military news dominated coverage. Because of this, many people missed an important shift in US policy toward Dynamic Capitalism. In 2018, under economic and societal assault from China and Russia, the United States began erecting more barriers around one of its biggest assets, its large domestic market. The erection of additional trade barriers against China and the development of the first US industrial policy in a generation were the most significant shifts in our business policy since 1957, when Sputnik threw America into a frenzy of scientific research that resulted in the invention of the silicon chip and the creation of Silicon Valley. The protectionist stance embraced by President Donald Trump during his first term was extended in the Biden administration, and ramped up to nearly unprecedented levels in the second Trump administration.

For much of the 20th century, the United States was a global hegemon. It retains an advantage for now, precisely because previous eras distributed wealth broadly. America's GDP per capita is nearly $82,000; China's is under $13,000. But US leaders of both political parties are already shifting away from the hegemon's mindset: rethinking tariffs, new immigration policies, foreign aid, and overseas military and trading alliances are all part of Dynamic Capitalism, whether they're championed in a Trumpian shock-and-awe Truth Social post or delivered by the rank-and-file diplomats of the Biden administration.

Pendulum Swings

After two decades in which US companies saw their trade secrets swiped by Chinese cyberattacks and government-fueled competition from People's Republic–sponsored companies, the American business community, which has been lockstep behind free trade policies for decades, has now adopted a more nuanced set of views on the subject. Even the US Chamber of Commerce, a stalwart supporter of free trade, tacitly acquiesced to some trade barriers erected by the Trump administration and extended by Biden, though it has since spoken out against Trump's spring 2025 tariffs.[7]

Nation-states often define themselves in terms of an enemy. When you're trying to pull together a continent's worth of people, it can be convenient to contrast your way of life with someone else's as "foreign." Because so much of America's power resides in its economy and its companies, and because what Washington, DC, calls "kinetic" war in a nuclear-armed world is so unthinkable, conflicts starting in the latter half of the 20th century took on an economic cast. Ronald Reagan turned the entrepreneurs of Silicon Valley into soldiers of a sort, innovating against communism. In the 1980s and early 1990s, Japanese companies were considered the greatest and potentially most dangerous competitors to US business interests. Ultimately, the threats from the USSR and Japan turned out to be overblown. Communism produced weak economies and discontented people, and the USSR, though a nuclear power, was a house of cards that collapsed in a matter of months in the early 1990s. However, lingering suspicion meant that the politicians of the 1980s missed what historians believe were serious opportunities to begin disarmament of nuclear arsenals that could destroy the world many times over. Today, Japan and the United States share innovation in business processes, and Japan is now among the United States' key trading partners and military allies.

These shifts in thinking remind us of the fallacy of an overly simplistic and hubristic approach to the world. Is it possible, then, that the economic and military threat from China, or its leadership's aggressive intentions, are, in turn, overblown? That question is at least worth considering as we grapple with what form our economic engagement with China will take and how we'll react to its expanding global political ambitions.

We believe the United States must engage with China, including on issues such as climate change and global economic development. Dynamic Capitalism, with its emphasis on nuance, cooperation, and coalition building, will be better suited to engagement with a near-peer competitor—and potential enemy—than the black-and-white thinking of neoliberalism. Early in its second term (as we write this), the Trump administration seems to be falling into the trap of zero-sum thinking and is pushing China (and other nations) away, rather than engaging with them. Business leaders, whether or not they are directly involved in US or state government policies and actions, have roles to play in establishing fair and profitable relationships with companies in other countries. Webs of human relationships help countries remain at peace. The past two decades have taught us that trade barriers designed to safeguard American institutions, including the rule of law, are clearly called for. At the same time, the Chinese example shows us that capitalism exists in many forms and can flourish even within a state-controlled political system.

Where Capitalism Is Working

US business leaders and policymakers should not be blind to other countries in the world that have found ways, if on smaller scales, to create capitalist systems different than our own. "These capitalist success stories maintain the key balance of government, providing help for their most vulnerable citizens without narrowing economic freedom," wrote Ruchir Sharma, an influential emerging markets investor, in *Foreign Affairs* magazine.[8]

He held up Switzerland, Taiwan, and Vietnam as models. India, with its massive population and rising economic mobility, is emerging as well. Switzerland has been able to grow an export-led economy with government spending at 35% of GDP, relatively lean by European standards although still far above US rates. Its government benefits are generous but not what you'd call "rich"; the private sector delivers healthcare, which is subsidized for the poor; immigrants are welcome; and, without much government intervention, the country has built a powerful export economy. Taiwan keeps government spending even leaner, rejecting bailouts and, even during the COVID pandemic, refraining from large state spending to support the economy. Rather, it has focused on worker productivity and building innovative companies—not just huge multinationals but also smaller businesses that manufacture parts for foreign corporations. Vietnam, meanwhile, has also created an export-led economy by focusing on educating a skilled workforce. Like China, Vietnam is led by a free-market-embracing communist government.[9] India, with its favorable demographic trends, has been among the world's fastest-growing economies and may eventually rival China's economic influence.

Yet America faces burdens that no other nation has stepped up to shoulder. Through its treaties, it is responsible for the defense of about two billion people around the world, including nearly the entirety of the European continent. The United States has carried the lion's burden of paying for many of the multilateral organizations that have underpinned the global order since World War II, all while building the world's largest and most dynamic economy and spawning some of the most profitable, innovative companies ever created. This has all come with a cost to the people of the United States, who often suffer individually in the chaotic but intensely innovative and fast-growing tumult of the American economy. It has also left us with a heavy debt load and a sharp debate about the limits that should be placed on continuing this global burden.

The Dynamic Capitalism Imperative

Indeed, one reason our economic system is evolving is because the US debt burden has become untenable. Politically, it's expedient to be a progressive or a populist and to call for lowering taxes and boosting spending. Both political persuasions imagine that spending can go on forever. But on this count, we believe traditional conservatives have laid out the most compelling argument. Government spending in the United States is climbing toward 25% of GDP, the US national debt is rapidly approaching $40 trillion, and debt service—the interest we pay on this debt—is nearing $1 trillion annually, on track to becoming the largest line item in the national budget.[10]

Simple financial literacy suggests that this situation is unsustainable. Holders of US government bonds, which include foreign governments and large investment firms, as well as many US citizens, may well demand higher interest rates in exchange for the risk of holding an investment underwritten by an increasingly overburdened and fractious United States. Solving the debt problem will require both domestic political will, which will need to come from new coalitions, and skillful diplomacy, requiring leadership from people who aren't steeped in ideas of American hegemony reinforced by rigid neoliberal thinking. If the American experiment is to survive, the United States has to find a path forward to a more equitable, environmentally sustainable means of economic growth. The alternative is to become a country that we no longer recognize.

Unquestionably there are sources of economic growth to be tapped, including the transition to a new energy economy and the adoption of new technologies such as AI, that can lead us to a different future. If they are successful, these investments may—like those made in Silicon Valley 70 years ago—start new industries that result in rapid economic gains.

Whichever country controls the energy source for the next iteration of capitalism will have a huge strategic advantage. Fossil fuels laid the foundation for America's dominance in the 20th century. If we're going to continue to be a strong actor in the world, we need a strong new energy policy. This doesn't mean ripping up all our fossil fuel infrastructure—China certainly isn't—but we do need to get past our internal political squabbles and develop a practical strategy for developing more renewable energy, including more nuclear power. This is part of an overall industrial policy we're finally starting to reckon with.

Investing in the Middle Class

None of this work is easy. Dynamic Capitalism will require some of the leaders and winners of the age of neoliberal capitalism to share power and wealth while abandoning familiar ways of thinking and working. The path forward requires a particular emphasis on our beleaguered middle class, recognizing that it is among our most important assets, and investing more deliberately in strengthening it. We need to create an economy that enables not just broad economic growth but also individual economic mobility and greater economic opportunities across income and class. America has shown a propensity for the former—we continue to enjoy an economy that leads the world. However, we must also recognize that the underlying source of this economic growth is human capital. With technology set to unleash another wave of disruption on the labor markets, individual economic mobility has been, and continues to be, under threat. What was once a wildly dynamic and mobile economy has become much more static, where only relatively few can truly climb the economic ladder. Regaining this dynamism will require new thinking and new ideas. This is the basis for Dynamic Capitalism and the reason it is so desperately needed.

Section IV

NEW BARGAINS, NEW POSSIBILITIES

Chapter 14

MORE MIDDLE-CLASS CAPITALISTS

In 2020, Rick Plympton and Mike Mandina reflected on the company they had built over the past 30 years. Since its 1991 founding, Optimax had achieved remarkable success. Companies around the globe were adopting their high-end optical lenses, including NASA, which was using Optimax products in space. Over the years, the company had generated about $500 million in revenue, with more than half of that paid out to employees as payroll, benefits, and profit sharing, supporting the community the men loved: Rochester, New York.

They founded Optimax after meeting as workers on the production line at Kodak—by coincidence, Marion Folsom's former employer. The company decided not to pursue a product the men invented because managers there thought the market potential was too small. Striking out on their own to pursue rapid delivery of prototype optics, the men built Optimax in line with their blue-collar roots. They took a risk at the beginning and believed it was appropriate to be compensated for that risk, as well as for their hard work over the years. But what they saw among some company owners and CEOs across America bothered them. "It's frustrating that you can have a company where they pay their workers as little as possible, and the leaders take boatloads of money," Plympton said. "That's a perversion of capitalism."[1] In contrast to most businesses, Optimax is run open book—meaning that corporate financials are shared with employees. Each month 25% of the profit is distributed to employees who have been with the company for at least five years.

Now, as they considered the next chapter in their lives, it was time to look at succession plans. Should they sell the company? Would a buyer treat their employees—400 by that time—fairly and keep the company's sharp reputation for quality? "We didn't like the conventional ways to sell your business," Plympton said. Looking for a different path, they eventually discovered a model called an Employee Ownership Trust (EOT). Popular in the United Kingdom (where there are tax incentives that privilege this structure) and in a few other countries, EOTs remain relatively obscure in the United States.

But EOTs and other models of ownership—especially Employee Stock Ownership Plans (ESOPs), which we'll discuss in a few paragraphs—hold great promise. As we researched ways in which the capital and labor classes can come together, we were struck by the potential of creating a larger class of "owners" in America and the role that various forms of employee trusts and stock plans might play in this transition.

EOTs permit companies to transfer ownership into a benefit trust on behalf of its employees. They are one example of a growing movement in America to expand ownership in ways that move outside the economic paradigm of neoliberal capitalism and its emphasis on the differences between capital and labor. In the norms and structures of the past 50 years, "capital" has been central. In the neoliberal style of capitalism, shareholders are the first and most important beneficiaries of companies' activities. Shareholder earnings are taxed differently than labor, and government policies—not to mention social status—generally skew heavily toward the capital class. However, more and more people are looking for new economic frameworks that seek to rebalance capital and labor. Strikingly, many of the leaders of this movement come from working-class backgrounds. As in the case of Optimax's owners, they are aligning incentives and broadening ownership while still compensating capital (investors) for the risk they take. At the same time, these new structures allow employees to turn the value of their time into ownership. In Dynamic Capitalism, the power that individuals have to choose where to contribute their labor, and the risk they take with their future earnings, is valuable too.

This trend is not about creating a welfare system or altruistically imposing one set of values across the business ecosystem. Instead, it is about creating mechanisms to rethink how profits are shared within an organization. A growing number of people—including the two of us—advocate for expanding the idea of ownership as one of the best mechanisms for closing the gap between the capital class and the middle class and creating better alignment between the two. The more members of the capital class our economy creates, the more the economy will thrive.

The Mechanisms of Wealth Sharing

Kodak is a convenient symbol of the story of American capitalism. Built on groundbreaking advancements in film technology, the company was a mechanism for distributing the profits of that innovation because such a large workforce was required to earn them. Kodak was famous for paying wages and providing benefits that helped elevate families into the middle class. Yet when another innovation came to the fore—the digital camera—Kodak failed to adapt. And though other companies arose to produce the cameras consumers wanted, those companies didn't require the same-sized workforce. Take, for example, Apple. It had 161,000 employees in 2023, sales of $383.3 billion, and profits of nearly $100 billion.[2] At its peak, in the early 1990s, Kodak had 145,000 employees, sales of $19 billion, and profits of $2.5 billion (or roughly $40 billion and $5.3 billion, respectively, in 2003 dollars)—nearly 10 times more employees per dollar of revenue. On one hand, it's positive for America that we have built some of the most profitable companies in the world. On the other hand, part of what drives that profitability is that many businesses no longer need large numbers of workers to generate their revenue. We're not suggesting that companies should look to become less profitable by hiring more workers than they require. But we must recognize that the pathways to the middle class are different than they were for prior generations of workers.

If you focus on individual companies, what you see looks like a series of deaths and rebirths, inventions and reinventions, and new market entrants surpassing entrenched and older businesses that failed to adapt. If you look at capitalism as a system, you see companies as mechanisms for delivering value and profits. Firms provide value to consumers and make profits, which they distribute to workers as wages and to owners as returns. Through this lens, you can see that the old mechanism for creating and distributing economic gains throughout society started changing in the 1980s. This served to accelerate income inequality and, more perniciously, wealth inequality.

America's innovation engine is still working, something we see every day in our jobs as a venture capitalist and a business journalist. Optimax is just one example of many in which ingenuity combined with risk-taking resulted in a new technology that created value. However, companies are no longer the mechanisms of profit sharing between owners and workers that they once were. This profound change in our economy has disproportionately hit the middle class.

You can see the trend by comparing the growth of wages versus corporate profits—a rough measure of how corporate revenue gets distributed between workers and shareholders. For most of the last century, wages and profits have grown roughly in line, meaning the relationship between return to capital and return to labor was relatively static. Starting in the mid-1990s, however, these trend lines diverged, with profits growing at a significantly higher rate than wages, according to data compiled by the Federal Reserve (see figure 5).[3] This once fundamental mechanism of economic mobility and stability has broken down. Capital has been favored over labor in ways that have been detrimental to the long-term health of our overall economy.

Labor Productivity vs. Wages 1973-2023*

[Chart showing Labor productivity and Real hourly compensation from 1973 to 2023, Log of index (1973 = 100), y-axis from 4.5 to 5.7]

* non-farm business sector

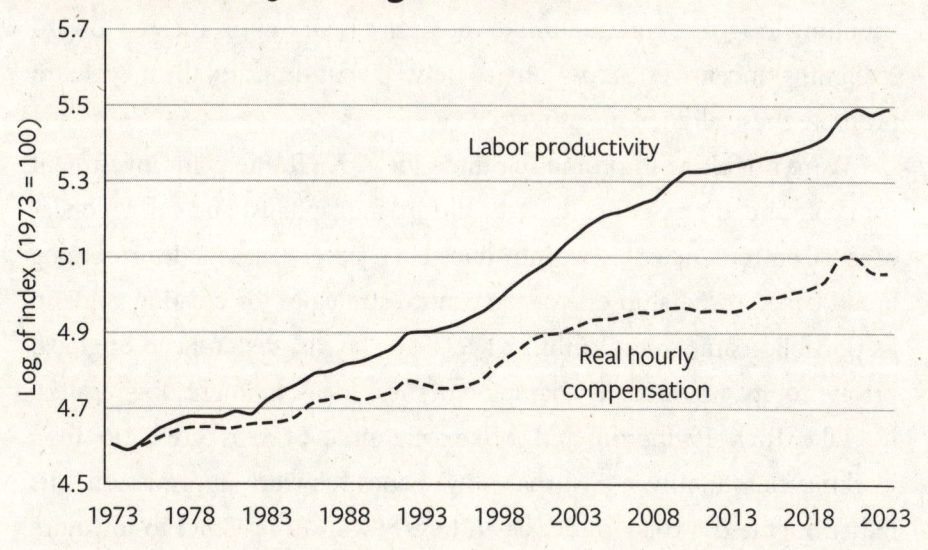

Figure 5. Source: US Bureau of Labor Statistics.

Dynamic Capitalism challenges us to rethink the mechanisms that enable the economic mobility that neoliberalism not only failed to deliver but actually reduced. Politicians tend to talk about aggressively redistributive tax policy, typically favoring particular interest groups or the people they see as their most important constituents. You could write a whole book on tax policy, which is not our purpose here, but three things are clearly true: (1) A complex tax code creates perverse disincentives,

(2) those disincentives hamper economic fairness and growth, and (3) the US government will need more revenue in the coming years, not less. Whatever your view on the specifics of tax policy, building a stronger middle class whose incomes are rising faster than their taxes are going up is essential and will create an overall stronger economic base upon which to build.

To allow more workers into the capital class, we should build greater legal and tax incentives to encourage owners to share the risks and rewards of ownership. Turning workers and consumers into owners with a corresponding long-term orientation to the future is an important step toward realigning incentives across our society. Dynamic Capitalism seeks to promote these aligned incentives.

We're not alone in promoting these ideas. KKR, the giant investment firm cofounded by George Roberts, the ardent capitalist and early pioneer of social entrepreneurship we introduced in chapter 8, has made promoting broad-based ownership one of the central strategies for creating value in its portfolio companies. Within KKR, Pete Stavros, the co-head of global private equity, was an early champion of these ideas, to interesting results.

Like Rick Plympton and Mike Mandina, Stavros grew up in a working-class family, a past that now shapes his work and mission. His father operated a road grader as an hourly worker in Chicago for more than 40 years.[4] "He used to talk about this misalignment of incentives: If you work too fast, your hours go down, your paycheck goes down. There is this weird, perverse incentive to not try that hard, but to work steady. And my parents are both absolute workaholics." At one point, the company stopped paying workers for their lunch hour. In protest, his father's union arranged to have road aggregate delivered at lunchtime. "My dad would look at his watch and say, 'We don't work now,'" Stavros explained. "They would refuse deliveries and the job would run out of material and have to shut down for the day."

Witnessing his father's frustration with the company left a deep impression on Stavros. For one thing, it highlighted the need to better match incentives to work and how paying employees only by the hour was shortsighted. Today, equity-based compensation for top executives has become commonplace, yet nearly 70 million people in America are paid hourly. "There is a lot of pushback that regular workers won't understand equity—it's too complicated, they won't appreciate it," Stavros told us, waving his hand derisively. For him, the business rationale is simple: "It's crazy to me that you wouldn't want the folks on the front lines—the people interacting with customers and ensuring quality and on-time delivery—motivated by the company's success."

So when Stavros became the head of the industrial manufacturing group of KKR's Americas private equity business, he began an experiment—initially with a small handful of companies, then more broadly across KKR's investment portfolio. Working with management, he helped the companies modify equity plans traditionally reserved for senior managers and expanded them to include all employees.

When KKR sells companies that have implemented these ownership plans, employees share in the gains from that sale, in some cases receiving payouts that are multiples of their annual wages. Based on its early success with broad employee ownership, KKR has supported the implementation of employee equity structures across more than 55 companies, including Ingersoll Rand, CHI Overhead Doors, Minnesota Rubber and Plastics, Fortifi, and CIRCOR International. Managers found that employee retention and engagement go up, and in the best cases, employees can earn life-changing payouts. When KKR sold CHI Overhead Doors in 2022, the average worker received $175,000.[5]

Of course, workers may not see these gains. Not all the companies in KKR's portfolio do well enough to sell for a profit. And the strategy isn't altruistic, Stavros reminded us. If KKR can turn a company around faster, it will make more money, and the bulk of the gains still go to the owners of KKR itself. (Anyone can become an owner of KKR these days; the company is publicly listed.)

This type of widespread ownership model has long been common among venture-capital-backed startups in Silicon Valley and beyond. Fairchild Semiconductor, founded in 1957, pioneered the use of stock options in technology startups. The practice spread through the 1960s and 1970s as technology companies laid the foundation for what would become decades of innovation. Early tech companies such as Intel Corporation and eventually Microsoft, Apple, Oracle, and others made wide use of stock options to incent employees, and the practice has become nearly ubiquitous. Today, nearly all technology startups—whether located in Silicon Valley, Boise, or Stockholm—provide stock options to employees to align corporate interests and share the "upside" of their business performance. The result has been many high-profile successes where large numbers of employees see a meaningful windfall when a business either goes public or sells. When Facebook went public in 2012, a reported 600 employees became millionaires. Mark Cuban has boasted that more than 90% of his employees became millionaires when he sold his company, Broadcast.com, to Yahoo in 1999.[6] Perhaps it is due to the risk-taking culture of tech startups, but the result has been a system that nearly ubiquitously rewards employees as owners and allows everyone from senior executives to hourly workers at these businesses to share in a company's success. This labor-to-capital pathway is one that a broader set of business leaders can learn from.

As of 2021, 11 million employees participated in equity compensation plans such as restricted stock, stock options, and employee stock purchase plans.[7] Many are ESOP plans, which, next to stock option plans, are the most common way for owners to share equity with their employees. Other workers are employed in worker cooperatives, and still more are beneficiaries of EOTs like the one at Optimax, which distribute profits on an ongoing basis to workers, rather than through a one-time sale as in the case of the companies owned by KKR. Approximately 18% of US employees have an ownership stake in their employers.[8] That's a great start and something we should aggressively build upon. Employee ownership doesn't need to be unique to technology businesses or to a handful of forward-looking companies outside of the tech sector. It is something that we can and should embrace more broadly, and a practice that has a long, if often forgotten, history in the United States. In the early 20th century, employee profit participation was much more common, and many companies, including Sears, Pillsbury, S. C. Johnson, Hallmark, and US Steel, shared earnings with their workers. We can learn from the past.

The AI Disruption Is Coming

ESOPs and stock options are models that supplement the other ways Americans can own companies, either through the stock market or by becoming entrepreneurs. These models are becoming more important now as the pace of technological change accelerates. We don't know how machine learning or AI will change the job market or economy of the United States (or other countries), but surely it will have an effect, just as automation did in the 1990s. Innovations create economic value, but Dynamic Capitalism is not only concerned with aggregate economic growth; it also considers how that growth is shared.

What we can say with certainty now is that the last wave of automation, unleashed as neoliberal capitalism took a stranglehold on the United States, devastated many American families—especially those in which the head of household didn't have a college degree. AI is likely to replace jobs that have what researchers call a "routine cognitive" component, meaning they involve mental tasks that are fairly repetitive, rule-based, and predictable. The RAND Corporation analyzed patents as one way to predict the potential disruption from AI. Their conclusion was that AI and machine learning were likely to affect lab technicians, web and social media administrators and marketers, and document management specialists. The researchers also noted that these are jobs dominated by college-educated women.[9] This is just the tip of the iceberg in terms of job disruption and displacement, and in our own experiences we have already witnessed disruption in many other job segments. This will likely be a boon to productivity, much as manufacturing automation led to greater and more efficient industrial throughput. And some workers will greatly expand their capacity for work with the benefit of AI copilots and agents. However, the disruptions these changes will impose on our economy are very real, and we expect the list of jobs impacted to expand meaningfully as the power of AI becomes more fully understood and new use cases are implemented.

When automation hit the manufacturing economy, the convenient go-to prescription was to implement retraining programs to help people whose jobs had been automated out of existence find work in the new economy. History suggests it's a mistake to count on this idea; the displacement of losing a job or profession is profoundly disruptive to people's identities and communities. Our experience with prior periods of technological dislocation shows us that technology not only disrupts specific sectors and occupations but that, over time, it shifts where and how labor is needed across the entire economy. This can be an economic boon when viewed at the level of the entire country, but it can cause massive displacements at local or regional levels. These are powerful realities that we must come to terms with and address. In many respects, the rise of economic populism can be seen, at least in part, as a reaction to the economic dislocation of the past 50 years, as well as a widespread fear that additional changes to our economy are looming on the near horizon.

In its heyday, Kodak distributed wealth to its workers through the standard mechanisms of the time. Output—the number of film canisters processed in Kodak's case—was easily quantified and served as a good proxy for a worker's time and value. Today, the processes employed at

Optimax require higher speed, less physical plant, and more creativity and brainpower. The connection between time and output, so crucial to distributing the profits of large corporations in the Golden Age, is no longer an appropriate way to measure productivity or value that contribution. We must think in different and more wholistic ways.

It's noteworthy that the trend of employee ownership emerged from within the business community itself. It shares some of the ideology of the "woke left"—the idea that the wealthy should share the wealth and that companies have a greater responsibility to their employees—as well as the ideology of the "new right," which holds that we ought to be paying more attention to the experiences of people in the middle of the country. Widespread adoption of broader employee-ownership practices will require a growing number of business leaders and owners to embrace shared ownership—and importantly, it will require government incentives and new laws that make it easier for them to do so.

Limits to Employee Ownership

Obviously, employee ownership isn't a panacea, and structural changes don't happen quickly. Bringing the US system back into balance will also require changes in the traditional labor markets. The pandemic brought the value of physical labor back into focus. Just as the advent of America's Industrial Revolution in the early 1900s brought a wave of labor activism, the shift toward Dynamic Capitalism will include rebalancing traditional means of sharing wealth within companies. In surveys of public opinion by Just Capital, worker pay tops the list of the more than 20 factors that Just uses to measure the impact of America's largest businesses. "The resounding refrain from the public is that America's largest companies should put workers squarely at the heart of just business practice," it declared.[10]

The year 2023 saw renewed labor activism—fortunately, not accompanied by the labor violence of the early 1900s. That year, the Teamsters won a contract for 340,000 workers that its leadership called the richest in the company's 40-year history, after the companies with whom the Teamsters negotiated had posted years of record profits.[11] Television and movie actors and writers went out on strike, ultimately reaching a deal, and the United Auto Workers struck as well, lobbying for a share of company profits after years in which executives' pay climbed as workers' pay stagnated or fell. In our new politics and shifting economics, labor is seeing a surge of empowerment.

Consumer Ownership

A change in capitalism doesn't only come from leadership or even leadership and labor combined. It also comes from the ground up. In a market-driven, consumption-driven society like ours, there is another powerful force: Consumers, especially those under 40, are demanding a different approach.

The conventional wisdom used to be that most people preferred to buy from a "sustainable" company—*as long as that company also offered the lowest price.* This dynamic is shifting. When Gen Z or millennial customers believe a brand cares for people and the planet, they are more likely to buy from it—by a significant margin (15%–27%, depending on the brand's specific qualities). As young consumers begin to comprise a greater portion of overall consumer purchasing, companies are spending more time and resources projecting a good corporate-citizen image.

While consumer demand alone can't spur the move to Dynamic Capitalism, it is certainly a powerful force. Take the example of Publix, one of the country's largest employee-owned companies. As a 2023 *Harvard Business Review* article describes:

[Publix] ranks #1 in customer trust of 11 peer grocery brands . . . This difference is even more pronounced with Gen Z and Millennial customers, who score Publix as 83% and 95% higher than the number-two player, respectively. As a result, trusting customers are 54% more likely to purchase from Publix than from competitors. And this is even more pronounced with Gen Z and Millennial customers, who are 162% more likely to purchase from Publix than from competitors.[12]

Reframing Labor

Nearly 135 million people are employed full time in the United States. Through the neoliberal lens, they have largely been viewed as a cost center to be minimized. Dynamic Capitalism encourages us to see them as a resource instead. How we better balance capital and labor and how we shape an economy that creates more owners and more capitalists are critical questions to consider as we seek an economy that continues to thrive while sharing more of its gains with a broader number of Americans.

Chapter 15

POLICIES AND LEADERSHIP

This isn't a book on policy, but in the course of interviewing dozens of CEOs, academics, researchers, investors, workers, and others thinking about the future of capitalism, we came across many ideas for how to encourage the shift in thinking that we've outlined in this book. We thought it would be useful to share a few of them, organized around three central themes: increasing economic mobility, addressing our rapidly changing environment, and broadening worker prosperity and ownership. Each of these is an area where our current systems are coming up short. Dynamic Capitalism is shifting power toward the business community, which offers an opportunity for private-sector or public–private solutions to some problems that have proven intractable to government action. For decades, the knee-jerk approach to policy has been to pass changes at the federal level. But many of the new norms of Dynamic Capitalism are more likely to be established first in companies, then by communities, and then by state and local governments.

Increasing Economic Mobility— Creating More Capitalists

Fifty years ago, those born into the bottom 25% of the wealth scale in the United States had about a 25% chance of ending their lives in the top 25%.[1] While there were plenty of obstacles to economic mobility, the US economy was significantly more dynamic than it is today. The American Dream was alive, and those who worked hard and strived could expect to be rewarded for their ingenuity and grit. While certainly far from perfect, our economic system was at least something of a meritocracy.

Today, things in the United States are quite different. While we continue to celebrate stories of self-made entrepreneurs who grew up in impoverished circumstances and, through grit, determination, and luck, were able to create a social and economic legacy for themselves and their families, the truth is that these stories are no longer representative of our economy. Of those born today into the bottom 25% of the wealth scale, only about 5% will rise to the top 25%.[2] We've awakened from the American Dream to a much harsher reality. Some of the trends we've discussed throughout this book suggest the root causes of this deterioration in economic mobility—from changes in the global manufacturing economy to the move away from labor-intensive extractive energy sources to the rise of AI. The United States was once a leader in economic mobility—a shining city on the hill, as Ronald Reagan liked to describe it. While this is no longer the case, and the United States is actually now lagging other nations in terms of economic opportunity, we don't have to accept this as a new, permanent reality.

Lower Barriers to Starting a Business

There is certainly a role for appropriate safeguards governing business activity, but the amount of red tape and regulation—especially around starting a company—has become untenable. A patchwork of regulatory and licensing requirements across cities, counties, and states is preventing economic mobility and stifling economic growth. These are especially problematic across many job categories that are predominantly occupied by those in the middle class. Many during the COVID-19 pandemic were unable to take their skills as a hairstylist, manicurist, nurse, accountant, plumber, electrician, or any number of other jobs from one state to another—or sometimes even from one city or county to another. One solution could be greater reciprocity between states, whereby being licensed in one state automatically gives you a license in other states, or by nationalizing licensure in some of these categories. (Federal law often has limited authority to override local laws in many of these areas, so local participation will be key.) Our intent isn't to trample on "states' rights," but to recognize that we have the ability to offer consumer protections at a national level in a different way than was practical 150 years ago when many of these regulatory frameworks were first adopted. Nor do standards always need to be the purview of the government; in many professions where small businesses are common—including medicine and accounting—licensure and enforcement are managed by a combination of professional associations, industry standards, and state-level regulators.

More generally, the overall regulatory burden of starting a new business is too high. Businesses of all sizes regularly cite regulation and compliance as one of their top three or four challenges.[3] While we're certainly not arguing for the elimination of all regulations—there is an appropriate role for the oversight of health, safety, worker protections, and so forth—we believe that the long-term trend in federal and local regulations is headed in the wrong direction and argue for the easing of barriers to business activity more generally, and starting a business more specifically.

Retirement Savings for All

As US employers have shifted away from pension-style retirement plans (called "defined benefit" plans because they pay out a specific percentage of an employee's pre-retirement wage) to plans that are effectively savings accounts that vary in size based on the contributions made into them (called "defined contribution" plans), the number of Americans who have effectively saved for retirement has decreased.[4] Additionally, many Americans simply don't have access to a retirement plan to fund in the first place. The vast majority of retirement plans are administered through employers, but by some estimates, 56 million Americans don't work for employers that offer such plans.[5] And for those that do, the default is almost universally set to not participating in them, meaning that employees need to act to sign up, rather than being enrolled from the start with the choice to opt out.

Both of these issues can easily be addressed. More and more states are now setting up state-sponsored retirement plans. This is a positive trend and one that should be broadened, either by states or nationally by the federal government. Appropriately structured, these plans shouldn't cost the government much, as they are relatively cost-effective to operate and cover administrative costs via fees. If there were an appetite to supercharge this idea, the federal government could match a portion of the contributions, as many employers do, to create more incentive for participating. Over the long run, this would likely save the government money, as citizens would be better prepared for retirement and less reliant on government social programs as they age. Also, setting participation in these plans as the default choice would ensure broader participation. As the Nobel-winning behavioral economist Richard Thaler has argued repeatedly, making such plans opt-out is the best way to increase the retirement savings rate.[6] Combining broader access to retirement plans, adding the potential for matching funds, and setting enrollment as the default will significantly boost savings across our population, making more Americans "investors" in the process.

Capitalists from Birth

One idea that has been floated for years, and which we wrote about in our last book, *The New Builders,* is for the United States to implement a so-called baby bond. The idea is simple but powerful: Every child born in the United States would have an investment account set up for them by the federal government. This account would grow tax free through investments in a selection of low-cost investment funds overseen by the US Treasury. Money in this account couldn't be accessed until the recipient turns 18, after which the funds could be used, but only for certain purposes (say, for education or starting a business). At some point, the funds would become freely available for account owners to do with as they please. If such an account grew at 7% annually (below the annualized market return since the end of the Great Depression), it would be worth nearly $17,000 when that child turned 18. If they waited to pull the money out until they were 30, they would have nearly $40,000.

The beauty of these accounts is what everyone from Ben Franklin to Jack Bogle has called "the miracle of compound interest"—the multiplying effect of earning returns upon returns. Another benefit is that it would encourage others—family and friends—to contribute to the child's account as well. Even a small amount of contributed capital makes a significant difference, and having an account already set up for this purpose makes it easy. Contributing just $150 annually would increase the value of a baby bond account to more than $22,000 at age 18, for example.

The cost of such a program would be relatively modest compared to the overall size of the US budget. Approximately four million children are born in the United States each year, meaning that the cost of the program would be in the neighborhood of $20 billion annually.[7] That represents less than half of 1% of the current federal budget. If that was too much for politicians to swallow, the program could be structured as a loan, where participants had to pay the original principal back when they turned 18. The point is to turn every American into a member of the capital class and to provide each child with a nest egg upon which they can build. However they choose to use this money, an entire generation could reap the benefits of investing in themselves.

This is yet another solution that is already being experimented with at the state level. And there is no barrier to individuals or individual company owners setting up a version of this idea for their children, family, or employees. In fact, a few foundations have begun to implement similar models in their communities. Opening a savings account on behalf of a newborn, or perhaps for a niece's birthday, is a great way to start them on the path to savings and ownership. While it doesn't yet enjoy the tax benefits of the broader idea we've outlined, it can serve as a decisive first step to creating owners, even if the initial deposit is relatively modest.

Further Democratize Access to Investing

With few exceptions, ordinary Americans historically have been unable to participate in most private investment opportunities. This started to change in 2012 as the Jumpstart Our Business Startups (JOBS) Act opened the door to new investors and new investment opportunities by lifting a number of restrictions on private investments while still maintaining reasonable controls and protections. The result has been the chance for more people to invest in the kinds of businesses and funds that, prior to the JOBS Act, were only available to the wealthy (so-called accredited investors). We should double down on these opportunities and further ease the barriers to a wide range of investment opportunities. This would benefit not only individual investors but also businesses and private investment funds, which would benefit from a broader set of potential investors.

Expanding Financial Literacy

The unequal access to educational opportunities at the primary level (kindergarten through 12th grade) creates a drag on the nation's economic vitality, especially its economic mobility. We do an especially poor job of preparing citizens to manage their finances. Decades ago, most high school students participated in "home economics" classes, which, while not exactly what we have in mind, provided some basic understanding of how to manage a household, including personal finances. Society has largely given up on this idea—presumably due to greater focus on topics that are covered by standardized testing combined with funding constraints. Our failure to prepare our citizens for the basic tasks of managing their financial affairs is an oversight with dire repercussions. We send students into the world unprepared for the realities of managing their financial lives at our societal peril. Instead, every student should graduate from high school with a basic understanding of the US financial system, stocks and bonds, investing, credit, and budgeting. This minimum understanding would go a long way toward empowering more Americans to better handle their finances and take advantage of some of the other proposals we've outlined here.*

Environmental Protections

How and why reasonable environmental protections went from near bipartisan consensus to stark division is outside the scope of this book. But despite the partisan bickering over the environment, it seems clear that environmental risk is becoming business risk, to paraphrase BlackRock's Larry Fink. As we argued previously, companies cannot be expected to tackle these problems on their own. Where, how, and the form environmentally friendly actions take is perhaps at the bottom of the partisan disagreement, although there is plenty of climate change denial in today's politics as well. That those on either side of the argument might disagree with some of what we suggest next perhaps drives home the point that we

---

* A great example of this idea in practice is the Delaware Money School, a free program that teaches financial literacy to students across that state.

need to carve out a reasonable middle ground if we are to make progress in time to avoid catastrophic environmental consequences.

The Nuclear Option

The move away from fossil fuels underpins Dynamic Capitalism. While neoliberal capitalism was built on the back of extractive power, Dynamic Capitalism will see the transition away from fossil fuels as our primary energy source in favor of cleaner technologies. We applaud research and investment into a broad set of renewable energy alternatives. However, nuclear power continues to be underweighted in its potential as a long-term, environmentally friendly, safe power source. Actually, that statement is not entirely correct, as countries outside of the United States are leaning heavily into a nuclear future. China alone has 25 nuclear power plants under construction, adding to the 35 that they've brought online in the past 10 years (by contrast, the United States added two during that period).[8] New developments in reactor technology can and should cause us to think differently about the safety and efficacy of nuclear power, which—despite several high-profile incidents—has a surprisingly good safety record.[9]

Building more reactors will require both capital and a different approach to regulation, as well as rising above our current divisive political environment. With the vast majority of the cost of producing energy from nuclear sources coming from the construction costs of nuclear power plants rather than their ongoing operating expenses, addressing the regulatory and approval processes can meaningfully change the economics of nuclear power.[10] We must effectively balance community safety with the reasonable streamlining of nuclear regulations to lower the cost of bringing more nuclear power online in the United States. The estimated life of a nuclear power plant is about 60 years, according to the US Nuclear Regulatory Commission, and much of our generation stock is nearing its end of life. With most US nuclear power generation coming from plants built in the 1970s and 1980s, we will need to act quickly to expand our generating capabilities before these older plants become obsolete.

Carbon Frameworks

Creating a "price" for carbon and adopting market-based principles for managing carbon's impact once enjoyed widespread bipartisan agreement, and there remain proponents of carbon markets on both sides of the political aisle. It's also an example of where government intervention into private markets not only makes sense but is likely a requirement for creating the framework and guardrails necessary for the market to function. However, such action needs to be a global effort, not just an American one. To date, much of the focus in the United States has been around voluntary carbon markets. Readers may have experienced these early carbon markets when booking an airline ticket or ordering an item to be shipped when a vendor provides the ability to buffer a purchase's carbon footprint by buying an offset. These voluntary markets—with their limited scale and, typically, lack of certification of the carbon capture promised—are a positive but incomplete start. In our view, these efforts should be extended through thoughtful government oversight of carbon markets as well as mandatory participation requirements. There is also work to be done in certifying carbon credits—that is, making sure that those selling carbon sequestration are actually providing the benefit they claim (not to mention making sure that an individual offset only gets sold once).[11]

The limitations of current carbon markets notwithstanding, participating in the existing voluntary carbon markets is a real (and relatively easy) way for readers to support their greater adoption and increase their efficacy. While the political cost of mandatory carbon market participation may ultimately prove to be too high, the power of consumer behavior can be harnessed to increase the efficiency of existing voluntary markets, to pressure companies to participate in them, and ultimately to lay the groundwork for more widespread—and possibly required—participation. That same consumer pressure can also be brought to bear on companies who have made pledges about their carbon footprints. These pledges are just that—public promises—rather than carrying any real consequences. With few companies actually on track to reach their carbon emission goals, increased scrutiny and public pressure could help tip the scales.[12]

Broadening Worker Prosperity and Ownership

One theme that has come up repeatedly in our research, as well as in many of the interviews we conducted for this book, is the idea of further extending employee ownership and giving more workers a way to participate in the fruits of their labor beyond just a paycheck. Sharing ownership broadly within companies remains the exception instead of the rule. However, we believe a significant opportunity exists to change this mindset, broaden economic prosperity, and create better alignment between business owners and their employees.

For this effort to have an impact, these ownership ideas need to be implemented broadly and meaningfully. Ideally, much of this change will be driven by market economics. KKR, the private equity firm we profiled in our earlier discussion about employee ownership, isn't acting altruistically when it spreads ownership more broadly at the companies it owns. They've found that sharing ownership makes them and their investors more money. The most scalable ideas do exactly that—create larger economic returns for everyone involved. That said, a nudge in the right direction could speed up the adoption of these ideas and broaden their appeal.

Easy ESOPs

ESOPs, EOPs, and other similar programs take different forms and can vary in their purpose, from purchasing a business from an existing owner to facilitating profit sharing to providing broader ownership across a business that pays out in some later acquisition of the company. All should be expanded. These programs carry many business benefits and, in some cases, tax advantages, but they're not nearly as widely adopted as they can or should be.

While we support streamlining the process of setting up employee stock plans, the main barriers to their adoption are simply education and awareness. Most business owners—especially small business owners—are unaware of their existence or how to leverage them to benefit their company and employees. Perhaps the simplest and most direct way of addressing this would be to set up an Employee Ownership Office under the Small Business Administration (SBA), whose job would be to educate businesses about employee ownership programs; help companies set up stock plans; and be a conduit for information, connection, and assistance around all things related to employee stock plans.

Employee Ownership Trusts, in particular, represent an area of opportunity for growing employee ownership. While less well known and much less widely adopted (as of this writing, there are only 31 EOTs in existence across the United States), they hold several advantages over ESOPs.[13] Because EOTs are not governed under the Employee Retirement Income Security Act, they are less complex to set up and operate, and they offer more flexibility than other forms of ownership plans. Here again, one of the major barriers to adoption is simply education and access, something the new SBA Employee Ownership Office could address.

Incentives for Broadening Ownership

While we believe that broader employee ownership ultimately drives better overall investment returns, we recognize that the markets, broadly speaking, have been slow to move in this direction. One way to accomplish this is to pair broader, meaningful employee ownership with capital gains treatment for carried interest—the profit share that private equity investors and venture capitalists receive after their funds return capital to their investors (sometimes after generating a minimum return). Whether the IRS should treat carried interest as a capital gain or ordinary income has been the subject of debate and scrutiny for a number of years, and Congress has tightened the rules around what returns qualify for the favorable carried-interest tax treatment (e.g., by lengthening the holding time required of the underlying assets). Across the private equity and venture capital industries, the treatment of carried interest as capital gains remains a charged and important topic. Given this focus, one idea to incent broader ownership would be to tie carried-interest treatment to employee ownership (in addition to, not replacing, existing rules). To qualify, companies would need to spread ownership across a broader range of employees beyond their senior management team. This would be relatively simple to implement and provide a significant incentive to private equity and venture capital investors to broaden company ownership and participation. Similar incentives could be adopted for businesses that are not funded by venture or private equity investors.

Investing in the Care Economy

America (and the world) has a global blind spot when it comes to the economic value of caregiving. Part of being human is caring for our elders, our children, and others who need our help. Yet the high value of this work is unrecognized, in large part because so much of it is in the hands of women whose work is unpaid or informal.

What gets measured gets changed and improved, and coming up with an estimate for the value of this work is a good place to start to understand its impact on our economy. To this end, global organizations such as the International Labour Organization are establishing standards to more accurately measure an economy's informal and unpaid labor by including questions about the use of time rather than just the value of goods and services in economic surveys. This policy change isn't expensive but has the potential to be meaningful if adopted more broadly, providing a more accurate representation of the economic value of these sectors and informing policy decisions. Some countries, most notably Japan, that have lived through stagflationary environments and declining populations, have already recognized that investments in creating innovations and companies in the care economy have a multiplier effect—freeing up resources to be better allocated to other areas of their economies.

Policy ideas that could serve to unlock the value in the care sector include programs at federal, state, and local levels that better support caregiving—especially universal pre-kindergarten programs, full-day kindergarten, rules and norms around flexible hours, and time off for caregiving (such as the current Family and Medical Leave Act). These programs aren't meant to be altruistic, but rather to unlock the talents of some who have been left out of the workforce due to caregiving obligations. Just as embracing women moving into the workforce drove the better allocation of talent and GDP growth in the middle and end of the twentieth century, these programs are likely to create a similar stimulus to our economy today.[14]

Employee Board Representation

The composition of corporate boards has been much debated in recent years, with several states and the major stock exchanges now requiring representation from certain groups historically underrepresented in the boardroom. Several large investment banks have publicly stated that they will no longer take businesses public if they lack board diversity.* And in 2020, for the first time, every company in the S&P 500 had at least one female board member.[15] These requirements have focused on the demographic makeup of boards—specifically requiring that women

---

* This is another area that has been targeted by the Trump administration in its second term, the result of which has been a number of banks and others backing away from their diversity pledges.

and people of color be given literal seats at the table. Plenty of research backs up why these requirements are actually good for companies and their shareholders (and given that is the case, it is clearly a perversion of capitalism in favor of entrenched interests that this hasn't happened on its own already). The same can be said for giving employees the opportunity to participate on boards. While research into employee board participation is still relatively scarce, several studies indicate that including employees on corporate boards leads to greater worker productivity and higher wages.[16] This is practical only for companies of a certain size and scale, but it is something that we suspect will become best practice across an expanding range of US industries, as it has already in many countries around the world.

Just the Beginning

Neither of us is a policy wonk, and these ideas are not intended as an exhaustive list of proposals. We included this chapter in the hopes that it would pique many readers' interest in Dynamic Capitalism and ensure its broad and deep adoption across our economy. In each of the three categories we've just outlined—increasing economic mobility, addressing our rapidly changing environment, and enabling workers—there are many additional ways to foster continued progress. We organized our policy thinking along these three axes because we believe they each represent a critical yet distinct area of focus for Dynamic Capitalism. Our hope is that these ideas will spark further discussion, debate, and ideas.

Chapter 16

RECLAIMING DYNAMISM

Change is rarely easy—and almost never linear. That's certainly true of the transformation underway in the US economy. After five decades dominated by one version of capitalism, we are now witnessing the emergence of a new model, Dynamic Capitalism. For many, this shift feels disorienting, threatening, or even painful. And without a doubt, some who benefit from the current system will be asked to relinquish power as we move toward a more balanced relationship between capital and labor.

Still, we believe the system taking shape has the potential to serve society far more—broadening prosperity and reigniting the ideal of meritocracy that for so long propelled American innovation and the US economy. We have many choices before us, and our actions over the coming few years will determine if we are to truly chart a new path. Ultimately, Dynamic Capitalism is about creating the environment for a resurgence of the American Dream. This book is a call to action for people in the business world, who are in the best position to help establish new norms, standards, and institutions that both enable Dynamic Capitalism and that put appropriate guardrails around it.

Dynamic economies are complicated, and the policies and conditions that enable them can't be boiled down to catchphrases or slogans. Dynamism requires giving more people opportunities to succeed, and the chance at economic security if they do. A dynamic economy needs governments that support and govern markets without overstepping so that entrepreneurs and companies can innovate and grow, and a national security policy that secures our borders without falling too far into protectionism.

If America is to continue to be the world's leading economic power, we need to navigate these complex questions—together. We see the potential for an economy with greater balance between labor and capital, that gives more people the ability to receive income through ownership, that functions with a reasonable but limited government, and where we recognize the economic value in protecting the environment for the long term. Sustainable economic growth that is shared by the middle class is a priority. Many people reading this book are in positions to help create new systems that reduce inequality, whether immediately, by changing compensation structures like Dan Schulman of PayPal, or longer term, by helping to establish new paths for people to take on the mantle of ownership, like Rick Plympton and Mike Mandina of Optimax.

Dynamic Capitalism isn't socialism, and while there is a role for government action—sometimes a critical role—we believe that this role should be limited in nature and scope. Centralized planning, price controls, and similar government interventions in the economy never work and serve only to slow economic growth and ultimately reduce prosperity. The United States is flirting dangerously close to some of these ideas. The policies of the past several decades have created huge budget deficits and ballooned our national debt. The military, government, and government-adjacent workforce (meaning jobs whose existence relies on government procurement) have expanded to unsustainable levels, requiring a difficult reckoning. Our aging population means more than half the US federal budget is consumed by entitlement programs. Basic common sense tells you that we need a larger, better-paid, taxpaying population in order to sustain reasonable levels of support and spending across our economy.

During the time we were researching this book, Javier Milei, the Argentinian president, gave a speech at the World Economic Forum worth highlighting. In it, he offered a forceful defense of capitalism against what he termed "collectivism" (a broad term that refers to various socialist and communist ideologies). A century ago, Argentina was among the top economies of the world, and its capital, Buenos Aires, was known as the "Paris of South America." But starting after the First World War, the Argentinian economy was upended by political instability, the rise of socialism, and a vastly expanded social welfare state. Starting in the 1980s, the economy experienced hyperinflation that at times reached more than 3,000% per year, devaluing the Argentinian currency, wiping out savings, and lowering living standards dramatically. "[I'm] here to tell you that collectivist experiments are never the solution to the problems that afflict the citizens of the world," Milei proclaimed. "Rather, they are the root cause. Do believe me: No one is in a better place than us, Argentines, to testify to these two points. Thirty-five years after we adopted the model of [economic] freedom, back in 1860, we became a leading world power. And when we embraced collectivism over the course of the last hundred years, we saw how our citizens started to become systematically impoverished, and we dropped to spot number 140 globally."[1]

Our divisive political system is yielding leaders that swing from one extreme—collectivism—to another—authoritarianism. The former results in a stagnant economy; too much of the latter results in an economy governed by the whim of an individual (or small cartels who wield all the power). Neither collectivism nor authoritarianism creates the conditions for the next capital evolution. Dynamic Capitalism requires people to participate in their economies, to move with agency, and to have reasonable faith that their success and hard work will be rewarded.

Dynamism and its by-products of sustained growth must be our goal. Achieving this will take different thinking, different skills, and a different mindset.

Leadership Through Action

Capitalism is evolving to put businesses and business leaders into ever more powerful positions as other centers of power decline. At the same time, companies and leaders are evolving to embrace values-driven, employee- and community-centered ways of doing business. Today's corporate and startup leaders are forging ahead despite the political opposition and general uncertainty that often accompanies their actions. We've seen this in the actions of company leaders that put religion, the environment, or communities above short-term profits. Some of these leaders fly the banner of social entrepreneurship, benefit corporations, or impact. Others prefer not to put a label on their actions. None are perfect solutions, but all are examples of how the norms are changing and of the slow evolution of entrenched systems. We need more of these movements to help create the new norms and institutions of Dynamic Capitalism.

The movement to Dynamic Capitalism remains diffuse and isn't yet fully defined. In fact, this is in large part our motivation for writing this book—to recognize the shift that is occurring and to consider its implications. Many of the corporate executives we spoke to highlighted the need for intelligent leadership, especially from the public sector. However, the movement lacks a high-profile figurehead. A "Milton Friedman" for Dynamic Capitalism has yet to emerge. We need a few figures of that stature who will speak loudly and consistently, who have the gravitas and reach to pull together people from across the political spectrum, and who hail from both the public and private sectors.

Being a transformational leader takes courage. It's also complicated.

Companies need to make money to survive, and there's no formula that can be shared in its entirety from one business to the next. Stepping onto the podium in today's charged political environment is fraught with personal and business risks. That said, what we observed in our interviews and learned directly from many of the business leaders we spoke with is that positioning businesses for success involves much more than thinking about the bottom line. As Dick Parsons told us about his time running a small bank before he took the helm of two of the country's largest companies, Citibank and Time Warner,

> I started preaching the gospel of responsible corporate leadership. This was back in a time when people strongly believed that a CEO's job—only job—was to look after shareholders. I said that's not really true. You have employees (because without them, you don't have a business)—if you don't take care of your people, you're going to suffer. And you have the communities you serve because if those communities sink, you're going to sink with them because you can't just pick up the bank and move it someplace else. I still believe these things. Now, back in the 1990s, early 2000s, that was not a popular thing to say, but it's becoming more popular.[2]

Large numbers of executives are finally coming around to Parsons's thinking.

Dynamic Capitalism reflects a shift from a short-term to a longer-term mindset—from the cost-cutting and often ill-conceived acquisition sprees of GE's Jack Welch to the more values-driven leadership of JPMorgan's Jamie Dimon. As Dimon told us, "We don't need to separate rapacious capitalism from humanity."[3]

In the short term, there are trade-offs between profits and values. In the long term, that's less likely to be true. Greg Curtis, former Deputy General Counsel of Patagonia, described their approach to us this way: "We were comfortable with the tension between profitability and giving back. We didn't feel like we were making a trade-off but rather investing for our future."[4] In organizations like Patagonia and JPMorgan, values-based decision-making occurs across the organization. Mid-level managers are empowered to make decisions guided by the longer-term value they believe will be created by them, not just with an eye toward short-term profits.

As our Dynamic Capitalist economy takes shape, different attributes will be rewarded and valued. While the Friedman economy embraced black-and-white thinking, Dynamic Capitalism will reward a different set of skills across the labor force, including among CEOs. Values-based leadership, coalition building, and an ownership mentality are all key attributes of Dynamic Capitalism's leaders. While it may seem quaint to suggest this in 2025, Dynamic Capitalism will reward the avoidance of overtly partisan politics in business. Business operations are being debated too frequently in the political sphere. This is a sign of the transition we're in, but we must guard against it becoming entrenched thinking or allow the principles of Dynamic Capitalism to be weaponized and politicized by those who would prefer to divide the country rather than bring it together.

We have highlighted a values-driven approach to management. The most effective practitioners of Dynamic Capitalism will look for the line *between* values and politics. They will lean on their values and use them to inform decision-making at their businesses while trying to avoid taking overtly political stances. They will look to others to push their thinking, embrace debate and discourse, and build broad coalitions across many sectors of our society. This will include a pragmatic approach to engaging with the government and the realization that government can be a partner, not just a hindrance. State and federal leaders also must recognize that while the government can be a powerful actor in some instances, it can also stifle needed changes, especially at the speed required to solve some of society's most significant challenges. If government intervention is called for, public–private partnerships that leverage the scale of government with the speed of private businesses are often the best solution.

Dynamic Capitalism will reward not just these coalition builders but also individuals with dynamism and grit. People who are willing to learn new skills and adapt to new markets and new environments. That's been the case for a while, as the United States has endured 30 years of rapid change brought on by the deindustrialization of our workforce and the computer and internet revolutions. These changes have the potential to be dwarfed by those of the next 30 years, led by AI, quantum computing, and other new technologies just beginning to take hold. Neoliberals understood the need for retraining but ultimately didn't provide the support and infrastructure for people to successfully accomplish this—nor did they recognize that some people simply get left behind. We should learn from those mistakes and chart a different path.

Neoliberal capitalism was skeptical of government and actively sought ways to limit its power and involvement in society. The result of this diminished role was the rise of corporate power, sometimes disguised within government. Not only was this the inevitable outcome of decades of neoliberal policies, it was also their intent. Our current systems of finance and governance aren't set up to check the power of corporations, or of parts of the government that have been co-opted by them. As companies, including the world's giant asset managers, play a greater role in Dynamic Capitalism, we need mechanisms to keep them in check.

One of the themes that threads its way through this book is the role of information in Dynamic Capitalism. In fact, along with heralding Dynamic Capitalism, another reason we turned to writing this book was because it is so hard to trust information about our economic and political systems. The information exists, but it takes time and effort to ferret out accurate sources and piece together a coherent sense of America today. The role of data—so critical to decision-making—will increase in importance under Dynamic Capitalism as companies and their leaders and employees are forced to make quicker and more consequential decisions more frequently. One of the strengths of any capitalist system where free markets are working properly is that it moves quickly to solve problems. We don't despair of better solutions for accurate information; those may not take the form of journalism as we know it, but new, probably more local, information systems will evolve to replace the broken social media "news" universe. That universe, in turn, has enabled the rise of populists and fascists. In this sphere, we desperately need leaders who recognize that a healthy economic system requires accurate information and who have the vision to establish new sources and platforms that support truth, accuracy, and accountability.

Flexible thinking and the ability to reconsider deeply held beliefs is a fundamental requirement of Dynamic Capitalism. We experienced this ourselves in writing this book, as some of the ideas we came into this work with changed as we opened ourselves to the perspectives of people different from us. As we talked to more people and, especially, as we sifted through our notes and started to turn our initial thinking into paragraphs, sections, and chapters, we found ourselves reassessing preconceived notions and more thoroughly considering ideas from those with differing views. We benefited from the interplay between the two of us, and we took the time to debate the views expressed by the many people we spoke with or whose writing we analyzed while researching this book. We didn't always agree with them, but their thinking and prodding forced us to sharpen our minds and reconsider our positions.

Diversity of thinking and open-mindedness ultimately lead to innovation. When we consider the daunting challenges confronting us, we must acknowledge that we benefit from synthesizing different ways of thinking and ideas. Dynamic Capitalism will reward those who can collaborate and find the balance between effective advocacy for their views and the flexibility to consider those of others.

Dismissing all forms of capitalism is just as ill-conceived as arguing that the United States has become a socialist country—both tactics are tools of those trying to weaponize this moment. These politicized labels are counterproductive to developing the language and coalitions of Dynamic Capitalism, especially those that enable more middle-class capitalists—people who participate in the economy not just by their labor, but through ownership and the agency that being a shareholder brings.

We also need to recognize that policy reforms need to be undertaken in a global context. The institutions that grew up in the last half of the 20th century, from the Golden Age into the Neoliberal Age, won't serve our current moment, but the United States still needs to be part of a global community. Hubris and isolationism go hand in hand. History suggests that a United States that ignores the rest of the world will eventually be doomed to try to save it.

Values = Freedom

We live in an increasingly complex world in which there are very few absolutes. Binary thinking and rigid ideologies won't work in this dynamic global environment. Many nations' power structures are under ever more vicious attack, and it's no coincidence that would-be authoritarians use the power of black-and-white narratives and the divisiveness that results from them to cement power. In some ways, this is the natural evolution of neoliberal capitalism. Far from fostering liberal traits as its name suggests, it has led to economic disparity; entrenched thinking; and ultimately the rising polarization, populism, and authoritarianism that we are witnessing across the world.

Dynamic Capitalism can be about greater freedom and decision-making. Attacks on values-driven capitalism are actually attacks on individual liberty and freedom. Those attacks aim to restrain the ability of business leaders to freely make decisions about their business operations while obscuring investors' ability to base their investment decisions on the attributes and values they believe will lead to better long-term economic performance. By being open and transparent about the factors guiding their decisions, leaders driving Dynamic Capitalism are actually fostering a purer, if not more purposeful, form of capitalism. One of the fallacies of neoliberal capitalism is that most participants in the economy are acted *upon*, with the world simply happening around them. This lack of agency—both individual and collective—was never really the case, although that narrative served the entrenched leaders of neoliberalism well. The world is moving beyond this way of thinking. Americans are ready to embrace new ideas and a new direction.

We are at the precipice of a new future, one in which businesses and innovation are more important than ever and can be turned to greater good. But this future is not guaranteed. The time to embrace Dynamic Capitalism is now. Business leaders and people who see business as a vehicle for change have a critical role to play. People who have the skill and vision to see beyond labels and politics need to step up.

Every meaningful transformation in society is fraught with uncertainty and pushback from those who either benefit from the current way of thinking or are simply scared. Don't listen to them. Our economy and society must change to move forward. It must evolve.

EPILOGUE

July 2025

When we started this book, we had some hope that the US federal system would play an important role in shaping Dynamic Capitalism, moving us toward a more equitable and sustainable future. It's now clear that the hard and constructive work of establishing new norms and institutions will have to be done in the private sector, in industry groups, business communities, and labor unions, with support from philanthropies, and at state and local levels, or in new forms of collaborations between states and other nations. At least for now.

No form of capitalism can survive without two essential pillars that uphold the functioning of free markets: the rule of law and reliable access to information. Amid the turbulence of 2025, it's critical that business leaders stay focused on these core principles. If these foundations erode at a national level, the viability of the American free market system itself could be at risk. And yet, the first months of the Trump administration have exposed just how fragile these underpinnings have become—not only in the United States but also across much of the world.

Because Americans—especially those in business—have benefited from the rule of law for so long, many no longer recognize its fragility. We take it for granted, treating it as a given rather than what it actually is: the foundation upon which private property rights, contract enforcement, and the broader functioning of markets all depend. That's why the Magna Carta is displayed alongside the US Constitution in the National Archives. It represents a foundational underpinning of the American experiment. When thirteenth-century English barons compelled King John—an erratic and tax-hungry monarch—to sign the Magna Carta, they weren't just protecting their own interests. They were asserting a revolutionary idea: Executive power must be subject to the law, and the state could not arbitrarily strip individuals of their lives, property, or livelihoods. Centuries later, these principles were expanded through the US Constitution to protect freedoms like speech, privacy, and due process—cornerstones of our modern, rules-based society. These documents belong side by side.

But today, as the old system declines and a new one struggles to emerge, the rule of law—always imperfect—is under growing strain. The use of government institutions to target political opponents, threats against judges and law firms, and attempts to erode the legitimacy of independent education and media are all alarming signs of a broader breakdown. These aren't just isolated incidents; they reflect a dangerous erosion of respect for the norms and guardrails that make a democratic capitalist society possible.

The rule of law doesn't function simply because rules exist—it depends on broad societal adherence. People must obey not just out of fear of punishment but out of shared belief in the system's fairness and necessity. This collective agreement is, in many ways, more important than the laws themselves. Without it, the fabric begins to unravel. No state, however powerful, has the resources to govern purely through enforcement.

Warnings about a weakening respect for the rule of law in the United States have been growing for years. In 2025, those warnings have become impossible to ignore. Over the first six months of this year, cracks in many of our foundational norms have widened dramatically. The arbitrary and often chaotic imposition of tariffs, the erratic swings of trade policy, threats to the independence of the Federal Reserve and the Securities and Exchange Commission, and the weaponization of government resources to penalize private companies for their hiring or investment decisions all point to a troubling politicization of institutions once seen as neutral and essential.

This erosion of trust has profound implications for the business world. Contracts lose meaning if they can be overturned at will by the more powerful party. Entrepreneurs and investors will hesitate to take risks if regulators cannot curb market manipulation by dominant players. And consumers are less likely to engage in commerce if they can't trust the reliability of products and services. At the national level, we are drifting toward a system where unchecked power—held by a few through luck, inheritance, or raw aggression—undermines the very framework that supports both democracy and capitalism.

One of the essential traits of successful capitalists is their ability to see the world as it is, not as they wish it to be. Across both the Golden and Neoliberal Ages of post–World War II capitalism, a shared commitment to uncovering truth defined our progress. Whether through science, journalism, or literature, society sought clarity amid noise—an honest reckoning with reality. Where disagreements arose, we relied on processes like peer review, judicial proceedings, and editorial oversight to get closer to the truth.

Capitalism cannot function without truth. Nor can it flourish without the broad availability of reliable information. Nowhere is this more evident than in public markets, where the flow of information underpins value. When a company faces a crisis, those who know first act first. But beyond markets, the broader economy relies on a shared belief in the integrity of information and the fairness of access to it. If only the wealthy have the time, resources, and channels to access verified, fact-checked content, they will accumulate even more power while others fall behind. This creates a world where innovation is stifled because the most promising ideas, sometimes born in overlooked communities or under-resourced schools, never get a chance to emerge. The erosion of informational equality doesn't just threaten fairness—it cripples dynamism and undermines meritocracy, two pillars of America's historical economic success.

The danger is clear: If our system serves only the powerful and well-connected, it ceases to function for the rest. Protecting the rights of *all* Americans, supporting institutions that ensure the flow of trustworthy information, and rebuilding the structures that uphold economic and social mobility—these efforts may not offer immediate rewards, but they are essential.

As business becomes the most powerful force in modern society, it must also shoulder more responsibility. We're encouraged to see business leaders taking public stands, as Jamie Dimon did in his 2025 annual letter to shareholders (released just as we were writing this epilogue). "Today, it is clear this system needs serious reform and strengthening," he wrote. We agree.

We hope others will join this fight—people at all levels of business, academia, and government. We see a future beyond this current crisis. We believe capitalism is best positioned to allow us to continue achieving prosperity. Yet we also recognize the need to reform it. To allow for greater economic mobility, for a more robust middle class, and for increasing, not decreasing, dynamism. We can't take American prosperity for granted. It must be earned.

Seth Levine
Elizabeth MacBride

ACKNOWLEDGMENTS

We hope you'll take a moment to read this section, as tempting as it can be to skip it. There are many people who contributed to the effort behind *Capital Evolution* and to whom we owe a debt of gratitude. This book was truly a passion project for each of us, and it was one in which we frequently came across data or ideas that changed or expanded our thinking. We quickly learned to let go of preconceived ideas and be willing to be challenged by new perspectives. The two of us benefited from our now decade-long working relationship and enjoyed many spirited discussions and debates about the wide range of topics that became part of the research for this book.

In working on *Capital Evolution*, we were fortunate to have had the opportunity to talk with dozens of interesting and thoughtful people from varying disciplines, backgrounds, and political persuasions. We benefited greatly from the generosity of their time. Many are voices that were quoted in these pages. Others provided background information, connected us with others, or served as sounding boards for our ideas as they developed. We are deeply grateful to the many people who took the time to talk with us as part of this project.

We had the great fortune of having a team surrounding us as we worked through early drafts of *Capital Evolution* and researched the underlying data we relied upon to tell the story of the changing nature of capitalism in the United States. In particular, Megan Salmida provided invaluable help in managing the logistics behind the book. Everything from helping us make sure our citations were correct to the logistics of setting up interviews to helping us create order out of the chaos that is fact-checking and collecting releases for the material we used. This was essential to ensure the book you have in your hands actually came together.

During the writing of this book, Elizabeth was working on a mid-career master's degree at the Johns Hopkins School of Advanced International Studies. During her two-year program, she took classes only from women business professors. As it is still harder to be a woman university professor, she reasoned that this would give her the chance of learning from the best thinkers among a group of great ones. This proved to be the case in classes taught by Lisel Hintz, Melissa Griffith, Mary Sarotte, Kristin Diwan, Narges Bajoghli, and Elly Rostoum. Their wisdom, knowledge, and the space created by SAIS to learn from them is hereby acknowledged.

Our agent, Alice Martell, was an early believer in this work and helped encourage us to pursue it (this is our second book with Alice). It was Alice who introduced us to Matt Holt of BenBella, our publisher. We are incredibly grateful to Matt and the entire team at BenBella for their immediate and strong support. We are grateful for Matt's belief in us. Indeed, the entire BenBella team was incredibly supportive. Lydia Choi, our editor, was an extremely helpful sounding board and helped us turn *Capital Evolution* into a well-organized and logically laid out book. James Fraleigh, our copy editor, was increasingly important to our work as we finalized the manuscript. His attention to every detail never ceased to amaze us. Brigid Pearson designed the cover and jacket for the book and was kind enough to suffer through our early iterations and ideations. Jessika Rieck developed all the charts for the book and was always happy to accommodate our changes and ideas for them. We were thrilled to have Kerri Stebbins help us think through our marketing and sales strategies to ensure as many people as possible knew about *Capital Evolution*. And Seth's wife, Greeley, came up with the title for the book.

We benefited from feedback on early drafts of the manuscripts and are indebted to a number of friends and colleagues who provided critical feedback on our work. Perhaps no one more so than Seth's partner, Brad Feld, who was the first person to see an early version of the book and provided feedback and advice at a critical time. Nate Wong was another early and helpful reader. A number of other friends also contributed important feedback, especially Tom Healey (who helped completely reshape what is now the Introduction), Canyon Kornicker (who encouraged us to add new voices to a number of our key arguments), and Sharon Matusik (who provided critical feedback as we neared the end of the editing process). We are grateful for your contributions.

Writing a book—especially while holding down full-time jobs—is an all-consuming effort. Late nights and weekends to start with. But a project like this also has a way of taking over mindshare and conversation, poking its way into discussions over dinners, walks, and whenever else the spirit might strike. Our families not only endured this constant in our lives for several years but embraced and encouraged it. Thank you!

NOTES

Introduction

1. Chris Vercase et al., "World Reimagined: The Rise of the Global Middle Class," Nasdaq, July 9, 2021, https://www.nasdaq.com/articles/world-reimagined%3a-the-rise-of-the-global-middle-class-2021-07-09; Joe Hasell et al., "Poverty," *Our World in Data*, https://ourworldindata.org/poverty; Steven Pinker, *Enlightenment Now: The Case for Reason, Science, Humanism, and Progress* (Viking, 2018).
2. Pew Research Center, "Modest Declines in Positive Views of 'Socialism' and 'Capitalism' in US," September 19, 2022, https://www.pewresearch.org/politics/2022/09/19/modest-declines-in-positive-views-of-socialism-and-capitalism-in-u-s/.
3. Anna-Louise Jackson, "Young People Aren't Completely Anti-Capitalist, but the Future of Capitalism Depends on Them," *Fast Company*, January 17, 2024, https://www.fastcompany.com/91010958/gen-z-young-people-anti-capitalism-future-davos-2024.
4. Will Daniel, "'We May Be Looking at the End of Capitalism': One of the World's Oldest and Largest Investment Banks Warns 'Greedflation' Has Gone Too Far," *Fortune*, April 5, 2023, https://fortune.com/2023/04/05/end-of-capitalism-inflation-greedflation-societe-generale-corporate-profits/.
5. Jiaquan Xu et al., "Mortality in the United States, 2021" (NCHS Data Brief No. 456), Centers for Disease Control and Prevention, December 2022, https://www.cdc.gov/nchs/products/databriefs/db456.htm.
6. Jackson, "Young People Aren't Completely Anti-Capitalist."
7. Mark Muro, "No Matter Which Way You Look at It, Tech Jobs Are Still Concentrating in a Few Cities," Brookings, March 30, 2020, https://www.brookings.edu/articles/tech-is-still-concentrating/.

Chapter 1

1. Jamie Dimon, interview by Elizabeth MacBride and Seth Levine, March 21, 2023.
2. Dan Ennis, "Texas Ramps Up Probe into JPMorgan, BofA, Wells Fossil Fuel Ties," *Banking Dive*, October 18, 2023, https://www.bankingdive.com/news/texas-ag-net-zero-climate-jpmorgan-stanley-bank-america-wells-td-state-street-rbc-barclays/696941/.
3. John F. Cogan, "Some Thoughts on the Business Roundtable's Statement of Corporate Purpose," Harvard Law School Forum on Corporate Governance, October 7, 2020, https://corpgov.law.harvard.edu/2020/10/07/some-thoughts-on-the-business-roundtables-statement-of-corporate-purpose/.
4. Jamie Dimon, interview by Elizabeth MacBride and Seth Levine, March 21, 2023.
5. Business Roundtable, "Business Roundtable Redefines the Purpose of a Corporation to Promote 'An Economy That Serves All Americans,'" August 19, 2019, https://www.businessroundtable.org/business-roundtable-redefines-the-purpose-of-a-corporation-to-promote-an-economy-that-serves-all-americans.
6. Jim Himes and Bryan Steil, *Bridging the Divide: Building an Economy That Works for All*, Bipartisan House Committee on Economic Disparity and Fairness in Growth (US Government Printing Office, 2022), https://himes.house.gov/_cache/files/5/a/5a60990d-1f35-4764-8877-37c58a7d9a20/07094705142D4EF70AD3F1A5D46A6879.scedfg-report.pdf.
7. Business Roundtable, "Business Roundtable Redefines."

Chapter 2

1. "PayPal Holdings, Inc. Number of Employees 2013–2023," *Macrotrends*, https://www.macrotrends.net/stocks/delisted/PYPL/PayPal/number-of-employees.
2. Dan Schulman, interview by Elizabeth MacBride and Seth Levine, May 23, 2023.
3. Dan Schulman, interview by Elizabeth MacBride and Seth Levine, May 23, 2023.
4. There are about 6.1 million businesses in the country that employ people. US Census Bureau, "The Number of Firms and Establishments, Employment, and Annual Payroll by State, Industry, and Enterprise Employment Size: 2021," December 12, 2023, https://www2.census.gov/programs-surveys/susb/tables/2021/us_state_naics_detailedsizes_2021.xlsx.
5. Milton Friedman, "A Friedman Doctrine—The Social Responsibility of Business Is to Increase Its Profits," *The New York Times*, September, 13, 1970, https://www.nytimes.com/1970/09/13/archives/a-friedman-doctrine-the-social-responsibility-of-business-is-to.html.
6. Lanny Ebenstein, *Milton Friedman: A Biography* (Palgrave Macmillan, 2007).
7. Mont Pelerin Society, "About the Mont Pelerin Society," accessed August 2024, https://www.montpelerin.org/About.html.
8. David Harvey, *A Brief History of Neoliberalism* (Oxford Academic, 2005).
9. Brian Doherty, "Best of Both Worlds: An Interview with Milton Friedman," *Reason*, June 1995, https://reason.com/1995/06/01/best-of-both-worlds/.
10. Friedman, "A Friedman Doctrine."
11. Lewis F. Powell Jr., "Powell Memorandum: Attack on American Free Enterprise System," *Washington and Lee School of Law Scholarly Commons*, August 23, 1971, https://scholarlycommons.law.wlu.edu/powellmemo/1/.

12 Harvey, *A Brief History of Neoliberalism*.
13 Michael C. Jenson et al., "Theory of the Firm: Managerial Behavior, Agency Costs and Ownership Structure," *Journal of Financial Economics* 3, no. 4 (October 1976): 305–60, https://www.sciencedirect.com/science/article/pii/0304405X7690026X.
14 Harvey, *A Brief History of Neoliberalism*.
15 Mark J. Perry, "Only 52 U.S. Companies Have Been on the Fortune 500 Since 1955, Thanks to the 'Creative Destruction' That Fuels Economic Prosperity," *AEI*, June 3, 2021, https://www.aei.org/carpe-diem/only-52-us-companies-have-been-on-the-fortune-500-since-1955-thanks-to-the-creative-destruction-that-fuels-economic-prosperity-2/.
16 GE, "About Us," accessed January 27, 2025, https://www.ge.com/about-us.
17 "Jack Welch 1935–", Reference for Business, https://www.referenceforbusiness.com/biography/S-Z/Welch-Jack-1935.html.
18 David Gelles, *The Man Who Broke Capitalism: How Jack Welch Gutted the Heartland and Crushed the Soul of Corporate America and How to Undo His Legacy* (Simon & Schuster, 2022).
19 Malcolm Gladwell, "Was Jack Welch the Greatest CEO of His Day or the Worst?," *The New Yorker*, October 21, 2022, https://www.newyorker.com/magazine/2022/11/07/was-jack-welch-the-greatest-ceo-of-his-day-or-the-worst.
20 Cogen, "Some Thoughts."
21 Lawrence Summers, "The Great Liberator," *The New York Times*, November 19, 2006, https://www.nytimes.com/2006/11/19/opinion/19summers.html.
22 Dan Schulman, interview by Elizabeth MacBride and Seth Levine, May 23, 2023.
23 Dan Schulman, interview by Elizabeth MacBride and Seth Levine, May 23, 2023.
24 Dan Schulman, interview by Elizabeth MacBride and Seth Levine, May 23, 2023.

Chapter 3
1 Andrew Ross Sorkin, "World's Biggest Investor Tells C.E.O.s Purpose Is the 'Animating Force' for Profits," *The New York Times*, January 17, 2019, https://www.nytimes.com/2019/01/17/business/dealbook/blackrock-larry-fink-letter.html.
2 Aspen Institute Forum, "An Interview with Larry Fink: The BlackRock Chairman and CEO Sits Down with David Rubenstein, Co-founder and Co-chairman of the Carlyle Group," 2023.
3 Davide Barbuscia, "BlackRock Assets Hit Record $11.6 Trillion in Fourth Quarter," *Reuters*, January 15, 2025, https://www.reuters.com/business/finance/blackrock-assets-hit-record-116-trillion-fourth-quarter-2024-2025-01-15/#:~:text=Assets%[…]0third%20quarter; "BlackRock Is Wrestling with Succession Planning. Here's the Latest News on the Biggest Money Manager," *The Digital Banker*, January 11, 2024, https://thedigitalbanker.com/blackrock-is-wrestling-with-succession-planning-heres-the-latest-news-on-the-biggest-money-manager/.
4 Larry Fink, "Larry Fink's 2019 Letter to CEOs: Purpose & Profit," May 22, 2019, https://www.wlrk.com/docs/LarryFinksLettertoCEOsBlackRock.pdf.
5 Aspen Institute Forum, "An Interview with Larry Fink: The BlackRock Chairman and

CEO Sits Down with David Rubenstein, Co-founder and Co-chairman of the Carlyle Group," 2023.
6. Larry Fink, "Larry Fink's 2020 Letter to CEOs: A Fundamental Reshaping of Finance," January 14, 2020, https://www.BlackRock.com/corporate/investor-relations/2020-larry-fink-ceo-letter.
7. Visit Orlando, "Regional Economic Impact from Orlando Tourism Increases 6.4%," November 18, 2019, https://www.visitorlando.com/media/press-releases/post/regional-economic-impact-from-orlando-tourism-increases-6-4/.
8. Florida House of Representatives, "CS/CS/HB 1557 (2022) Parental Rights in Education," https://www.myfloridahouse.gov/Sections/Bills/billsdetail.aspx?BillId=76545.
9. Ashley Woo et al., "Walking on Eggshells—Teachers' Responses to Classroom Limitations on Race- or Gender-Related Topics: Findings from the 2022 American Instructional Resources Survey," RAND Corporation, January 25, 2023, https://www.rand.org/pubs/research_reports/RRA134-16.html.
10. Chick-fil-A, "Our Purpose," accessed January 27, 2025, https://www.chick-fil-a.com/careers/culture.
11. Chick-fil-A, "Our Purpose."
12. Haley Peterson, "'Chick-Fil-A Is About Food': How National Ambitions Led the Chain to Shed Its Polarizing Image," *Business Insider*, August 6, 2017, https://www.businessinsider.com/chick-fil-a-reinvents-itself-liberal-conservative-2017-5?r=DE&IR=T.
13. Ian Miles Cheong (@stillgray), "Chick-fil-A has gone woke," Twitter (now X), May 30, 2023, 6:34 a.m., https://twitter.com/stillgray/status/1663524241621532673.
14. Nathaniel Meyersohn, "Target Sales Fall for the First Time in 6 years After Pride Month Backlash," *CBS News*, August 16, 2023, https://www.cbsnews.com/boston/news/target-sales-pride-month-backlash-quarter/.
15. Jamie Dimon, interview by Elizabeth MacBride and Seth Levine, March 21, 2023.
16. Amanda Carpenter, "GOP Wants Corporations to Shut Up and Put Up," *The Bulwark*, April 8, 2021, https://www.thebulwark.com/gop-wants-corporations-to-shut-up-and-put-up/.
17. Cheyenne Ligon, "BlackRock CEO Larry Fink Says He No Longer Uses Term 'ESG': 'It's Been Totally Weaponized,'" *Pensions & Investments*, June 26, 2023, https://www.pionline.com/esg/blackrock-ceo-larry-fink-says-he-no-longer-uses-term-esg.
18. Tom Krantz, "The History of ESG: A Journey Towards Sustainable Investing," *IBM* (blog), February 8, 2024, https://www.ibm.com/blog/environmental-social-and-governance-history/.

Chapter 4

1. Emma Goldberg, "Have the Anticapitalists Reached Harvard Business School?" *The New York Times*, November 28, 2022, https://www.nytimes.com/2022/11/28/business/business-school-social-justice.html.
2. Debora Spar, interview by Elizabeth MacBride and Seth Levine, July 18, 2023.
3. Debora Spar, interview by Elizabeth MacBride and Seth Levine, July 18, 2023.
4. Bruce R. Scott, "The Political Economy of Capitalism," Working Paper No. 07-037, December 2006, https://www.hbs.edu/ris/Publication%20Files/07-037.pdf.

5   Scott, "Political Economy."
6   Adam Smith, *The Wealth of Nations* (W. Strahan and T. Cadell, 1776).
7   Elizabeth interviewed Bogle about a half dozen times for CNBC.
8   Economic Policy Institute, "The Productivity-Pay Gap," last modified December 2024, https://www.epi.org/productivity-pay-gap/.
9   Kimberly Amadeo, "Historical U.S. Unemployment Rate by Year," *The Balance*, December 6, 2022, https://www.thebalancemoney.com/unemployment-rate-by-year-3305506; Lawrence Mishel et al., "Wage Stagnation in Nine Charts," Economic Policy Institute, January 6, 2015, https://www.epi.org/publication/charting-wage-stagnation/.
10 Barry M. Leiner et al., "A Brief History of the Internet," Internet Society, 1997, https://www.internetsociety.org/internet/history-internet/brief-history-internet/.
11 Pew Research Center, "Beyond Distrust: How Americans View Their Government, 1. Trust in Government: 1958–2015," November 13, 2015, https://www.pewresearch.org/politics/2015/11/23/1-trust-in-government-1958-2015/.

Chapter 5

1   Kate Williams, interview by Elizabeth MacBride and Seth Levine, December 16, 2022.
2   Angel E. Navidad, "Stanford Marshmallow Text Experiment," *Simple Psychology*, September 7, 2023, https://www.simplypsychology.org/marshmallow-test.html#.
3   Nitin Nohria, "Leading Business Education," *The Harvard Gazette*, October 12, 2011, https://news.harvard.edu/gazette/story/2011/10/leading-business-education/.
4   Rakesh Kochhar and Stella Sechopoulos, "How the American Middle Class Has Changed in the Past Five Decades," Pew Research Center, April 20, 2022, https://www.pewresearch.org/short-reads/2022/04/20/how-the-american-middle-class-has-changed-in-the-past-five-decades/.
5   Alina K. Bartscher et al., "Modigliani Meets Minsky: Inequality, Debt, and Financial Fragility in America, 1950–2016," *Federal Reserve Bank of New York Staff Reports* (Report No. 924, 2020), www.newyorkfed.org/medialibrary/media/research/staff_reports/sr924.pdf.
6   Ronald Reagan, "Inaugural Address," Ronald Reagan Presidential Foundation & Institute, January 20, 1981, https://web.archive.org/web/20210401000851/https://www.reaganfoundation.org/ronald-reagan/reagan-quotes-speeches/inaugural-address-2/.
7   George Monbiot, "Neoliberalism—the Ideology at the Root of All Our Problems," *The Guardian*, April 15, 2016, https://www.theguardian.com/books/2016/apr/15/neoliberalism-ideology-problem-george-monbiot.
8   Monbiot, "Neoliberalism."
9   Chris Matthews, "The 'Invisible Hand' Has an Iron Grip on America," *Fortune*, April 13, 2014, https://fortune.com/2014/08/13/invisible-hand-american-economy/.
10 George Monbiot, "How Ayn Rand Became the New Right's Version of Marx," *The Guardian*, March 5, 2012, https://www.theguardian.com/commentisfree/2012/mar/05/new-right-ayn-rand-marx.

Chapter 6

1. Arco, "World's 100 Largest Philanthropic Organizations List," March 12, 2024, https://www.arcolab.org/en/worlds-100-largest-philanthropic-foundations-list/; Elizabeth MacBride, "The Son of a Single Mom, He Rose from Poverty to Lead One of the World's Largest Foundations," *Forbes*, December 15, 2022, https://www.forbes.com/sites/elizabethmacbride/2022/12/15/diversity-in-america-isnt-just-about-race-its-also-about-class/.
2. Jim Himes and Bryan Steil, *Bridging the Divide: Building an Economy That Works for All*, Bipartisan House Committee on Economic Disparity and Fairness in Growth (US Government Printing Office, 2022), https://himes.house.gov/_cache/files/5/a/5a60990d-1f35-4764-8877-37c58a7d9a20/07094705142D4EF70AD3F1A5D46A6879.scedfg-report.pdf.
3. Bradley Hardy and Dave Marcotte, "Education and the Dynamics of Middle-Class Status," *Brookings*, June 30, 2020, https://www.brookings.edu/articles/education-and-the-dynamics-of-middle-class-status/.
4. Gloria Guzman and Melissa Kollar, "Income in the United States: 2023" (Report No. P60-282), United States Census Bureau, September 10, 2024, https://www.census.gov/library/publications/2024/demo/p60-282.html.
5. Hardy and Marcotte, "Education and the Dynamics."
6. Alyssa Fowers et al., "How Americans Define a Middle-Class Lifestyle and Why They Can't Reach It," *The Washington Post*, February 15, 2024, https://www.washingtonpost.com/business/2024/02/15/middle-class-financial-security/.
7. Wikipedia, "Hazelwood (Pittsburgh)," accessed April 2024, https://en.wikipedia.org/wiki/Hazelwood_(Pittsburgh).
8. Aaron O'Neill, "Life Expectancy (from Birth) in the United States, from 1860 to 2020," Statista, August 9, 2024, https://www.statista.com/statistics/1040079/life-expectancy-united-states-all-time/.
9. United Nations Human Rights Office of the High Commissioner, "OHCHR Assessment of Human Rights Concerns in the Xinjiang Uyghur Autonomous Region, People's Republic of China," August 31, 2022, https://www.ohchr.org/en/documents/country-reports/ohchr-assessment-human-rights-concerns-xinjiang-uyghur-autonomous-region.
10. "The Deaths-of-Despair Narrative Is Out of Date," *The Economist*, December 23, 2023, https://www.economist.com/united-states/2023/12/23/the-deaths-of-despair-narrative-is-out-of-date.
11. Anna Fleck, "The Most Popular TED Talks of All Time," Statista, accessed April 17, 2023, https://www.statista.com/chart/29742/most-popular-ted-talks/#.
12. Based on media accounts, including from *The New York Times*, CNN, and many others.
13. Coleman Hughes, "Why Is TED Scared of Color Blindness?" *Coleman's Corner*, September 28, 2023, https://colemanhughes.substack.com/p/why-is-ted-scared-of-color-blindness.

Chapter 7

1. Erik Kreil, "United States Produces More Crude Oil Than Any Country, Ever," Today In Energy, U.S. Energy Information Administration, March 11, 2024, https://web.archive.org/web/20240312015235/https://www.eia.gov/todayinenergy/detail.php?id=61545.

2   Worldometer, "Oil Consumption by Country," accessed September 2024, https://www.worldometers.info/oil/oil-consumption-by-country/.
3   Darren Dochuk, *Anointed with Oil: How Christianity and Crude Made Modern America* (Basic Books, 2019).
4   Ron Chernow, *Titan: The Life of John D. Rockefeller, Sr.* (Random House, 1998).
5   Robert B. Tomasson, "Marion Folsom Is Dead at 82; Architect of the Social Security Act," *The New York Times*, September 29, 1976, https://www.nytimes.com/1976/09/29/archives/marion-b-folsom-is-dead-at-82-architect-of-social-security-act.html.
6   Ron Chernow, *Titan: The Life of John D. Rockefeller, Sr.* (Vintage 2004), 494.
7   Chernow, *Titan*.
8   Peter Turchin, *End Times: Elites, Counter-Elites, and the Path of Political Disintegration* (Penguin Press, 2023).
9   Mark Blyth, "Death of the Carbon Coalition," *Foreign Policy*, February 12, 2021, https://foreignpolicy.com/2021/02/12/carbon-coalition-median-voter-us-politics/.
10 Darren Dochuk, interview by Elizabeth MacBride and Seth Levine, May 17, 2023.
11 Darren Dochuk, interview by Elizabeth MacBride and Seth Levine, May 17, 2023.

Chapter 8

1   Baba Shiv and Matt Abrahams, "Feelings First: How Emotion Shapes Our Communication, Decisions, and Experiences," Stanford Graduate School of Business, November 20, 2020, https://www.gsb.stanford.edu/insights/feelings-first-how-emotion-shapes-communication-decisions-experiences#.
2   Lisa Green Hall, interview by Elizabeth MacBride and Seth Levine, January 26, 2023.
3   "10 Million Reasons for the Private Sector to Invest in Social Enterprise," World Economic Forum, Trade and Investment, January 18, 2024, https://www.weforum.org/agenda/2024/01/10-million-reasons-for-the-private-sector-to-invest-in-social-enterprise/#.
4   Melinda Tuan, interview by Elizabeth MacBride and Seth Levine, January 6, 2023.
5   Jed Emerson, interview with Elizabeth MacBride and Seth Levine, January 27, 2023.
6   "ANNUAL SURVEY: In an Unstable Economic Environment, Workers and Wages Are More Important Than Ever to the American Public," *Just Capital* (blog), September 15, 2022, https://justcapital.com/reports/2022-survey-workers-and-wages-are-more-important-than-ever-to-the-american-public/; Alison Omens and Kelley Fenelon, interview by Elizabeth MacBride and Seth Levine, December 9, 2022; "2024 Overall Rankings," Just Capital, February 5, 2024, https://justcapital.com/rankings/.
7   Dick Parsons, interview by Elizabeth MacBride and Seth Levine, June 22, 2023.
8   Dick Parsons, interview by Elizabeth MacBride and Seth Levine, June 22, 2023.
9   Morgan Stanley, "Sustainable Funds Outperformed Peers in 2023," February 9, 2024, https://www.morganstanley.com/ideas/sustainable-funds-performance-2023-full-year.
10 Chang-Tai Hsieh et al., "The Allocation of Talent and U.S. Economic Growth," *The Econometric Society* 87, no. 5 (2019): 1439–74, https://www.econometricsociety.org/publications/econometrica/2019/09/01/allocation-talent-and-us-economic-growth.
11 "Video: $50B Pledged for Fossil Fuel Divestment as Rockefeller Heirs Join

Growing Movement," *Democracy Now!*, September 24, 2014, https://www.democracy now.org/2014/9/24/rockefeller_foundation_divests_from_fossil_fuels.

Chapter 9

1. Elizabeth MacBride, "The Strange Illusion of the Lone Hunter," *Forbes*, August 31, 2018, https://www.forbes.com/sites/elizabethmacbride/2018/08/31/strange-illusion-lone-hunter/.
2. Kenichi Hori, interview by Elizabeth MacBride and Seth Levine, April 19, 2023.
3. "The Carbon Majors Database: Launch Report," *CarbonMajors*, April 2024, https://carbonmajors.org/briefing/The-Carbon-Majors-Database-26913.
4. "Emissions from Oil and Gas Operations in Net Zero Transitions," *World Energy Outlook 2023*, May 2023, https://www.iea.org/reports/emissions-from-oil-and-gas-operations-in-net-zero-transitions.
5. Oxy, "Climate Report 2023: Leading the Way in Carbon Management," 2023, https://www.oxy.com/siteassets/documents/publications/oxy-climate-report-2023.pdf.
6. ExxonMobil, "Corporate Citizenship Report 2013," 2013, https://corporate.exxonmobil.com/-/media/global/files/sustainability-report/publication/2013-ccr-highlights.pdf.
7. Christopher M. Matthews, "Exxon Mobile Resists Write-Downs as Oil, Gas Prices Plummet," *The Wall Street Journal*, June 30, 2020, https://www.wsj.com/articles/exxon-mobil-resists-write-downs-as-oil-gas-prices-plummet-11593521685.
8. "*Held v. State*: Montana Court Holds That Montana Youth Can Access Equitable Relief for Climate Impacts," *Harvard Law Review* 137, no. 5 (March 2024), https://harvardlawreview.org/print/vol-137/held-v-state/.
9. Molly Quell and Raf Casert, "Verdict Saying Switzerland Violated Rights by Failing on Climate Action Could Ripple Across Europe," *AP News*, April 9, 2024, https://apnews.com/article/europe-eu-climate-court-human-rights-3b540a965aff7e2b49f1451c7a328e77.
10. Kenneth P. Vogel, "Leonard Leo Pushes the Courts Right. Now He's Aiming at American Society," *The New York Times*, October 12, 2022, https://www.nytimes.com/2022/10/12/us/politics/leonard-leo-courts-dark-money.html.
11. "Watch Leonard Leo Talk About Teneo," Vimeo video, 0:38, posted by documented.net, March 9, 2023, https://vimeo.com/806310279.
12. "Project 2025 Publishes Comprehensive Policy Guide, 'Mandate for Leadership: The Conservative Promise,'" *Project 2025*, April 21, 2023, https://www.project2025.org/news/press-releases/project-2025-publishes-comprehensive-policy-guide-mandate-for-leadership-the-conservative-promise/.
13. David Armiak, "Fossil Fuel Consultant and Leonard Leo Lieutenant Lobby ALEC Lawmakers on 'Stopping ESG,'" *Exposed by CMD*, August 2, 2023, https://www.exposedbycmd.org/2023/08/02/fossil-fuel-consultant-and-leonard-leo-lieutenant-lobby-alec-lawmakers-on-stopping-esg/.
14. There are many sources documenting the funding pipeline for these and other groups, all of which are readily found online.
15. "Recognizing the Duty of the Federal Government to Create a Green New Deal," H.Res.

109, 116th Cong., Congress.gov, February 7, 2019, https://www.congress.gov/bill/116th-congress/house-resolution/109/text.
16   Christian Spencer, "FBI Investigating 41 Cases of Eco-sabotage in Washington," *The Hill*, July 30, 2021; Dharna Noor and Aliya Uteuova, "Tens of Thousands in NYC March Against Fossil Fuels as AOC Hails Powerful Message," *The Guardian*, September 17, 2023.
17   "Funding Trends 2021: Climate Change Mitigation Philanthropy," ClimateWorks Foundation, October 7, 2021, https://www.climateworks.org/report/funding-trends-2021-climate-change-mitigation-philanthropy/; Jessica Glenza, "Overwhelming Majority of Young Americans Worry About Climate Crisis," *The Guardian*, October 17, 2024, https://www.theguardian.com/environment/2024/oct/17/young-americans-climate-change.
18   Ashley Reichheld et al., "Research: Consumers' Sustainability Demands Are Rising," September 18, 2023, https://hbr.org/2023/09/research-consumers-sustainability-demands-are-rising.
19   Kate Williams, interview by Elizabeth MacBride and Seth Levine, December 16, 2022.
20   Andy Kroll et al., "Inside the 'Private and Confidential' Conservative Group That Promises to 'Crush Liberal Dominance,'" *ProPublica*, March 9, 2023, https://www.propublica.org/article/leonard-leo-teneo-videos-documents.
21   Paul Ryan, "A Conversation with Paul Ryan, Former Speaker of the U.S. House of Representatives," interview by Kevin Kajiwara, *Teneo Insight Series*, November 30, 2023, https://www.teneo.com/insights/teneo-insights-series/a-conversation-with-paul-ryan-former-speaker-of-the-u-s-house-of-representative.

Chapter 10
1   Bethany McLean and Luigi Zinzales, "A Defense of the Neoliberal Order with Glenn Hubbard + Big Tech Antitrust Bills," podcast format audio, 52:51, July 9, 2022, https://www.capitalisnt.com/episodes/putting-the-liberal-back-in-neoliberal-with-glenn-hubbard-big-tech-antitrust-bill/transcript.
2   Manreet K. Bhullar et al., "Trends in Opioid Overdose Fatalities in Cuyahoga County, Ohio: Multi-drug Mixtures, the African-American Community and Carfentanil," *National Library of Medicine*, June 15, 2022, https://www.ncbi.nlm.nih.gov/pmc/articles/PMC9948855/#.
3   Paul A. Einsentein, "From 'Ruin Porn' to High-Tech Incubator; Ford's Michigan Central Is Helping the Automaker Reinvent Itself—and the City of Detroit," *The Detroit Bureau*, April 26, 2023, https://www.thedetroitbureau.com/2023/04/from-ruin-porn-to-high-tech-incubator-fords-michigan-central-is-helping-the-automaker-reinvent-itself-and-the-city-of-detroit/.
4   Tim Smart, "The Ten Largest Economies in the World," *U.S. News*, February 22, 2024, https://www.usnews.com/news/best-countries/articles/the-top-10-economies-in-the-world#.
5   GEM 2024/2025 Global Report, Global Entrepreneurship Monitor, accessed May 9, 2025, https://www.gemconsortium.org/file/open?fileId=51621.
6   Lane Gillespie, "Bankrate's 2024 Annual Emergency Savings Report," *Bankrate*, June 20,

2024, https://www.bankrate.com/banking/savings/emergency-savings-report/#sudden-bill.
7   Federal Reserve, "Survey of Consumer Finances (SCF)," October 18, 2023, https://www.federalreserve.gov/econres/scfindex.htm?mod=article_inline.
8   Juliana Uhuru Bidadanure, "The Political Theory of Universal Basic Income," *Annual Review of Political Science* 22 (2019): 481–501, https://doi.org/10.1146/annurev-polisci-050317-070954.
9   Dan Pilat and Dr. Sekoul Krastev, "Why Do We Mispredict How Much Our Emotions Influence Our Behavior? The Empathy Gap, Explained," *The Decision Lab*, accessed January 28, 2205, https://thedecisionlab.com/biases/empathy-gap.
10 Joseph Stiglitz, "Opinion: Time Is Up for Neoliberals," *The Washington Post*, May 13, 2024, https://www.washingtonpost.com/opinions/2024/05/13/stiglitz-captialism-economics-democracy-book/.

Chapter 11

1   "Apollo to Announce First Quarter 2025 Financial Results on May 2, 2025," Apollo Press Releases, April 2, 2025, https://www.apollo.com/insights-news/pressreleases/2025/04/apollo-to-announce-first-quarter-2025-financial-results-on-may-2-2025-3054235.
2   Sovereign Wealth Fund Institute, "Rankings by Total Managed AUM," accessed April 2024, https://www.swfinstitute.org/fund-manager-rankings/asset-manager.
3   Lisa Hall, interview by Elizabeth MacBride and Seth Levine, January 26, 2023.
4   Dean Hand et al., *GIINsight: Sizing the Impact Investing Market 2022*, The Global Impact Investing Network, October 12, 2022, https://thegiin.org/publication/research/impact-investing-market-size-2022/.
5   US SIF Foundation, *2022 Report on U.S. Sustainable Investing Trends*, December 2022, https://www.ussif.org/Files/Trends/2022/Trends%202022%20Executive%20Summary.pdf.
6   US SIF Foundation, *2022 Report*.
7   John C. Bogle, "Bogle Sounds a Warning on Index Funds," *The Wall Street Journal*, November, 29, 2018, https://www.wsj.com/articles/bogle-sounds-a-warning-on-index-funds-1543504551.
8   Lucian Bebchuk and Scott Hirst, "The Specter of the Giant Three," *Boston University Law Review* 99 (2019): 721–41.
9   Lisa Hall, interview by Elizabeth MacBride and Seth Levine, January 26, 2023.
10 Colin Marshall, interview by Seth Levine, May 2020.
11 Gallup, "What Percentage of Americans Own Stock," *The Short Answer* (blog), May 24, 2023, https://news.gallup.com/poll/266807/percentage-americans-owns-stock.aspx.
12 Gillian Tett, "The Magnificent Seven Is Not the Only Concentration America Should Worry About," *Financial Times*, January 5, 2024, https://www.ft.com/content/35ea40d1-3c83-4e9b-b202-f648a5192866.
13 Larry Fink, "Larry Fink's 2024 Annual Chairman's Letter to Investors," BlackRock, 2024, https://www.blackrock.com/corporate/investor-relations/larry-fink-annual-chairmans-letter.

14 Apollo, "Investing in Tomorrow, Today: Annual Sustainability Report, Volume 14," 2022, www.apollo.com/content/dam/apolloaem/documents/insights/apollo-2022-sustainability-report-June-19-2023.pdf.
15 Fink, "Annual Chairman's Letter."
16 Marc S. Gerber et al., "Social Responsibility and Enlightened Shareholder Primacy: Viewsfrom the Courtroom and Boardroom," Skadden, Arps, Slate, Meagher, & Flom LLP, February 4, 2019, https://www.skadden.com/insights/publications/2019/02/social-responsibility/social-responsibility-and-enlightened-shareholder#.
17 Armanino, "B Corp Certification Guide," September 13, 2022, https://www.armanino.com/articles/b-corp-certification-guide/.
18 B Lab, "Make Business a Force for Good," accessed April 2024, https://www.bcorporation.net/en-us/.
19 Andrew Kassoy, interview by Elizabeth MacBride and Seth Levine, January 25, 2023.
20 María Jesús Contreras, "OpenAI Could Be a Force for Good If It Can Address These Issues First," *The New York Times*, October 14, 2024, https://www.nytimes.com/2024/10/14/opinion/open-ai-chatgpt-investors.html.
21 Aspen Institute Forum, "An Interview with Larry Fink."
22 Keith Marzilli Ericson, "What Do Shareholders Want? Consumer Welfare and the Objective of the Firm" (Working Paper No. 32064), National Bureau of Economic Research, January 2024, https://www.nber.org/papers/w32064.

Chapter 12

1 "Our Story," Hobby Lobby Newsroom, accessed June 10, 2024, https://newsroom.hobbylobby.com/corporate-background.
2 Brian Fung and Sean Lyngaas, "CEOs of OpenAI, Google and Microsoft to Join Other Tech Leaders on Federal AI Safety Panel," *CNN Business*, April 26, 2024, https://www.cnn.com/2024/04/26/tech/openai-altman-government-ai-safety-panel/index.html#.
3 Jamie Dimon, "Chairman and CEO Letter to Shareholders," *JPMorgan Chase & Co. Annual Report 2022*, https://reports.jpmorganchase.com/investor-relations/2022/ar-ceo-letters.htm.
4 Dan Schulman, "PayPal Withdraws Plan for Charlotte Expansion," *PayPal Newsroom*, April 5, 2016, https://newsroom.paypal-corp.com/PayPal-Withdraws-Plan-for-Charlotte-Expansion.
5 Dan Schulman, interview by Elizabeth MacBride and Seth Levine, May 23, 2023.
6 Dawn Chmielewski, "The 68 Companies (Including Apple) That Are Taking North Carolina's Anti-LGBT Law to Court," *Vox*, July 8, 2016, https://www.vox.com/2016/7/8/12128698/apple-cisco-intel-salesforce-68-companies-north-carolina-anti-lgbt-law-hb2.
7 Martin Armstrong, "The Size of the Company 'Given Away' to Save the Planet," *Statista*, September 15, 2022, https://www.statista.com/chart/28257/patagonia-inc-revenue-company-db/.

Chapter 13

1. John Buckman, "Westinghouse's Steve Tritch Talks About the Company's Latest Moves," *Pittsburgh Quarterly*, May 6, 2007, https://pittsburghquarterly.com/articles/westinghouse-ceo-steve-tritch/.
2. Ben Buchanan, *The Hacker and the State: Cyber Attacks and the New Normal of Geopolitics* (Harvard University Press, 2020).
3. "About George Westinghouse," Library of Congress Digital Collections, https://www.loc.gov/collections/films-of-westinghouse-works-1904/articles-and-essays/the-westinghouse-world/about-george-westinghouse; "Unleashing the Power of Human Ingenuity," Westinghouse, accessed January 28, 2025, https://www.westinghousenuclear.com/about.
4. Council on Foreign Relations, "What Happened When China Joined the WTO?" February 6, 2025, https://world101.cfr.org/global-era-issues/trade/what-happened-when-china-joined-wto.
5. Buchanan, *Hacker and the State*.
6. Zeyi Yang, "How China Takes Extreme Measures to Keep Teens Off TikTok," *MIT Technology Review*, March 8, 2023, https://www.technologyreview.com/2023/03/08/1069527/china-tiktok-douyin-teens-privacy/.
7. American Chamber of Commerce in the People's Republic of China, "2022 American Business in China Paper," 2022, https://www.amchamchina.org/wp-content/uploads/2022/05/WP2022-Final.pdf.
8. Ruchir Sharma, "Where Capitalism Is Working," *Foreign Affairs*, September 17, 2024, https://www.foreignaffairs.com/united-states/capitalism-switzerland-taiwan-vietnam.
9. Sharma, "Where Capitalism Is Working."
10. Congressional Budget Office, "An Update to the Budget and Economic Outlook," June 18, 2024, https://www.cbo.gov/publication/60039; Peter G. Peterson Foundation, "What Are Interest Costs On The National Debt?," last updated March 25, 2024, https://www.pgpf.org/budget-basics/what-are-interest-costs-on-the-national-debt.

Chapter 14

1. Rick Plympton and Mike Mandina, series of interviews by Elizabeth MacBride, June 2023.
2. Statista, "Apple's Number of Employees in the Fiscal Years 2005–2023," Statista, https://www.statista.com/statistics/273439/number-of-employees-of-apple-since-2005/.
3. Federal Reserve Bank of St. Louis, "Corporate Profits Versus Labor Income," August 9, 2018, https://fredblog.stlouisfed.org/2018/08/corporate-profits-versus-labor-income/.
4. Peter Stavros, interview by Elizabeth MacBride and Seth Levine, October 17, 2023.
5. Claudia Zeisberger and Jean Wee, "KKR and CHI Overhead Doors (A): Sharing Profits Fairly Through Broad Equity Ownership," Insead Publishing, March 8, 2023, https://publishing.insead.edu/case/kkr-chi.
6. Alex Koller, "Mark Cuban Turned 91% of His Employees into Millionaires When He Sold a Company for $5.7 Billion," CNBC, June 7, 2024, https://www.cnbc.com/2024/06/07/mark-cuban-how-i-turned-most-of-my-companys-employees-into-millionaires.html.
7. Joseph Blasi and Douglas Kruse, "Employee Ownership and ESOPs: What We Know

from Recent Research," Rutgers School of Management and Labor Relations, April 2024, https://smlr.rutgers.edu/sites/default/files/Documents/Centers/Institute_Employee_Ownership/ResearchBriefs/APRIL2024_RB_Employee_Ownership_ESOPs_What_We_Know_Recent_Research.pdf.

8   National Center for Employee Ownership, "Employee Stock Ownership Plan (ESOP) Facts," accessed June 12, 2024, https://www.esop.org/.
9   Elie Alhajjar et al., "Leading with Artificial Intelligence," RAND, October 2024, https://www.rand.org/content/dam/rand/pubs/perspectives/PEA3400/PEA3414-1/RAND_PEA3414-1.pdf.
10 Jennifer Tonti, "ANNUAL SURVEY: In an Unstable Economic Environment, Wages Are More Important Than Ever to the American Public," Just Capital, September 15, 2022, https://justcapital.com/reports/2022-survey-workers-and-wages-are-more-important-than-ever-to-the-american-public/.
11 International Brotherhood of Teamsters, "Teamsters Ratify Historic UPS Contract" (press release), August 8, 2023, https://teamster.org/2023/08/teamsters-ratify-historic-ups-contract/.
12 Ashley Reichheld et al., "Research: Consumer Sustainability Demands Are Rising," *Harvard Business Review*, September 18, 2023, https://hbr.org/2023/09/research-consumers-sustainability-demands-are-rising.

Chapter 15

1   *America's Burning*, directed by David M. Smick (Ian Michaels, 2024), movie.
2   *America's Burning*.
3   Chris Edwards, "Entrepreneurs and Regulations: Removing State and Local Barriers to New Businesses," CATO Institute, May 5, 2021, https://www.cato.org/policy-analysis/entrepreneurs-regulations-removing-state-local-barriers-new-businesses#regulations-businesses.
4   Congressional Research Service, "A Visual Depiction of the Shift from Defined Benefit (DB) to Defined Contribution (DC) Pension Plans in the Private Sector," December 27, 2021, https://www.congress.gov/crs-product/IF12007; US Government Accountability Office, "Growing Disparities in Retirement Account Savings," August 24, 2023, https://www.gao.gov/blog/growing-disparities-retirement-account-savings#.
5   John Sabelhaus, "The Current State of U.S. Workplace Retirement Plan Coverage," *Scholarly Commons*, March 1, 2022, https://repository.upenn.edu/prc_papers/726/.
6   Shlomo Benartzi and Richard Thaler, "Heuristics and Biases in Retirement Savings Behavior," *Journal of Economic Perspectives* 21, no. 3 (Summer 2007): 81–104, https://www.aeaweb.org/articles?id=10.1257/jep.21.3.81.
7   Statista, "Number of Births in the United States from 1990 to 2022," Statista, September 5, 2024, https://www.statista.com/statistics/195908/number-of-births-in-the-united-states-since-1990/.
8   "China Is Building Nuclear Reactors Faster Than Any Other Country," *The Economist*, November 30, 2023, https://www.economist.com/china/2023/11/30/china-is-building-nuclear-reactors-faster-than-any-other-country.

9. Angela Dewan et al., "New-Wave Reactor Technology Could Kick-Start a Nuclear Renaissance—and the U.S. Is Banking on it," *CNN*, April 26, 2024, https://www.cnn.com/2024/02/01/climate/nuclear-small-modular-reactors-us-russia-china-climate-solution-intl/index.html.
10. Brian Potter, "Why Does Nuclear Power Plant Construction Cost So Much?," IFP, May 1, 2023, https://ifp.org/nuclear-power-plant-construction-costs/.
11. Antoine Rostand, "Trust in Voluntary Carbon Markets Has Been Consistently Low: What Needs to Change?" World Economic Forum, June 12, 2024, https://www.weforum.org/agenda/2024/06/building-trust-in-carbon-markets/.
12. L.E.K. Consulting, *Putting Sustainability at the Heart of Strategy: L.E.K. Corporate Sustainability Survey*, 2022, https://www.lek.com/sites/default/files/PDFs/LEK-global-corporate-sustainability-survey.pdf.
13. Joseph Blasi and Douglas Kruse, "Employee Ownership and ESOPs," Aspen Institute, April 2024, https://www.aspeninstitute.org/wp-content/uploads/2024/04/Employee-Ownership-and-ESOPs-What-We-Know-from-Recent-Research-1.pdf.
14. Gaurav Chiplunkar and Pinelopi K. Goldberg, "Aggregate Implications of Barriers to Female Entrepreneurship" (Working Paper 28468), National Bureau of Economic Research, July 2024, https://www.nber.org/system/files/working_papers/w28486/w28486.pdf.
15. Judy Samuelson and Miguel Padró, eds., *A Seat at the Table: Worker Voice and the New Corporate Boardroom*, Aspen Institute, August 23, 2021, https://www.aspeninstitute.org/wp-content/uploads/2021/08/Final-Worker-Voice-and-the-Corporate-Boardroom.pdf.
16. Simon Jager et al., "Labor in the Boardroom" (Working Paper No. 26519), National Bureau of Economic Research, August 2020, https://www.nber.org/papers/w26519.

Chapter 16

1. "Davos 2024: Special Address by Javier Milei, President of Argentina," World Economic Forum, January 18, 2024, https://www.weforum.org/agenda/2024/01/special-address-by-javier-milei-president-of-argentina/.
2. Dick Parsons, interview by Elizabeth MacBride and Seth Levine, June 22, 2023.
3. Jamie Dimon, interview by Elizabeth MacBride and Seth Levine, March 21, 2023.
4. Greg Curtis, interview by Elizabeth MacBride and Seth Levine, January 13, 2023.

INDEX

A
ability to scale, 118
Accenture, 121
Advanced Research Projects Agency, 66
Affordable Care Act, 186–187
Agricultural Adjustment Act, 107
agricultural industry, 154
allocation of talent, 127
Alphabet, 179
Altman, Sam, 159
Amazon, 179
American Airlines, 185
American exceptionalism, 118
Anthropic Corporation, 174
anti-apartheid movement, 55
anti-woke movement, 138
Apollo Global Management, 115, 125, 163–164, 165, 170
Apple, 179, 185, 205–206, 210
APT1, 191
Argentina, 233
artificial intelligence (AI), 80–81, 148–149, 174, 180, 199, 211–213
Aspen Ideas Festival, 43–44, 124

asset bubble, 125
asset managers, 165–166, 167
assets, private control of, 59–60
automation, 157, 159, 211–212
automobile industry, 65, 107, 135, 152
Aveda, 173

B
B Certification movement, 173
B Corporation movement, 172–174
B Lab, 173
baby bond, 221–222
Baehr, Evan, 144
Bank of America, 121
banking, 14, 122
Barra, Mary, 16–17
Bears Ears National Monument, 186
Bell Labs, 154
Ben and Jerry's, 119
benefit corporations, 172–173
Bill of Rights, 190
Black Americans, 3, 93–94, 96, 103, 108
BlackRock, 43, 45–46, 55, 113, 124, 165, 166, 170

Blyth, Mark, 107–108
Bogle, Jack, 63, 165, 221
Boxed Water, 70, 71
British Petroleum, 109, 134
Broadcast.com, 210
Brookings Institution, 106
Budweiser, 52–53
Buffett, Warren, 45, 134, 183
Business Roundtable (BRT), 14, 15, 16, 17, 19–20, 33, 38, 117
businesses/companies
    benefit corporations and, 172–173
    change in, 10, 19, 35, 112–113
    customer-owned structure of, 63–64
    deaths and rebirths in, 206
    distractions of, 33–34
    domination of, 15
    economic power of, 179
    erosion of trust in, 243
    externalities of, 55, 74–75
    government partnership with, 152
    greed in, 62–63
    licensing requirements for, 218–219
    long-term effects of decisions of, 44
    long-term sustainability of, 34–35
    lower barriers to starting, 218–219
    optimism of, 152
    as political, 44
    politicization of, 47, 54, 181
    profit investing by, 122–124
    public opinion of, 66
    public *versus* private, 51
    purpose in, 45–46
    reciprocity of, 219
    regulatory burdens of, 218–219
    responsibilities of, 28, 244
    shareholder primacy and, 16–17, 19
    short-term decision-making by, 34
    society role of, 43
    transparency, accountability, and reporting of, 55, 170
    values-driven approach by, 41, 116
    See also corporations

C

California, 47
cap and trade, 132
capital, 9–10, 23, 72, 73, 77–78
capitalism
    access to information in, 241
    assumptions of, 20
    changing of, 6–8
    communism as compared to, 1
    critiques of, 72–74
    defining, 58, 60, 107
    as exploitative, 69–83
    forms of, 6
    information availability in, 243
    measure of success in, 17–21
    people's implementation of, 116
    perversion of, 204
    pillars of, 59–61, 241
    as political bargain, 58–59, 60, 148
    private control of assets in, 59–60
    public opinion of, 2
    refresh of, 81–83
    rule of law in, 241
    selfishness in, 61–62
    shared commitment in, 243
    socialism as compared to, 73–74
    success in, 197–198
    truth in, 243
    See also Golden Age of capitalism; *specific types*
Capitalism and the State (CATS) course, 57–58, 59
capitalists, creating more, 218–223
carbon capture, 134
carbon credits, 132, 225
carbon frameworks, 225–226
care economy, 228–229
Carnegie Mellon University, 152
Case, Anne, 92
Cathy, Dan, 51
Cathy, S. Truett, 51
censorship, 95

Index

CEOs
    challenges of, 50
    compensation of, 5, 34
    as employee of owners of the business, 27
    engaging in political speech by, 184–185
    on front lines, 26
    function of, 17
    leadership model for, 235
    as long-term stewards, 20–21
    responsibilities of, 27
    on social media, 182
    threats against, 184–185
    values-based leadership of, 182–183
    vocality of values of, 181–182
    as weaponized, 54
Ceres, 134
Chapek, Bob, 48, 49
Chernow, Ron, 105–106
Chevron, 109, 134
CHI Overhead Doors, 209
Chick-fil-A, 50–53, 178
China, 148–149, 155, 165, 191–192, 193, 194–195, 196, 224
Chouinard, Yvon, 177, 187–188
CIRCOR International, 209
Citibank, 235
Citigroup, 121
Citizens United v. Federal Election Commission, 181
Civil Rights Movement, 32, 67
Civil War, 102–103
class, 88, 89–94. *See also* middle class
Clean Air Act, 130
Clean Water Act, 130
climate crisis
    capitalism as enemy of, 142–143
    change in, 112–113
    consumer power in, 140–142
    denial of, 137–139
    extremism in, 140
    fallacy in, 142–143
    fossil fuels and, 101, 108
    globalization and, 196
    government and, 131–132, 135, 136–137, 189
    greenwashing and, 141–142
    individual action *versus* collectivism in, 132
    as investment risk, 169
    liberals in, 140
    oil and gas industries and, 133–134
    overview of, 129–133
    public opinion regarding, 140
    shared future in, 143–144
Clinton, Hillary, 89, 91
coalitions, 107–108, 126–127, 130, 137
collective power, 110–112
collectivism, 29, 233
color blindness, 94–95, 96–97
communication systems, 103
communism, 1, 67, 72, 73, 195–196
Communist Revolution, 111
communities, 122–124, 132–133, 157
Community Redevelopment Act (CRA), 122
companies. *See* businesses/companies
compensation, 5, 25–26, 34, 39–41, 65, 206–207, 209, 210–211
competition, 17, 31, 40–41, 81–82, 148, 186–188, 192
compound interest, 221
computer revolution, 237
Coney Island, 123
ConocoPhilips, 92
conscription, 30
consensus-building, 107
Consumers' Research, 139
consumers/consumption, 78, 80, 118, 124, 140–142, 214–215
corporations
    assumptions of, 20
    benefit, 172–173
    boards of, 172, 229–230
    centrality of, 31
    change in, 35

distractions of, 33–34
importance of, 179
influence of, 14–15
interests of, 46–47
lack of accountability of, 178–179
long-term sustainability of, 34–35
Milton Friedman's viewpoint of, 31–32
multinational, 180
power check of, 237
purpose of, 15–17
rethinking role of, 121
as shaped by leadership in, 182
shareholder primacy and, 16
short-term decision-making by, 34
social responsibility of, 32, 52
values of, 181–183
See also businesses/companies
Cotopaxi, 70
COVID-19 pandemic, 154–155, 158, 219
credit card debt, 79–80
Cuban, Mark, 210
culture wars, 144
Curtis, Greg, 235–236
customer-owned structure, 63–64

D

Danone, 173
data, role of, in Dynamic Capitalism, 237–238
data science, 110–111
Deaton, Angus, 92
debt, 78–80, 198–199
decision-making, human emotions in, 116
defense, United States, 197–198
defined benefit plans, 219–220
defined contribution plans, 220
deindustrialization, 237
Delaware, 171–172
Delaware Money School, 223
Department of Defense, 154
Department of Energy, 135, 138
Department of Homeland Security, 180
DeSantis, Ron, 48–49

Detroit, Michigan, 152
Dime Savings Bank, 122–123
Dimon, Jamie, 13–14, 15–17, 20, 45, 54, 178, 183–184, 235, 244
displacement, job, 211–213
diversification, 126–127
diversity, in values-driven approach to business, 126
Dochuk, Darren, 101, 109
"Don't Say Gay" bill, 48, 49, 50, 185
Dow Jones Industrial Average, 36
Dynamic Capitalism
backlash against, 113
benefit corporations and, 173
capital and labor balance in, 158
characteristics of, 232
complications of, 232
data role in, 237–238
decision-making in, 239–240
defined, 7, 231
diversity and, 126
emergence of, 231
energy alternatives in, 224–225
engagement in, 75
Environmental, Social, and Governance (ESG) movement and, 124
environmental protections in, 223–226
flexible thinking in, 238
fossil fuels and, 127–128
founding principle of, 158
free markets in, 117, 190, 192
freedom in, 239–240
government role in, 148, 158, 232, 236–237
imperative of, 198–199
individual power in, 204–205
information role in, 237–238
innovation in, 238
leadership through action in, 234–239
legal and tax incentives in, 208
market-based systems in, 15
measurable outcomes of, 189

middle class in, 199–200
myths of, 118–119, 124, 126
need for, 21–23
neoliberal capitalism as compared to, 116
power shifting in, 217
reconsideration of beliefs in, 238
reframing labor in, 215
rewards of, 8, 236–237
safety net in, 156–157, 158
short-term to long-term mindset shift in, 235
social entrepreneurship and, 118–119
US policy toward, 194
values *versus* politics in, 236–237
wealth sharing in, 213
woke capitalism and, 128
dynamism/dynamic economies, 18

E

Eastman, George, 104
economic diplomacy, 153–155
economic growth, inclusion and, 126–127
economic mobility, 218–223
economic pragmatists, 116–117
economy of the United States
allocation of talent in, 126
businesses as actors in, 7
decline of dominance in, 18
dominance of, 153–154
foundational norms of, 242–243
GDP of, 65, 155, 194–195
in Golden Age of capitalism, 65–67, 102
hidden pain in, 3–6
insecurities in, 5
as meritocracy, 89–91
middle class in, 77
personal consumption in, 78
questioning of, 2
rule of law and, 242–243
statistics of, 18, 218
success of, 2
unease regarding, 80

Edison, Thomas, 36
education, 4, 18, 48, 49, 50, 66, 78, 89
Eisenhower administration, 106
Elaine Massacre, 103
elites, 103, 111
Emerson, Jed, 121
emotions, in decision-making, 116
empathy/empathy gap, 116, 160–161
employee ownership approach, 204, 208, 210, 211, 213–215, 226–230
Employee Ownership Trust (EOT), 204, 210–211, 227
Employee Retirement Income Security Act, 168, 227
Employee Stock Ownership Plans (ESOPs), 204, 210–211, 226–227
employees, as competitive advantage, 40–41
energy, 129, 134, 169, 181, 199. *See also* fossil fuels; *specific industries*
Engels, Friedrich, 72
entitlement programs, 232–233
entrepreneurship, 118, 119–122, 155–156, 157
environment, 61, 70–71, 72, 75, 108, 130, 223–226. *See also* climate crisis
Environmental, Social, and Governance (ESG) movement, 55, 124, 125, 139, 164, 166–167, 175
Environmental Protection Agency, 138
Erickson, Keith Marzilli, 176
Etsy, 119
European Court of Human Rights, 136–137
European Union, 148–149, 175
exceptionalism, 118
executives, 27, 28, 34, 54, 179, 209. *See also* CEOs
exploitation, in capitalism, 69–83
externalities, 55, 74–75, 82
ExxonMobil, 109, 134–135

F

Facebook, 180, 210
failure, 155–156

Fair Labor Standards Act of 1938, 65
Fairchild Semiconductor, 154, 210
Family and Medical Leave Act, 228
Federal Reserve, 158, 207, 243
Federalist Society, 138, 143
feminism, 33
fiduciary standard, 172
financial literacy, expanding, 222–223
financial sector, importance of, 165
Fink, Larry, 43–44, 45–46, 55, 124, 125, 166, 169, 170, 175
First Amendment, 181, 187
Florida, 48, 185
Floyd, George, 48
Folsom, Marion, 104–106, 111
Ford Foundation, 121
Ford Motor Company, 152
Fortifi, 209
fossil fuels
   American dominance in, 199
   capitalism of, 143
   in climate crisis, 101, 112–113, 133
   climate crisis and, 108
   in Golden Age of capitalism, 100
   neoliberal capitalism and, 127–128
   in social compact, 110
   woke capitalism and, 46
France, 18
Francis (pope), 159
Franklin, Ben, 221
free markets
   challenges to, 61
   competition in, 148, 192
   doctrine of, 108
   in Dynamic Capitalism, 117, 190, 192
   in dynamic economies, 18
   importance of, 190, 238
   innovation and, 193
   interference in, 139
   leveraging of, 117
   limitations of, 82
   self-interest and, 62
   as unfettered, 151, 192
   See also markets
Free to Choose (Friedman), 34
free trade, 193–194
freedom, 161, 239–240
freedom of speech, 152
Friedman, Milton
   background of, 28–29
   doctrine of, 27–28
   economic conditions during time of, 31
   embrace of, 110
   in historical context, 28–32
   influence of, 6, 26, 67
   influences to, 38
   meaning of, 38–39
   public opinion of, 27
   on self-interest, 62
   on shareholding, 168
   on universal basic income (UBI), 160
   writings of, 30
Friedman Doctrine, 34, 35–38, 39, 41
Friedman-style economics, 6, 26, 74
front lines, 26

G

gains, distribution of, 73
gas industry, 133–134, 181
Gay, Edwin, 77
Gen Z, 214–215
General Electric, 35–38
General Motors, 107
Germany, 18, 29
GI Bill, 66
Global Entrepreneurship Monitor, 155–156
Global Reporting Initiative, 55
globalization, 17, 157, 180, 192
Golden Age of capitalism, 65–67, 99, 100, 101–102, 103, 104–106, 107–108, 109–110, 112
Goldman Sachs, 125
Goodwill, 119
Google, 179, 180

government(s)
  business partnership with, 152
  climate crisis and, 131–132, 135, 136–137
  concerns regarding, 75
  consistent frameworks of, 162
  debt of, 198–199
  declining power of, 179–181
  in Dynamic Capitalism, 148, 158, 232, 236–237
  as the enemy, 150
  enforcement by, 150
  failure of, 189
  finding balance in, 162
  as forced to act, 136–137
  in Golden Age of capitalism, 65–67
  inflation role of, 61
  innovative technology investments of, 154–155
  lack of trust in, 182
  limits of, 8
  Milton Friedman's viewpoint of, 31
  monopoly policing by, 20
  in neoliberal capitalism, 139, 143, 147, 155, 237
  as partner, 150–153
  in political bargain, 148
  as the problem, 81, 150
  public opinion of, 66
  regulatory capture by, 149
  in socialism, 73
  societal engagement of, 66–67
  spending by, 198
  trust in, 66, 67
  as unfriendly, 150
Grand Staircase–Escalante National Monument, 186
Grant, Adam, 95
Great Depression, 105, 110, 132–133
greed, 62–63, 118
Green, David and Barbara, 177, 186–187
Green New Deal, 47, 140
greenhouse gas emissions, 131, 133

Greenspan, Alan, 83
greenwashing, 121, 141–142

H
Hall, Lisa Green, 115–116, 125, 163–164, 166, 170
Hallmark, 211
Hamm, Harold, 17
happiness, 92
Harvard Business School (HBS), 57–58
Hayek, Friedrich, 29
Hazelwood, Pennsylvania, 92
Hazelwood Coke Works, 92
Head Start, 66
healthcare, 40, 156–157
Heartland Institute, 46, 139
Heintz, Stephen, 128
Helena, Arkansas, 92
Heritage Foundation, 139
Hewlett-Packard, 121
Hobby Lobby, 177, 186–187
Hori, Kenichi, 130–131
House Bill 2 (HB2) (North Carolina), 184–185
housing, 80
Hubbard, Glenn, 151
Hughes, Coleman, 94–97
human capital, 77–78
hunting, 130

I
IBM, 185
identity, weaponizing of, 96
identity politics, 129–130, 144
Iger, Bob, 48
immigration, 103
impact investing, 125, 164–165, 171–174
Imprint Capital, 125
incarceration, 93
inclusion, economic growth and, 126–127
inclusivity, 184
index funds, 168
India, 193, 197

individual freedom, 29, 110
individual power, 110–112
individual retirement accounts (IRAs), 168
industrial policy, 148–150
Industrial Revolution, 100, 102, 106, 213
inequality, 5, 18, 77, 78
inflation, 30, 61, 233
information, 237–238, 241, 244
information ecosystem, 4–5
Ingersoll Rand, 209
innovation, 72, 152, 154–155, 206, 238, 244
Innovation District (Pittsburgh), 152–153
Instagram, 182
Institute for Government Research, 106
institutions, loss of trust in, 103
Intel Corporation, 121, 210
interest rates, 80
intermediaries, for fund management, 166
International Labour Organization, 228
internet revolution, 237
Interstate Highway System, 65
investing, 63–64, 222
Investment Advisers Act of 1940, 172
Investor Choice initiative, 170–171

J

Japan, 18, 153, 195–196, 228
Jensen, Michael, 33–34
job disruption, 211–213
John (king), 242
Jones, Paul Tudor, II, 121
JPMorgan Chase, 13–14, 15–16, 178, 183–184, 236
Jumpstart Our Business Startups (JOBS) Act, 222
Just Capital, 121–122, 213
just in time manufacturing, 154–155

K

Kassoy, Andrew, 173
Kennedy, John F., 33
Kennedy, Robert, 33
Keynes, John Maynard, 30

kinetic war, 195
King, Martin Luther, Jr., 33, 95, 160
Kiva, 119
Koch brothers, 109
Kodak, 104–105, 203, 205–206, 212–213
Kohlberg Kravis Roberts (KKR), 120, 208–210, 226

L

labor, 9–10, 65, 103, 104, 215
labor activism, 214
labor unions, 104–105
labor-to-capital pathway, 210
layoffs, 104
leadership, 178–179, 234–239. See also CEOs; executives
Leo, Leonard, 137–138, 139, 143
LGBTQ+ rights, 48, 51, 52–53, 181
libertarian view, 161
Licklider, J. C. R., 66
life expectancy, 3, 91–94
lobbying, 138
London, England, 75
long-term thinking/decision-making, 124–126, 131
low-income neighborhoods, 122
Ludlow Massacre, 103, 105–106

M

machine learning, 211–212
Magna Carta, 242
Mandina, Mike, 203, 208, 232
manufacturing industry, 89, 93, 107, 151–152, 154, 157, 192
market data, dependence on, 25–26
market-based systems, in Dynamic Capitalism, 15
markets, 58, 60, 61, 82, 102, 243. See also free markets
Marx, Karl, 72, 76–77
mass media, 103, 182, 194
McConnell, Mitch, 54
Me to We, 119

Meckling, William, 33–34
Medicare, 33, 65
meritocracy, 89–91
Michigan Central Station, 152
Microsoft, 180, 185, 210
middle class
    capital evolution and, 78–81
    characteristics of, 90
    as consumers, 78
    deaths of despair in, 92
    debt of, 78–80
    decline of, 90
    defined, 90
    development of, 108
    in Dynamic Capitalism, 199–200
    failures of, 156
    happiness and, 92
    investing in, 199–200
    manufacturing industry and, 89
    mechanisms of wealth sharing and, 205–211
    problems of, 90
    refocusing on, 97–98
    as resource, 77
    savings of, 156
    statistics of, 78, 79
    strength of economy and, 90
    suicide and, 92
    sustainable economic growth of, 232
Middle East, 165
Milei, Javier, 233
Millennials, 214–215
Minnesota Rubber and Plastics, 209
misinformation, on social media, 192–193
mission, into profit making, 120
Mitsui, 130
Monbiot, George, 81
monetary theory, 30
money managers, 167
Mont Pelerin Society, 29–30
Montana, 136
Musk, Elon, 150, 158, 180
mutual funds, 63

N

NASA, 203
Nathan Cummings Foundation, 121
National Association of Manufacturers, 33
National Bureau of Economic Research, 176
National Socialism, 29
nation-states, defining, 195
NBA, 185
NCAA, 185
neoliberal capitalism/neoliberalism
    competition in, 81–82
    defined, 6, 28
    Donald Trump and, 7, 22
    Dynamic Capitalism as compared to, 116
    embrace of, 81
    empathy gap of, 161
    end of, 7, 22
    fallacies of, 153, 240
    fossil fuels and, 127–128
    foundation of, 112
    government limitations in, 139, 143, 147, 155, 237
    lack of agency in, 240
    middle class and, 77
    origin of, 139
    overly simplified "beauty" of, 32–35
    personal responsibility in, 157
    public opinion of, 34
    reconsideration in, 60
    rigidity of, 116
    rise of, 110
    shareholder role in, 204–205
    Silicon Valley entrepreneurship and, 118
Nespresso, 173
net disposable income (NDI), 39–40
New Civil Liberties Alliance, 144
The New York Times (newspaper), 27
newspapers, influence of, 103
Nixon, Richard, 33, 67
North Carolina, 184–185

nuclear energy, 191–192, 224–225
Nvidia, 179

O
Occidental Petroleum, 133–134
O'Connor, Sandra Day, 127
oil industry, 100–101, 102, 106, 109–110, 127, 133–134, 139, 181
1% for the Planet, 70–71, 141
OpenAI, 174, 180
opioid epidemic, 92–93, 151
Optimax, 203–205, 206, 210–211, 213
Oracle, 210
Ostrom, Elinor, 132
ownership, ownership economy, 204, 208, 210, 211, 213–215, 226–230

P
Parental Rights in Education Act, 48, 49, 50
Paris Climate Accords, 134
Parsons, Dick, 122–124, 235
Patagonia, 70, 119, 173, 177, 186, 187–188, 236
PayPal, 25–26, 39–41, 113, 156, 184–185
Pearlstein, Steve, 15
people of color, 126, 229–230. *See also* Black Americans
Peto, John, 140
Pew brothers, 102, 109
Pigou, Arthur Cecil, 74–75, 77, 132
Piketty, Thomas, 73
Pillsbury, 211
Pittsburgh, Pennsylvania, 152–153
pluralistic society, 190
Plympton, Rick, 203–204, 208, 232
policies, 94, 217
political bargain, 58–59, 60, 148, 161–162
politics, 54, 178, 182–183, 236–237
populism, 5
poverty, reduction of, 1
Powell, Lewis F., Jr., 33
power, 20, 110–112, 165
profit-making potential, 118

profits
  automation and, 80–81
  in capitalism, 58
  carbon-intensive industries and, 112
  community investment of, 122–124
  compensation growth and, 206–207
  consequences of focus on, 36–37
  corporation role regarding, 16
  as distraction, 33–34
  distribution of, 204, 205, 226–227
  impact and, 122, 125
  investment of, 123
  middle class and, 77
  mission into, 120–121
  purpose and, 32, 41, 45, 58, 118–119, 130–131, 188–190
  short-term, 15, 19, 76, 130, 187–188
  of Target, 53
  values tradeoff with, 178, 188–190, 235–236
  wealth sharing and, 205–211
progress, balance in, 98
Progressive Movement, 103, 104
Project 2025, 138
property, 59–60
ProPublica, 143
Protestantism, 139
public health systems, 103
public markets, information availability in, 243. *See also* markets
public-private partnerships, 152–153
Publix, 214–215
purpose, 15–17, 32, 41, 45–46, 58, 118–119, 122–124, 130–131, 188–190

Q
quantum computing, 149–150

R
race, 94–95, 96
racism, 95, 122
radio, 103
Ramaswamy, Vivek, 166

Index

Rand, Ayn, 82–83, 150
RAND Corporation, 211
Reagan, Ronald, 6, 28, 30, 67, 81, 110, 118, 150, 195–196, 218
regulation, industrial policy and, 148–150
regulatory capture, 149
Reichheld, Ashley, 140
Reiman, Sam, 87–88, 96
relationships, insularity of, 4
Religious Freedom Restoration Act, 187
renewable energy, 134
reporting, goals of, 55
Republican Party, 4
Restaurant Revitalization program, 94
retirement savings, 219–220
retraining, 151–152, 212, 237
Richard King Mellon Foundation, 87
risk-taking, 155–156, 157, 184–185, 210
Ritthaler, Cory, 140
Roaring Twenties, 101–102
Robert Wood Johnson Foundation, 121
Roberts, George, 120, 121, 208
Roberts Enterprise Development Fund (REDF), 120
Robinhood, 169
Rochester Plan, 104–106
Rockefeller, John D., Jr., 103, 105–106, 109
Rockefeller, John D., Sr., 102
Rockefeller, Justin, 128
Rockefeller Brothers Fund, 127–128
Rockefeller Foundation, 106, 127, 128
Room and Board, 173
Roosevelt, Franklin D., 106
Rouen, Ethan, 57
routine cognitive component, 211
Rowan, Marc, 170, 171
Royal Dutch Shell, 134
rule of law, 241, 242
rules, focus on, 97–98
Russia, 29, 192–193, 194
Ryan, Paul, 83, 144

S

S. C. Johnson, 211
safety nets, rethinking, 155–158
San Pellegrino, 173
savings, statistics of, 156
Scaife, Richard Mellon, 34
Schulman, Dan, 25–26, 39–41, 156, 184–185, 232
Schwab, 124
Scott, Bruce R., 58, 60
Sears, 211
Securities and Exchange Commission, 37, 175, 243
self-absolution, 103
self-interest, 62, 72
selfishness, in capitalism, 61–62
semiconductor technologies, 154
shareholders/shareholder primacy
    assumptions of, 20
    as consumers, 175–176
    creating value for, 172
    defined, 16
    everyone as, 168–169
    influence of, 16–17
    limitations of, 116
    maximizing, 27
    minority, 170
    in neoliberal capitalism, 204–205
    responsibility in, 19
    serving, 43
    short-term happiness of, 35
    success in, 117–118
Sharma, Ruchir, 197
Shell New Energies, 134
short-term thinking/decision-making, 34–38, 74–75, 76–77, 131
Silicon Valley, 66, 118, 143–144, 159, 195–196
Singapore, 165
Skadden, Arps, Slate, Meagher & Flom LLP and Affiliates, 171–172
skills, labor market, 20
Smith, Adam, 61–62, 82

social entrepreneurship, 118, 119
social good, 124–125
social media, 182, 192–193
social responsibility, 32, 52
Social Security, 65, 106, 107
socialism, 72–74, 233
Socially Responsible Investing (SRI), 55
Spanish flu pandemic, 102
Spar, Debora, 57–58
Sputnik, 194
stakeholder capitalism, 44
stakeholders, 43, 172
Standard Oil, 109
Starlink, 180
State Street Global Advisors, 166
state-sponsored retirement plans, 220
Stavros, Pete, 208–210
steel industry, 107
Stern, Andrew, 159
Stiglitz, Joseph, 82, 161
stock markets, 102, 168–169, 204, 210, 211.
  See also markets
Strine, Leo E., Jr., 171–172
success, 7, 9, 17–21, 117–119, 156, 235, 243
suicide, 92
Summers, Larry, 38
supply-side economics, 30
sustainability, 141
Sustainable Investment Forum, 164
sustainable investment strategies, 164
Sweden, 18, 179
Switzerland, 137, 179, 197

T
Taiwan, 197
Target, 53
tariffs, 144
tax policy, 207–208
taxation, 108
Tea Party, 83
Teamsters, 214

technologies/technology sector
  artificial intelligence (AI) as, 80–81,
    148–149
  in China, 165
  government challenges with, 189
  influence of, 20
  open-armed approach to, 193
  power dynamic in, 180
  quantum computing as, 149–150
  regulatory frameworks of, 181
  risk-taking in, 210
  semiconductor, 154
  stock options in, 210
  universal basic income (UBI) and, 159
TED, 95–96
Teneo Network, 138, 139, 143
Tesla, 135
Thaler, Richard, 220
Thatcher, Margaret, 28, 30, 67
Thiel, Peter, 144
TikTok, 180, 193
Tillerson, Rex, 83
Time Warner, 123, 235
Toms, 120
Toshiba Corporation, 191–192
Total Energy, 134
trade, barriers to, 194
trade-offs, 161–162
Tragedy of the Commons, 132
transparency, goals of, 55
Treaty of Detroit, 107
Tritch, Steve, 191–192
Trump, Donald
  Ayn Rand and, 83
  campaign of, 89–90
  election of, 1–2, 7, 89–90, 139
  influence of, 7
  neoliberalism and, 7, 22
  populism of, 5
  Project 2025 and, 138
  protectionist stance of, 194
  symbolism of, 7
  travel ban of, 48

truth, in capitalism, 243
Tuan, Melinda, 120
Turchin, Peter, 111

U

underwriters, 47
unemployment, 30, 105, 158
Unilever, 119, 173
unions, 104–105
Unite the Right rally, 90–91
United Auto Workers, 107
United Kingdom, 204
United Nations Global Compact, 55
universal basic income (UBI), 158–160
University of Chicago, 29
University of Pittsburgh Medical Center, 152
US Chamber of Commerce, 33, 195
US Constitution, 181, 187, 190, 242
US Social Investment Forum Foundation, 55
US Steel, 211
USSR, 153, 195–196

V

values
    competing, 186–188
    as conflated, 54
    corporate, 181–183
    freedom in, 239–240
    politics and, 178, 182–183, 236–237
    profits tradeoff with, 178, 188–190, 235–236
    of public companies, 178
    See also specific companies
values-based leadership, 182–183
values-driven approach to business, 41, 125, 126, 131, 236
Vance, JD, 144
Vanguard, 62–64, 124, 165, 166, 170–171

Vietnam, 197
Vietnam War, 33, 67
von Mises, Ludwig, 29

W

wages. *See* compensation
Walmart, 179
Walt Disney Company, 47–50, 185
Warby Parker, 120
Washington Consensus, 6, 194
The Washington Post (newspaper), 15
water, 71
Watergate scandal, 67
wealth, 158, 169, 205–211, 213, 218. *See also* profits
Weber, Max, 59
Welch, Jack, 35–38, 235
Westinghouse Electric Co., 191–192
white population, suicides in, 93
white supremacy, 97
wildcat Christianity, 109–110, 139
wildcatters, 109–110, 139
Wilderness Act, 130
Williams, Kate, 70, 141–142
wishcycling, 71
woke capitalism, 21, 46, 52, 124, 128, 138
women, 118, 126, 212, 229–230
World Trade Organization, 192
World War II, 65, 108, 110, 194

X

X (formerly Twitter), 182

Y

Yahoo, 210
Young, Owen D., 37
Youngstown, Ohio, 151–152

Z

Zuckerberg, Mark, 17, 158

ABOUT THE AUTHORS

Photo by Lisa Helfert

Seth Levine

A longtime venture capitalist, Seth Levine works with venture funds and companies around the globe. His day job is as a partner at Foundry, a Boulder, Colorado–based venture capital firm he cofounded in 2006. As of 2025, Foundry had more than $3.5 billion in assets under management. He is also a cofounder of GoodBread, a lending platform focused on providing capital to Main Street businesses.

Easily distracted and a passionate advocate for entrepreneurship, Seth also spends time as an advisor to venture funds and companies around the world. The intersection of community and business has always been a driving force for Seth. He cofounded Pledge 1%, a global network of companies that have pledged equity, time, and product back to their local communities, and was the founding board chair of EforAll Colorado, an organization that promotes broad-based entrepreneurship in communities across the state and is part of the national EforAll movement. He was an early board member of StartupColorado, an organization that promotes entrepreneurship in areas of Colorado outside of the front range, and serves on the Investment Committee of Gary Community Ventures, which partners with local communities to reshape the arc of opportunity for Colorado children and families. Seth also serves as a trustee of his alma mater, Macalester College in St. Paul, Minnesota, where he helped found their entrepreneurship program as well as a popular student hackathon (the "Macathon"). He also works with a number of venture funds and companies around the world—especially in the Middle East and Africa—to help promote entrepreneurship and economic development.

His previous book, *The New Builders: Face to Face with the True Future of Business* (also coauthored with Elizabeth MacBride), was released in 2021.

A passionate cyclist, above-average skier, and general fan of all things outdoors, Seth and his wife live in Colorado with their three children.

Elizabeth MacBride

Elizabeth MacBride is a journalist, author, and public affairs expert with a long career working at the intersection of finance, technology, and civil society. She is an advocate for economic dynamism and the economic power of people who have historically had too little of it. She has been on the founding team of four startups, including Wealthfront, where she devised the language that helped launch the automated investment movement, giving middle-class Americans access to low-cost financial advice. A senior knowledge and advocacy consultant for the Women Entrepreneurs Finance Initiative, housed at the World Bank, she has written or edited for *Quartz*, *Forbes*, *The Atlantic*, the Stanford Graduate School of Business, CNBC, the BBC, *Newsweek*, and many others. She is also the coauthor of two previous books: *The Little Book of Robo Investing: How to Make Money While You Sleep*, the latest in the acclaimed Wiley series (published March 2024), and *The New Builders: Face to Face with the True Future of Business*. Research from *The New Builders* was used to reshape $250 billion in US government aid during the pandemic.

She is the proud daughter of a family with seven generations of military service, and the proud mother of two daughters. She's also a yoga enthusiast, gardener, reader, and traveler.